"Wonderful, practical, down-to-earth, and easy to read. . . .
I will recommend this book with great enthusiasm to my
colleagues and patients."

—Kathi Kemper, MD, MPH,
*chair for holistic and integrative medicine, professor of
pediatrics and public health science, and director of the
Second Opinion Clinic, Brenner Children's Hospital at
Wake Forest University Health Sciences*

"A must-read for anyone working with special-needs children."

—Leland R. Kaiser, PhD,
*founder and president of Kaiser Consulting, a health
care consulting firm in Brighton, Colorado*

"An important dialogue about our culture, the practice of medicine, and the emotional state of health of our children today.
This book is a much-needed guide to assist parents and practitioners to protect children and develop greater awareness of
how to treat them more safely. I recommend this book for anyone who chooses to look further than a label to know our children, and beyond drug treatments to manage the stress our
children are living with."

—Lawrence B. Palevsky, MD, FAAP,
*fellow of the American Academy of Pediatrics and past-
president of the American Holistic Medical Association*

"An excellent resource for any parent/caregiver who has a child
involved (or about to be involved) in our country's mental health
system. Using straightforward language and real-life examples,
Dr. Shannon speaks directly to parents and caregivers about
the potential pitfalls of accepting simplistic explanations for
problems our youth exhibit and the potentially damaging results
when these explanations lead to one-size-fits-all 'sledgehammer'
approaches."

—Richard J. Munschy, PsyD,
*psychologist and consultant in New Britain,
Connecticut*

"Informed, positive, and practical advice to help the mental health development of children. . . . Breaking from the traditional medical model, Dr. Shannon avoids using psychiatric diagnoses as the basis for understanding behavior. Instead he offers practical, professional guidance, from several perspectives, for nurturing emotionally healthy children."

—**Robert L. Hendren, DO,**
professor of psychiatry, executive director of the M.I.N.D. Institute, and chief of child and adolescent psychiatry at the University of California at Davis, and president-elect of the American Academy of Child and Adolescent Psychiatry

Please Don't Label My Child

Please Don't Label My Child

Break the Doctor-Diagnosis-Drug Cycle and Discover Safe, Effective Choices for Your Child's Emotional Health

SCOTT M. SHANNON, MD,
WITH EMILY HECKMAN

RODALE

© 2007 by Scott Shannon, MD

Rodale books may be purchased for business or promotional use or for special sales. For information, please write to: Special Markets Department, Rodale Inc., 733 Third Avenue, New York, NY 10017.

Printed in the United States of America

Rodale Inc. makes every effort to use acid-free ♾, recycled paper ♻.

Book design by Christina Gaugler

Library of Congress Cataloging-in-Publication Data

Shannon, Scott, MD.
  Please don't label my child : break the doctor-diagnosis-drug cycle and discover safe, effective choices for your child's emotional health / Scott M. Shannon with Emily Heckman.
      p.   cm.
  Includes index.
  ISBN-13 978–1–57954–682–3 hardcover
  ISBN-10 1–57954–682–X hardcover
  1. Child mental health—Popular works.   2. Child psychopathology—Popular works.   I. Heckman, Emily.   II. Title.
RJ499.34.S43   2007
618.92'89—dc22   2007020478

Distributed to the trade by Holtzbrinck Publishers

2 4 6 8 10 9 7 5 3 1 hardcover

I want to dedicate this book to my family, the source of all that I am.
To my parents, Howard and Pat, who gave me the experience of love;
to my wife, Suze, who taught me how to love; to my children, Sarah
and Noah, who uncovered new layers of love within me.

—S. S.

This is for Eamon, with love.

—E. H.

CONTENTS

ACKNOWLEDGMENTS

I would like to acknowledge the many people who helped make this book possible, especially my stellar agent, Gail Ross, who saw something in me many years ago. She has been steadfast and unwavering in her support of me ever since. My editors at Rodale have been patient and helpful in making this book occur. A big thank-you to the friends and professionals who reviewed many rough drafts and shared many rambling discussions, especially Jane, Charlie, Steve, Pat, Jeff, and Mark. I would like to acknowledge the many hours of hard work put in by Linda White on earlier versions of this manuscript. I am grateful for my mentors who inspired me to always honor the whole child—body, mind, and spirit. And I can't tell you how much I appreciate my partner on this project, Emily Heckman. She is smart, polished, insightful, and quite patient with my shortcomings. She understood what I wanted to share and made it better. Finally, to my wife and kids, who keep me whole and in my heart.

—*Scott Shannon*

With gratitude and love, I thank Christian and Eamon for taking such good care of each other—and me—while I wrote this book. Thanks also to David Black, my wonderful agent; Keith Berkowitz, MD; Heather Davis; Nancy Anderson Kane, MSW; Tami Booth; and my "mom posse," especially Cindy, Lisa, Jane, Linda, and all the other parents I know who said "you must write this book!" Thanks, too, to our fine team at Rodale Books. Finally, I want to thank Dr. Scott Shannon, a true visionary and loving child advocate whose empowering message will bring hope to millions of parents.

—*Emily Heckman*

INTRODUCTION

Too many of our children are not fitting in. Too many of them are not thriving. And too many of them are just not as happy as they ought to be. At least this is what I see in my daily practice, even in this age of "no child left behind." The rhetoric just isn't matching the reality. If no child is meant to be left behind, why are so many of our children being diagnosed with major psychiatric illnesses? Why are so many of our children on psychiatric medications? Why are so many of our children doing poorly in school or suffering socially? And why are so many of our families stressed by conflict and tension?

Even though I'm a medical doctor with a specialty in child psychiatry, I believe that the behavioral and emotional problems we see in our children today are too readily being considered and treated as medical problems rather than being addressed as the relational, nutritional, and environmental problems they are. Our children—all of whom have the capacity for strong mental and emotional health—are labeled and medicated at an alarming rate, yet they don't seem to be getting better.

In recent years, diagnoses such as attention deficit hyperactivity disorder (ADHD), depression, bipolar disorder, and even autistic spectrum disorders in children have skyrocketed. Why is this? Is it because more and more of our children are born with faulty brain chemistry or some other genetically related weakness that makes them more susceptible to these very serious illnesses? I highly doubt it.

Our children, though truly suffering, are being misdiagnosed at an alarming rate and consequently are not being properly treated. This isn't simply a problem with our health care system, which, in conjunction with the health insurance industry, puts a premium on doctors choosing a diagnosis—a label—as quickly as possible. This is a societal problem. True, the life stressors that burden our kids are greater than ever (and identifying and addressing these stressors is at the heart of this book). But we live in a society that tends to see things as being black or white, good or bad, right or wrong, and the sooner we find the right label for something, the better we all feel. All of us, that is, except our kids.

We're a culture that just isn't comfortable with the gray areas, with difference. We want things to fit into simple categories. We want things to be neat and tidy. We seem to want everything in our lives—even our kids—to conform to an ever-shifting—and shrinking—definition of "normal." We're even willing to medicate our children in order to achieve this mythical state.

What exactly is "normal" in children? Not that long ago, a child who now might be labeled as having ADHD would have been considered normal—just spirited, headstrong, or energetic. A child who was shy or functioned best on the edges of a group would once have been considered normal but is now likely to be labeled as having an anxiety disorder or depression. A child who became overly aggressive and oppositional would have been put in his place by a loving, involved, extended family. Today, we live in such isolation that many an overstressed and intimidated parent seeks an MD to label and medicate the problem away.

Even children who are thriving and achieving are being victimized by our overzealous need to label. Take the "gifted" child who lives with tremendous chronic anxiety because she is expected to excel academically at all times. Or the child we label "cooperative" who lives with terrible self-esteem because he fears that expressing himself in uninhibited ways (or even saying no) will cause that positive label to be replaced by a negative one.

Our tendency to want to label things has not only left our children without what they need most (our consistent, unconditional love and focused attention), it has also stripped them of the right to enjoy a childhood free of damaging and debilitating diagnostic labels.

It may seem that I'm stating the obvious, but parents need to be reminded of one simple fact: Our children are born with magnificent brains that are wired to function exquisitely well. Each child comes into this world with a unique brain, as rare as a thumbprint or a snowflake. That child's brain then interacts with the complex world around it and begins to develop and grow. The interplay of brain, nutrition, relationships, and environment creates what we come to know as that child's personality and mind, so we need to remember that no two kids are ever alike. Given this fact, why are we increasingly willing to pigeonhole our kids? Why do we wish to insist that they conform to such rigid ideas of what it means to be normal?

If a child doesn't "fit in," whether at school, at home, or in the larger community, we as a culture are too quick to assume that the child is somehow defective, that there is actually something wrong with her brain. When we make this assumption, we fall into what I call the doctor-diagnosis-drug cycle, a nearly inescapable progression of events in which the well-meaning parents of a suffering child find themselves seeking help and invariably being handed a prescription.

In truth, we've actually got it all *backward* when it comes to treating children. When one of our children is failing to thrive (socially, emotionally, or even physically), it's usually a sure sign to me that rather than something internal being at fault, something *external* is getting in the child's way. These external forces—or "brain stressors"—fall into six categories: relational, nutritional, environmental, familial, educational, and traumatic.

These stressors are the real culprits, and these are what we should treat when a child exhibits emotional or mental distress. In this book, I'll look at each of these brain stressors and share my approaches for solving emotional and behavioral problems—without labels and, typically, without drugs.

The practice of child psychiatry has so significantly narrowed that I hardly recognize it as the same field I embraced 25 years ago. As a profession, we fail to acknowledge and use the vast panoply of treatment options available to us. A number of years ago, I edited the first textbook on the emerging field of integrative psychiatry, which outlined a wide array of effective, evidence-based treatment modalities that were being unused. These safe, effective techniques are not taught to physicians, funded for research, or marketed to consumers, because they do not have the potential to make billions of dollars of profit. For the past 12 years, I have been on the road, speaking at medical conferences and hospitals all over the world, sharing my message of hope and choice. Every time I speak about how we're over-labeling and medicating our kids, I'm praised by my colleagues for offering a light at the end of the tunnel.

All of us who provide care for the growing throngs of stressed kids and families feel the pressure, the desperation to help. But too many of us still reach first for the prescription pad. The brilliant psychologist Abraham Maslow, PhD, said, "When all you have is a hammer, everything starts to look like a nail."

The truth is, there is very little science behind most psychiatric labels. Psychiatry is the only branch of medicine that has no biochemical test or form of imaging to verify clinical diagnosis. In fact, we know so little about the brain of an individual that we make our diagnosis based on patient history and personal judgment on the part of the clinician. A recent psychiatry journal article on the consistency of psychiatric diagnosis summarized the problem by stating that the reliability of psychiatric diagnosis remains poor in clinical practice. And this was in regard to diagnosing adults; everyone in the field acknowledges that diagnosing children, whose brains are still forming, is much more difficult.

The science behind the use of psychiatric medications in children is even more concerning. Most of the medications that we use in child psychiatry do not have FDA approval (which means they have not been adequately tested in terms of safety or effectiveness). Of all the medications that we use in child psychiatry, only stimulants have adequate evidence of long-term safety, and just last year, the FDA strengthened the warnings about the risks of some of these medications after a number of cases of sudden cardiac death in children. We have no body of research that addresses the use of multiple medications in children, and yet, in 2006, nearly 1.6 million American youths were prescribed two or more psychiatric medications simultaneously.

In an article in the *New York Times,* the director of the National Institute of Mental Health was quoted as saying, "There are not any good scientific data to support the widespread use of these medications in children, particularly in young children, where the scientific data are even more scarce." Yet all over America, overwhelmed doctors are besieged by overwhelmed parents, with a highly stressed child in tow, who demand "action." I understand this pattern well and see it all too often.

Things are finally beginning to change, however, and that's why I feel it's time to speak out more forcefully against the rigid doctor-diagnosis-drug cycle that has children, parents—and many of my well-meaning colleagues—caught in a terrible bind.

Our children are innately emotionally and mentally healthy. But they—and their brains—need our help in order to cultivate and maintain that health. It is our duty as parents and practitioners to do the hard work of identifying the stressors that are compromising the emotional and mental health of our children. We have to learn to see beyond labels and do the hard work of seeing things from our children's perspective.

My experience with the basic emotional and mental resilience of children has shaped my thinking as a psychiatrist and influenced my methodology as a healer in ways that many may perceive to be radical. I even sometimes joke that I am not a "normal psychiatrist," an oxymoron of sorts. I worked for 4 years as a primary care doctor in a rural area before specializing in child psychiatry. I am trained in acupuncture, nutrition, bodywork, herbal medicine, and Jungian psychotherapy as well as conventional psychiatry. I have twice been medical director of a psychiatric hospital, and I founded a holistic medical clinic at a local general hospital.

I joined the American Holistic Medical Association (AHMA) in 1978 as a founding member, and I have worked alongside and learned from such esteemed members as Andrew Weil, MD (my first mentor); Deepak Chopra, MD; Larry Dossey, MD; and Bernie Siegel, MD (a past president of the AHMA, like myself). I don't go to dinners on the tab of local drug reps; I won't even take one of their pens. Instead, I strive to find the least invasive form of treatment I can for every one of my patients, always preferring to recommend vitamins, bodywork, exercise, or other therapies instead of prescribing drugs. However, I feel it is important to state that I am not "anti-medication": I do prescribe medications, but cautiously.

I also strive to practice in a way that puts the power to heal squarely back into the hands of the children and parents I work with. When I am able to do this, both learn to see how strong the young brain is, how adaptable and resilient. Families begin to understand that children—and their minds and emotions—are wonderfully complex, ever-changing, and quite readily healed.

Instead of just aggressively treating symptoms and writing prescriptions, I view my job as being primarily that of an educator. My role is to encourage parents (and institutions) to look at children differently and to understand more fully how a child's brain actually works. When we do this actively and attentively, we help our children develop the mental and emotional resources they'll need for succeeding in life. My goal is to empower families to take ownership of their emotional and mental health, to learn the tools needed to identify and combat brain stress, and to learn how to effectively eliminate the offending stressors from their lives. When I'm able to facilitate this, I get to step back and watch the flowering of every member of a family, from the youngest to the oldest.

My approach is one of moderation and restraint. It is my firm belief that children—like all other living creatures—are designed to function at a high level of health and wellness without a whole lot of medical intervention. This includes functioning at a high mental and emotional level. But there is undoubtedly one kind of intervention our children *always* need, especially if they are suffering in any way: our loving, focused, and consistent attention. It is my great hope that this book will serve as a source of empowerment and encouragement for parents and enable them to look beyond labels; to break free of the doctor-diagnosis-drug cycle; and to truly see, support, love, and nurture their children toward strong mental and emotional health.

CHAPTER 1

The High Cost
of Labeling

A terrible epidemic is sweeping our country, and it's gaining momentum at a frightening pace. It's causing our children to suffer greatly, and it shows no signs of abating. No one can predict what long-term effects this trend will have on our kids' overall quality of life, but it's clear that the cost to their health and overall well-being right now is staggering. Our kids—millions of them—are being blighted every day. Their health, their self-esteem, their ability to thrive and fit in, and their capacity for joy and success are being undermined by a crippling foe called labeling.

LOST TO A LABEL

Labeling is what happens when our children show signs of distress and trouble and we, the well-meaning adults in their lives, intervene. On the face of it, we do the right thing when we are able to identify the symptoms of "dis-ease" in our children and turn to experts for help. But something curious happens when we defer—with the best of intentions—to doctors, psychologists, health care providers, educators, and other "experts" in order to help our children. Too often, the *relief of symptoms* becomes the sole goal of treatment, and our children wind up labeled and medicated but feeling no better.

I don't mean to be the voice of doom and gloom about this, and of course, it can be useful—even crucial—to first aggressively treat the symptoms a child exhibits. What does alarm me, however, is how many of our children are being treated *only* on a symptomatic level and thus become lost to their labels. When this happens, the true source of the upset often remains unidentified and unaddressed.

From 1987 to 1996, the number of children who were prescribed psychiatric medications in this country tripled. If this ominous trend continues, within a generation fully half of all American children will be on some kind of psychiatric drug. Everywhere you look the numbers of American children being prescribed psychiatric medications is reaching a crescendo that draws concern.

In one study published in 2006, called the National Ambulatory Medical Care Survey, researcher Mark Olfson, MD, of Columbia University found that the use of psychotropic medications for teenagers increased 250 percent between 1994 and 2001. More specifically they found the proportion of physician visits resulting in a prescription for a psychiatric medication rose from 3.4 percent to 8.3 percent. Sadly, by 2001 one in every 10 office visits by a boy resulted in a prescription for a psychotropic medication. One issue that concerned the researchers was a finding that about 25 percent of the cases that involved psychotropics did not have a mental health diagnosis. "That should alert physicians to the possibility of a trend toward casual prescribing of psychotropic medications to young people," Dr. Olfson commented.

Some of the most comprehensive current data comes from Medco Health Solutions (part of the drugmaker Merck). In

2004, it released its annual analysis of prescription drug users. In that report these startling facts were revealed: There was a 369 percent increase in spending on ADHD drugs for children under the age of 5 between 2000 and 2003. The number of prescriptions for autism and behavioral disorders rose by 71 percent. Spending for all psychotropics in children rose 77 percent in 3 years. Psychiatric medications for children were the fastest-growing prescriptions.

Express Scripts Inc. published the results of 5 years of study in 2004. These findings are no different: The use of antidepressant medications rose 100 percent in preschool girls and 64 percent in preschool boys (all kids under the age of 5).

The *Archives of General Psychiatry* published a study in 2006 that showed a sixfold rise in the use of antipsychotic medications in children between 1993 and 2002.

Anywhere from 3 to 10 percent of American children have ADHD, and this figure increases at an alarming rate each year. Why? I attribute it to a phenomenon known as diagnosis creep, which clinically captures our overwillingness to label and diagnose our children. Diagnosis creep has even been documented by the National Institute of Mental Health (NIMH). In a survey conducted from 2001 to 2003 and released in 2005, the NIMH postulated that more than 46 percent of the American population would meet the criteria used by the psychiatric industry for a mental illness. As the definitions we use for emotional and mental disorders expand, it seems inevitable that the range we allow for normalcy will shrink.

In 2003, the Medco study also pointed out, 65 percent of children and adolescents taking behavioral medicines were also on antidepressants. This is one of the most frightening aspects of overlabeling: More and more kids are on two or more psychiatric drugs at a time. This is true despite there being little or no research on what the effects of combining such drugs has on children. In late 2005, Medco Health released the alarming news that the fastest-growing population of prescription sleeping pill users in this country is made up of children between the ages of 10 and 19. The number of children taking sleeping pills is up a whopping 85 percent in just 4 years, despite the fact that the FDA has approved most popular sleep aids only for use in adults.

This points up one of the scariest facts of the labeling epidemic: There is no body of scientific research to prove that these drugs are safe for our children over the long term. In fact, in early 2004, the FDA insisted that manufacturers include warning labels on many antidepressants about their potential dangerous side effects, including increased risk of suicidal impulses in teens. (There is some slowdown in prescribing one category of these drugs, however. In late 2005, nearly a year and a half after drug companies were forced to include a "black box" warning on the labels of antidepressants, the number of prescriptions for antidepressants written for children dropped 20 percent.)

Other commonly prescribed drugs are finally coming under similar close scrutiny. In early 2007, the FDA directed the manufacturers of stimulants—including Ritalin (methylphenidate), Adderall (amphetamine-dextroamphetamine), Strattera (atomoxetine), and other brands—to issue guidelines alerting parents and patients to the serious risks involved in taking these medications, including psychiatric problems (hearing voices, manic behavior, and increased anxiety and suspiciousness) and heart problems (elevated blood pressure and even sudden cardiac death). These are big, serious, crucial steps in finally breaking the doctor-diagnosis-drug cycle, which will, I hope, lead to a decline in labeling.

Instead of spending my time diagnosing most kids I see, I try to *un*diagnose them, to free them from the labels that are hurting more than helping them. I work to figure out what leads to the symptoms and the label. Paradoxically, I often have to taper kids off medications to determine what is wrong.

How did we get into this situation of overlabeling our kids? I believe it's a problem of well-intentioned parenting colliding head-on with a rigid and label-oriented medical culture. Parents have kids who are suffering, and they want to find relief for them. They turn to a medical system that rewards quick diagnosis over thoughtful and reflective care and prizes the myth of "silver bullet" treatment over accurate understanding. This tendency to favor the "quick fix" is rapidly spreading into other areas of our culture, too. Look at our schools, for instance, where a child who prefers to move rather than sit still is flagged as a potential problem. Look into our homes, and you may find parents who are so temperamentally at odds with their own children that they can't resist seeing them as somehow being not quite normal. Labels, to many parents, appear at first glance to be a kind of lifeboat. Who wouldn't be relieved and hopeful when whatever ails their child is quickly and succinctly identified? But the long-term cost of labeling outweighs any short-term relief of symptoms.

Instead of stopping to contemplate what brain stressors might be undermining a child's ability to enjoy emotional and mental well-being, we parents have a tendency to panic at the signs of upset in our children, to become fearful in the face of serious symptoms. When this happens, our good parental intentions go bad.

How do I know this? First, I am a parent who has had to resist the urge to label my own kids whenever the going gets tough for them—or for me. Second, I am a child psychiatrist whose practice is bursting at the seams with children who have been aggressively (and often erroneously) diagnosed with and treated for major psychiatric problems but who are not getting better. Third, I speak to professional groups around the country, and I hear firsthand how frustrated and concerned my colleagues are with the current situation. Labeling our children often cripples them instead of liberating them. The very labels that we turn to in order to help our children can actually do more harm than good.

PSYCHIATRIC LABELS: HARD SCIENCE?

Unlike most branches of medicine, psychiatry does not rely on objective data to diagnose and treat illness. It is a soft science, not a hard science. There is no blood test or brain scan we can use to diagnose a condition like ADHD. Psychiatric diagnosis is based on the personal observation and judgment of the practitioner, which are colored by temperament, interest, skill, level of knowledge, degree of training, and innumerable other factors. In 2006, the journal *Psychiatry* explored this topic and found that despite much improvement over the past 50 years, "the reliability of psychiatric diagnosis among practicing clinicians remains poor," and this was in terms of diagnosing adults.

Psychiatry does very little research into the reliability of our diagnostic system in actual clinical practice. One reason may be that the results are so embarrassing and destructive to psychiatry that no one wants to consider them. Here is one such example reported in May 2006 in *Clinical Psychiatry News.* In this study 376 patients at a large psychiatric hospital in Tucson, Arizona, were readmitted within 30 days of their initial discharge, and very few received the same diagnosis. Fewer than half of the patients with bipolar disorder were given the same diagnosis. Ninety percent of patients with schizoaffective disorder got a new and different diagnosis. In this study 255 people had two admissions; only 50 of these (less than 20 percent) were given the same diagnosis. If they had three admissions, only 7 of 82 patients (9 percent) received the same label. When they were readmitted four times, only 2 of 27 (7 percent) got the same tag. The poor souls who were sick enough to be admitted more than four times batted zero for 12. The researcher who did this study gave this advice: "Take the prior diagnosis with a grain of salt because other diagnosticians may not be as careful as you." I don't think I could have said it better. Can you imagine what the diagnostic reliability would have been if these patients had been children? Everyone in the field of psychiatry knows that kids are much harder to diagnose, simply because they are "moving targets" as they constantly grow, change, and mature.

We psychiatrists have some understanding of how the human brain functions, but we have very little understanding of what causes the brain to malfunction in ways that cause emotional or mental disorders. In order to organize and "codify" the way we think about mental disruptions, psychiatry has evolved around an ever-expanding encyclopedia of terminology that gives a diagnostic name to a symptom or cluster of symptoms. These psychiatric terms are the labels I've been referring to, and they can be found in the *DSM*-IV *(Diagnostic and Statistical Manual of Mental Disorders),* which is the official handbook created by and for psychiatrists that names and defines mental disorders.

The *DSM,* which has been in existence for roughly a half century, is updated periodically (we're currently using the fourth edition, hence *DSM*-IV). When it was first published in 1952, the *DSM* contained 106 mental disorders. When it was updated in 1968, there were 182. Now, based on the most current edition, which was edited in 1994, there are more than 300 mental disorders identified in the *DSM.* Even I, a psychiatrist, must ask: Could the numbers of serious mental and emotional disorders really have *tripled* in 42 years? The answer is no. I believe the proliferation of mental and emotional disorders as created by the editors of the *DSM* reflects our tendency toward "diagnosis creep," toward our willingness to find illness where there may be simply difference.

The labels we most frequently give to kids include the acronyms for and names of some complex and serious mental, emotional, and social disorders. These disorders, though once thought to be very rare in children, are being diagnosed (and misdiagnosed) at alarming rates. (In the 1970s, ADHD was considered quite rare, and only about 150,000 American children were thought to have it. Today, nearly four million American kids are labeled with ADHD, and most of them are also being given very powerful drugs to "control" it.)

Before I begin to sound as though I am rigidly against all labeling, I must say that diagnostic labels do play an important role in terms of helping us identify what a child is experiencing. It would be foolhardy of me to say that I don't use the *DSM*-IV and the definitions it provides on a daily basis. I do use labels as insurance companies, other doctors, and many parents require them. But I always use them to the child's greatest benefit.

THE ADVANTAGES OF LABELS

Diagnostic labels were designed to facilitate healing. There is no doubt about this. Using such labels is not only crucial to guiding appropriate treatment, it also provides a source of much-needed relief for the parents of any child who is suffering. Once a diagnosis is made, parents experience an immediate sense of reassurance that the problems that plague their child are understood and will be addressed. With a diagnostic label in hand, parents can often break out of the isolation that comes with having a seriously troubled child. They can then find support among parents with kids who have been similarly diagnosed. They can also do research and learn more about the diagnosis, which, one hopes, will help them learn more about their child.

As a physician, finding a suitable diagnosis gives me a departure point, an entrée into treating a child, and this is a crucial first step in any good treatment. I turn to diagnostic labels daily in my own practice and use them to get a handle on the symptoms that may be debilitating a child under my care. I use these labels cautiously, however, as I'm aware of the tendency (even in myself) to become persuaded that the diagnosis—or the label—is the end point of treatment.

THE DISADVANTAGES OF LABELING

Of course, there are negative consequences of diagnostic labeling, even when the diagnosis is correct.

For one, a physician who has chosen a diagnosis may stop
looking for other causes of a child's symptoms. For example,
when a child is labeled ADHD, the adults around him may then
miss the fact that his symptoms indicate a stress reaction to
some traumatic experience or signal the stress brought on by an
undetected learning disability. The kind of myopic thinking that
an overreliance on labels promotes can have terrible consequences, including prolonged and unnecessary suffering for our
kids. Our current medical system (from insurance companies to
individual practitioners) has become diagnosis-oriented to the
extreme. Once a diagnostic label is applied, it is often understood
so rigidly that many potentially helpful treatment options are
ignored (or disallowed by insurers), much to the detriment of the
child in question.

Of course, the greatest cost of labeling is the effect on our
children. Children who are labeled in some way (however well
intentioned and therapeutically appropriate that label may be)
feel separated from their peers, which takes a terrible toll on
their self-esteem. Children have difficulty distinguishing a label
from who they are; they also believe that because they have
earned a label, they are somehow "less than," "broken," or "sick."

This tendency toward labeling is dangerous because it frac-
tures and fragments the way we look at things, particularly how
we view our kids. Instead of seeing robust, complicated, three-
dimensional people, we start to see our kids as being one-
dimensional. When we begin to identify and know our kids only
by the symptoms they exhibit, we have, however inadvertently,
abandoned them.

Even when a good diagnosis is made and a child is relieved of
terrible symptoms, the stigma surrounding the initial diagnostic

The Most Common Labels Given to Kids

The US Department of Health and Human Services estimates that one in every five children in America experiences some kind of mental health problem at any given time. Here are the most common labels our kids get today.

ADHD (attention deficit hyperactivity disorder). More than four million American children were diagnosed with this condition as of 2006, and most are on medication for it.

Anxiety disorders. It's estimated that 1 in 10 kids has an anxiety disorder.

Bipolar disorder. Experts believe that up to one-third of kids who have depression will develop bipolar disorder later in life.

Conduct disorder. The number of US kids estimated to have a conduct disorder is 1 in 10.

Depression. It's estimated that 1 out of 10 children suffers from a depressive disorder. This rate skyrockets to 2 out of 10 in adolescents.

label may prompt the child to view himself as being somehow defective or "bad." He may come to see himself as nothing more than a problem to be solved rather than as the lovable and breathtakingly complex human being he is. Putting a label on him distorts his—and our—perception of who he is.

There is also social stigma that comes with diagnostic labeling. I find the ADHD label to be particularly noxious for kids. Take Johnny, a pleasant and playful 9-year-old who came to me for an ADHD evaluation. His parents, who were very concerned about him, wanted to know if he indeed had ADHD, as diagnosed by his pediatrician. I actually did confirm the diagnosis and agreed with the use of stimulants to treat Johnny's symptoms. The drugs worked wonders in terms of allowing him to focus and concentrate, but it wasn't until I spent some time with Johnny in therapy and worked with him on the self-esteem issues brought on by the diagnosis that his performance in school began to improve. After a term of school under my care, Johnny brought home passing grades for the first time—even in math, his most difficult subject. I asked him what he thought had changed. "I used to think my brain was broken—isn't that what ADHD means?" he said. "Now I know it isn't, and so I can enjoy my schoolwork, even math."

Although labeling Johnny brought him symptomatic relief, he needed to refuse to identify himself with that label in order to thrive.

I encounter the shame children feel because of labels every day. It tears at my heart whenever I see this. Take Samuel, for example. I couldn't bear the thought that he was known in his family, his school, and his community as "that ADHD kid" rather than as Sam, the boy who rides a unicycle, collects Pez dispensers, plays the pennywhistle, and knows the name of every dog in the neighborhood.

Labels can also have a legacy effect. Once a child has been labeled and treated successfully, it's often difficult for those around the child (and the child herself) to let go of the label. Many psychiatric conditions, especially those found in children, run a variable course; they wax and wane and sometimes disappear altogether, and this is due to the fact that a child's brain is growing stronger and more resilient all the time. Let me give you a brief example.

Natalie

Natalie, a bright, willowy 17-year-old, and her mother showed up for our first meeting on time. Natalie's mother filled me in. "Natalie has had OCD (obsessive-compulsive disorder) for 6 years. Dr. Mendoza, her psychiatrist, diagnosed her at age 11 because of a severe compulsion to wash her hands. He started Natalie on

Prozac (fluoxetine), and almost immediately, her symptoms seemed to disappear. When Dr. Mendoza left town a couple of years ago, Dr. Howard, our family doctor, took over Natalie's care and continued to prescribe the Prozac. We felt like it might be time to check in with another psychiatrist since Natalie will be going to college in the fall."

I thanked Natalie's mom for the succinct history and then asked Natalie about herself. "My OCD doesn't seem to limit me at all, Dr. Shannon," she said. "I take only one shower a day, and I wash my hands only after using the bathroom or before a meal."

The young woman I spoke with for over an hour showed no signs of having OCD, so I recommended to her and her mom that we start to taper off on the medication. Within 4 months, Natalie was medication free, and no OCD symptoms returned. A year later, she remained symptom free. Both Natalie and her mother struggled with this, wondering if it was just a fluke and if the symptoms would reappear. Though I told them both that there were no guarantees, it was my experience that OCD in children often resolves itself. But what about the Prozac? they wondered. I told them that we will never know if the Prozac did or didn't "cure" Natalie's OCD, but it didn't matter. What mattered was that her symptoms were effectively treated, and they are still gone. Nevertheless, the specter of OCD remained with Natalie for some time.

Children often outgrow the psychiatric symptoms that plague them early on. Although this kind of spontaneous healing happens frequently, the stigma of the initial label may last a lifetime.

Multiple Labels

One of the true travesties of the epidemic of labeling is comorbidity, which, in plain English, means the application of more than one diagnosis. On average, every child who is seen by a child psychiatrist comes away with not one but three different diagnoses. This means that children who are identified as being ADHD are also tagged as being depressed. Or a child who has OCD may also be diagnosed as having mild bipolar disorder. Although one may find reassurance in this, thinking that our children are being looked at comprehensively, what co-morbidity indicates to me, more than anything else, is how profoundly complex our children are and how poorly our diagnostic system serves them.

Diagnostic Labels in the Wrong Hands

Since the year 2000, when the US Surgeon General's office conducted a study that showed that the mental health treatment system in the United States was in abysmal shape, things have only gotten worse. There are fewer beds available for children in psychiatric hospitals across the nation; health insurers have whittled down coverage for inpatient and outpatient treatment to unacceptably low levels; and though the country needs an estimated 30,000 child psychiatrists to treat our children adequately, as I write this, there are only 7,000 of us in business. In fact, child psychiatry has been cited as the medical specialty with the greatest shortage of practitioners in this country. Because of this shortage, parents are forced to turn to general practitioners, pediatricians, and other health care experts for help in treating their children's psychiatric problems.

In the best of hands, psychiatric diagnosis of children is a complex, confusing, and inaccurate art. In less specialized hands, it can become a real mess.

Say, for example, that a primary care doctor diagnoses 11-year-old Josh with ADHD and prescribes stimulants. A year and a half later, the school counselor meets with Josh, finds out that he is having suicidal thoughts, and refers him to me. My evaluation reveals that back when he was 11, his parents' frequent squabbling caused him to become depressed, and his depression triggered symptoms of ADHD. Because Josh kept his depressed feelings and thoughts to himself, the adults in his life never noticed that he was suffering in this way. The only outward expression of his depression was his poor performance in school, and this is what prompted the diagnosis of ADHD. His parents, believing that their pediatrician was right, unwittingly let Josh's depression go undiagnosed and untreated for 18 months, a terribly long time in the life of a child.

Even more troubling is the trend of educators—people with no formal medical training at all—taking on the authority to label and diagnose our kids based on their behavior in school. I have heard more than once of parents being threatened with the removal of their children from a school if they did not accept the school's diagnosis of the problem and begin treatment with medication immediately.

Incorrect Labels

Sometimes, kids are diagnosed with the wrong condition entirely. When this happens, you have a serious problem on your hands. Not only will the child not get the treatment she needs, she will continue to suffer—and so will her parents. The off-target treatment she does receive may not help at all, and it may even aggravate her symptoms. This happens very frequently with ADHD; I see kids all the time who are dealing with the effects of terrible, unacknowledged brain stressors. Instead of identifying the problem, someone slaps an ADHD tag onto these kids, and they continue to suffer, legitimately. If a child is anxious—and stress causes great anxiety in all of us—being given stimulants may make him more so. If he has endured an unspoken trauma, he will continue to suffer unless that trauma is acknowledged and addressed by the caregivers around him. All doctors—myself included—make this mistake at times. When a missed diagnosis misdirects treatment, I do my best to get back on track—and back in touch with the child—as quickly as possible. Here's an example of how damaging an inaccurate diagnosis can be.

Nick

When Nick was 6, he lived with his mother, who struggled to manage a busy job as an administrative assistant while raising three children on her own. Nick's father, a bright but under-achieving computer programmer who liked to drink, had finally left his wife—and their kids—in the rural small town he had taken them to in Idaho. Not long after the divorce, Nick's first-grade teacher called his mother to complain that the boy would not sit still and pay attention and that he was seriously disrupting the class.

Nick's mother took him to see their family doctor, who immediately became annoyed with Nick because he refused to sit still and insisted on rummaging through the doctor's supplies. The doctor promptly diagnosed ADHD and prescribed Ritalin. The medication seemed to help Nick to sit still and focus—for a few days. Then things got worse. His mother, who had been feeling isolated and overwhelmed since the divorce, became too depressed to be emotionally available to her children. Nick began to further act out at home and at school. The doctor upped the Ritalin dose, and after Nick failed to improve over the next few weeks, he raised it again. Nick began to hit kids at school and his siblings at home. When his teachers or his mother asked him to do something, he did the opposite, or he threw things and screamed. He became a tempest of a boy. In response, his doctor added the antipsychotic drug Risperdal (risperidone) to control the aggressive behavior.

On high doses of Ritalin and Risperdal, Nick was somewhat more manageable, although he became lethargic and began to gain weight. Because of his severe behavior and aggression, the school moved him into a classroom with other "high-needs" kids, most of whom had learning difficulties and poor social skills.

In the meantime, Nick's mother sought help for herself. She began taking antidepressants and started counseling. Once her

Flying Blind with
Antipsychotic Drugs for Children

Between 1992 and 2002, the use of antipsychotic medications in children in the United States increased sixfold. At the same time, Mark Olfson, MD, of Columbia University found that only 14.2 percent of the more than one million prescriptions for antipsychotics written for children were for psychotic problems. The majority were prescribed for disruptive behavior disorders and the remainder for developmental problems or mood issues. In perhaps the most striking finding of this study, the authors found that almost one in five visits to psychiatrists by children (18 percent) resulted in an antipsychotic prescription being given.

More than 90 percent of these medications have not been adequately tested in or approved for children. "There is a gap between what has been learned in carefully controlled studies and what is actually occurring in practice," Dr. Olfson noted. "We don't know enough about the metabolic effects of newer antipsychotics, particularly the long-term effects in young people."

This study confirmed for me what I have observed in current practice. We are way out in front of good science or safe practice when we use these potent psychiatric medications for our children.

head was above water, she decided to move back home to Colorado, where she had family and more friends.

Soon after she got here, she phoned me, and I made time to see Nick.

When I met him, Nick was 9 years old and obese (although his mother told me he had been thin most of his life). His clothes and hair were disheveled. He didn't seem to care how he looked; he didn't seem to care much about anything. To my astonishment, he related to me on the intellectual level of a teen. He could discuss politics and philosophy, electronics and computer programming. He compensated for an overall lack of social skills with a sharp and sarcastic sense of humor. When I asked about his medications, he jokingly compared himself to Jack Nicholson in *One Flew over the Cuckoo's Nest*. He was observant, intelligent, and a bit eccentric but clearly his own person. I liked him.

As we talked and I had the chance to watch Nick, I saw that he had some mildly compulsive traits. Specifically, he liked to order and count some of his possessions. I decided to taper his medications and do some testing. His IQ was over 140 for analytic skills, which is higher than all but about 1 percent of the population. Although he lagged in some academic areas, his greatest shortfall was in his social skills. The bottom line was that Nick didn't have ADHD at all. He was bored by school and had been extremely stressed by his family's turmoil and his father's abandonment.

Off medication, Nick was a handful: He was energetic, talkative, sarcastic, curious, testy, and stubborn. However, his mother, who now had more psychological ballast and generally felt better, was able to better cope with him. She realized that his "hyperactivity" surfaced mainly when he was bored or upset. At my urging, she agreed to put Nick into an educational program specifically designed for kids with two areas of uniqueness, which in his case were a high IQ coupled with poor social skills. His teachers encouraged his curiosity and intellect while providing special instruction in developing stronger social skills. They were also tolerant of his need for stimulation and movement.

Nick is now 11. He has lost some weight and makes more effort with his appearance and personal hygiene. The only medication he takes is a very low dose of a drug called Luvox (fluvoxamine) to help him with his compulsions. Relaxation training and calming herbs have helped him feel on more of an even keel. He enjoys his family and his home life and is loved by his mother, brother, and sister.

Nick is the perfect example of a child who became lost in a label. In his case, his hyperactive and frustrated behavior blinded the adults around him to his high intelligence and his thirst for knowledge, and he became known as "that ADHD kid" instead of the wonderfully complex and bright individual named Nick.

MINIMIZING THE HARMFUL EFFECTS OF LABELING: A HOLISTIC APPROACH

We need diagnostic labels in order to best identify and treat the symptoms of the stressors that are compromising our children's mental and emotional health, but it's our responsibility to minimize the harm these labels do. One way we can do this is to engage in a more holistic approach to evaluating our kids. We must be willing to look at any and all aspects of a child's life that seem to be off-kilter and not just focus on the symptoms that are most apparent to adults. In my practice, I sometimes find that I can do the most good if I don't apply any diagnostic label at all. That's what I did when Melanie's parents came to see me.

Melanie

I spent two sessions trying to understand 9-year-old Melanie, but I made little headway until I had the chance to spend some time with her parents. Both are engineers who work long hours, but they're devoted to their only child. The family came to me because Melanie was struggling with anxiety, sad moods, and a volatile temper. On the one hand, she could be intense, defiant, and contrary; on the other, she could be needy, weepy, and emotionally fragile. She had already been to see two other mental health professionals and had been given two very different diagnostic labels (depression, from the family doctor, and intermittent explosive disorder, from a psychologist). Melanie's parents were hoping I could resolve this diagnostic confusion for them.

After seeing the girl three times, I told her parents that she was somewhat fragile emotionally, which meant she needed a lot of support and attention from them. Then I outlined a very rich and holistic treatment plan for her. They seemed pleased by how comprehensive all this was, but I sensed some hesitation on their part. Finally, Melanie's mother spoke up: "But what is her diagnosis, Doctor?"

I believed that Melanie was feeling great stress due to the lack of a steady, consistent emotional connection with her busy and distracted though well-meaning parents. Of course, I couldn't say this out loud, so instead I told them that I would need their help in making a diagnosis. "Melanie could fall into one of five diagnostic categories," I said. "She is suffering from either a mood disorder, an anxiety disorder, oppositional defiant disorder, intermittent explosive disorder, or parent-child conflict." I asked both parents to watch her very closely and at the end of each day, to sit down with her and together decide which category she fell into on that day. I also asked them to keep a log and bring it the next time we met. I sent them out the door with the symptom checklist for each of the five disorders and a firm commitment to work hard on this assignment until we met the following week.

After five more sessions, this strategy bore amazing fruit. Melanie's parents were spending so much time with her—really connecting with her—that they declared that she really didn't fit into any of the five categories. They had given Melanie such high-quality attention and time over the 6 weeks that she had become much more relaxed and happy. She had also shed much of her anger. A bonus of this "treatment plan" was that her parents were working less and spending more time focused on their child and their home life. Both parents remarked about how well-rounded they found their daughter to be and how much happier they had all become.

Of course, I could have taken the easy route with Melanie and diagnosed her as having a mood disorder. I would have then prescribed antidepressant medication, which would have cleared up her symptoms. But the label—and the treatment—wouldn't have touched the true stress at the heart of Melanie's problem: her lack of connection with her overworked and emotionally unavailable parents. Sidestepping the doctor-diagnosis-drug cycle and resisting the urge to label her allowed her parents to look at her in new ways. They began to address the stress that was at the root of her problem. By doing this—without the aid of drugs or labels—they began a healing process that will strengthen Melanie's mental and emotional health for the long haul.

TOOLS FOR CHANGE: THE APPROPRIATE USE OF PSYCHIATRIC DRUGS WITH KIDS

Let me state plainly and right up front: Psychiatric medications can work wonders with children. I have seen some kids respond so well to medication that it is as if a switch had been turned on and they were brought back into sync with their own lives, simply by being given a pill. But these cases are not the norm. Most children who are put on drug therapy experience only mild improvement that is often compromised by the simultaneous onset of uncomfortable side effects. Many of these children are in a treatment situation where their medication is constantly being changed or their dosages are constantly being adjusted in a futile effort to reach some sort of reasonable balance between benefits and side effects. Many children simply experience no apparent improvement with drugs; others get *worse* with drug therapy.

A certain amount of roulette takes place when one turns to drugs to treat children with mental and emotional problems, and I for one don't like this kind of gambling. The brain is far too complex and unknown to us to flood it with drugs without first ruling out other, less invasive treatment options for our patients— especially children, whose brains are so very malleable and susceptible to change and damage.

I believe that drugs are risky enough that they are not

necessarily the wisest choice for a child—even one who, on initial observation, seems to have a serious problem like depression. For starters, we don't have enough meaningful scientific data on how such psycho-pharmaceuticals affect a child's brain over the long term or what kinds of side effects such drugs will elicit.

Clearly, the issue of safety and efficacy with drugs and children is a huge one, and thankfully, we are becoming more aware of this. Today, all antidepressants and the ADHD drug Strattera have black box warnings about the increased risk of suicide in children. The FDA has also recommended that children who are given these drugs be more closely monitored by their physicians.

Research is also emerging that shows that some antidepressant agents—particularly selective serotonin reuptake inhibitors (SSRIs), which include drugs like Paxil (paroxetine), Zoloft (sertraline), and Prozac—may distort neurological development in rats. This is also true of certain stimulants, such as Ritalin and Concerta (methylphenidate). In studies, rats were less able to learn and develop neurological connections after being given these drugs. Obviously, these studies were not done on people, but they do raise serious questions about how such drugs might affect any brain—human or otherwise—over time.

Whenever I face the question of whether it's in a child's best interest to introduce psychiatric drug therapy, I carefully weigh the pros and cons of the issue. This checklist will give you an idea of some of the factors I consider before I write a prescription.

Benefits of Using Medication to Treat Children

- **Power.** Medications are typically more powerful than natural alternatives.

- **Speed.** Medication often causes a response within days or weeks.

- **Precision.** Newer psychiatric medications can often target a specific problem with a high level of efficacy.

- **Research.** There is sometimes extensive research that documents a drug's effectiveness (though this research usually covers a short period of use and usually only the impact the drug has on adults).

- **Parental respite.** Medicating a child often provides a crucial break for overstressed parents and therefore helps facilitate ongoing treatment.

Drawbacks of Using Medication to Treat Children

- **Medical risk.** From allergic reactions, headaches, and insomnia to seizures and weight gain—and even sudden death—the effects can be severe.

- **Potential long-term effect.** There is no definitive research that tells us what effect—if any—these drugs will have on developing young brains over time.

- **Cost.** These medications, which are designed for daily use, are costly (some even as much as $200 to $300 per month). Insurance coverage for these drugs tends to be variable and is decreasing. This is a long-term issue, and the cost can make drug therapy a prohibitive choice for many families.

- **Dependence.** Children who use medications become dependent on their effects and often can't function without their daily doses.

- **Psychiatric risks.** Antidepressants may increase the risk of suicide or trigger bipolar-type cycling in children. Stimulants may cause depression, agitation, or even sudden cardiac death.

- **Superficial amelioration of the problem.** Drugs treat the symptoms of the core problem. By using them, are we avoiding or delaying getting to the true source of the problem and therefore delaying effective treatment?

■ **Labeling.** Often, a psychiatric drug is chosen according to the clinical diagnosis—the label—that's been given to a child. Labels can seriously impair a child's self-image. They can also narrow our view (as healers and parents) of the child. Most important, in my experience, the labels that children carry are all too often wrong.

First Do No Harm: Using Drugs to Treat Children

Although I'm sharing my ambivalence about using psychiatric medications on kids, I do use them on a daily basis in my practice. If I decide to add drug therapy to my treatment plan, I try to adhere to the following guidelines.

■ Whenever possible, I try less invasive, less risky treatment options first.

■ If I do choose to use drug therapy, I include other treatments that support the overall health of the child.

■ I use the lowest possible dose necessary to reduce symptoms.

■ I try to use medication on a short-term basis whenever possible. I tend to think of these drugs as tools for change rather than as long-term crutches for symptomatic relief. Because children are ever changing, and because many mental and emotional issues resolve themselves as the conditions within and around a child change, I frequently taper the use of medication or give a period of time off so I can reassess the child's state. If she does well without the medication, she stays off it.

■ I engage the child's natural ability to recover. Thoughts are powerful. If a person thinks a treatment will help, it probably will. I capitalize on this phenomenon and gain the trust and respect of the child I'm working with by showing her how much I trust and respect her. This encourages the child to trust her ability to heal and change.

■ I stress to the child that he is not a "label" even though he's being treated with drugs. Labels are for symptoms, not for people, and especially not for children.

HOW WE CAN AVOID LABELS AND DRUGS AND HEAL OUR KIDS

Every day, I see kids who are labeled, and every day, their parents ask me questions like these: "Does Johnny have ADHD?" "I was told Mary has bipolar disorder—will this ruin her life?" "My insurance company will pay for treatment only if Billy's diagnosis fits into one of these five categories. Do any of them fit him?" "My son wants to enlist in the Marines, but they say that since he was diagnosed with bipolar disorder, he can't. Why is this?"

These are important questions, but to my mind, the parents are not asking quite the right ones. Instead, they should be wondering: "Why is my child being labeled with such a serious disorder?" "Why has my child gone from being many things (a son, a student, a friend, an athlete) to being only this?" And finally, "What is keeping my child from enjoying the kind of mental and emotional health that she should have?"

Over the course of my practice, the greatest source of learning and truth about how to heal our children from emotional and mental problems comes not from a diagnostic manual or from a pharmacist but from our children themselves. Our kids, given the chance, can tell us (even in nonverbal ways) what's bothering them. It's our job to listen to them attentively and openly, to resist labeling them, and to work to remove the stressors from their lives that are blocking their mental and emotional health.

CHAPTER 2

How Your Child's Brain Grows

The brain is the most miraculous—and mysterious—organ in the human body. A damp, gray mass of trillions of cells that weighs roughly 3 pounds when fully grown, the brain is quite literally the most vital of all the vital organs, as it controls and regulates all of our bodily functions. Working in concert with the spine, the brain governs the nervous system, which in turn allows us not only to breathe, walk, and talk but also to think and feel. What also sets the brain apart from other organs is that it continues to grow, develop, and change throughout our lifetimes. Each human brain is exquisitely unique, but the most remarkable and least understood brain of all is the brain of a child.

During fetal development, an unborn child's brain undergoes explosive growth, and by the time a baby is born, she has all the brain cells she will ever have. Her brain is bursting with more than 100 billion neural cells (there are more than 1,000 types of neurons, which send and receive electrical signals from all over the body) supported by trillions of glial cells (nonconducting brain cells). These young brain cells are designed to store and

Fascinating Brain Facts: Did You Know?

- A child's brain is the most complex ecosystem in the universe.

- At the peak of fetal brain development, more than 250,000 new nerves are created each *minute.*

- Your child has twice as many brain cells as you do.

- Your child's brain is twice as active as yours.

- Your child's brain has twice the number of interconnections yours has.

- When neurons migrate in a child's brain, they can move up to a few centimeters. This is comparable to traveling the distance between New York and California.

- A single neuron of the human brain can have 10,000 different branches.

- A child's brain may have 1,000 trillion interconnections.

- The human brain at age 5 is more adept at building new synapses (i.e., learning) than at any other time in life.

- More than half of human genes (more than 50,000) are devoted to the child's brain.

- Early brain stimulation increases the number of blood vessels in the brain by 80 percent.

- A college graduate may have 40 percent more neural connections than a high school dropout.

- Trauma may decrease the size of a child's cerebral cortex by 20 percent or more.

- A child's brain needs almost twice the amount of sleep as an adult's brain does.

- Nobody has ever proven that a chemical imbalance exists in a child's brain.

transmit information, and they are poised to become interconnected in ways that will influence and shape her behavior for life.
By birth, many of these neural cells will have already begun to
form crucial early connections, but the newborn brain is far from
fully formed. It will continue to change and grow throughout the
baby's lifetime, with the most dramatic development occurring
during early childhood.

The human brain is the only organ in the body that is designed
to change in response to experience. And it's this dynamic, interactive nature of development that makes it so mysterious and
so difficult to understand. What is most notable about this new
brain is how active, flexible, and resilient—how *adaptable*—it is.

NATURE AND NURTURE: HOW A BRAIN GROWS

It is only within the past 15 years that researchers have come to
understand that the cells in the fetal and infant brain are not
automatically "predestined" to fulfill a particular function. In
the past 10 years alone, scientists have discovered that brain
cells are not as preprogrammed as they once thought. Now we
understand that it is external stimulation that influences which
brain cells will connect to each other and that a child's response
to that stimulation—*his experience*—is much more influential
than genes (biology) in terms of whether or not his brain builds
strong—or weak—neural connections.

Although genetics (the unique DNA coding of each child)
determines the basic quality of the brain cells each child is born
with, it's the stimulation the young brain gets that activates and
directs the cells as they become interconnected. In other words,
the cells that we get by luck of the draw can be thought of as the
bricks and mortar of the brain. The environment (including relationships, nutrition, and other factors) acts as the architect. A
high-quality environment can shore up and strengthen genetic
weaknesses, and similarly, strong genes can help a child better

withstand environmental stress. Brain development, like building a house, is the ongoing interplay of basic material (genes) and shaping (environment).

A child may be born with a brain that has some inherent weaknesses (all of us get a mixed bag in this regard), but these can be fortified by the right kind of environmental stimulation. Similarly, the strong parts of a child's brain may be weakened and damaged by negative stimulation. This is what makes understanding the brain so challenging and exciting: In order to fully understand it, we practitioners—and parents—must embrace a "nature and nurture" model rather than a "nature vs. nurture" model, or we'll miss the true story and be ill-prepared to help our children build the best brains possible.

Each child is born with some crucial brain cells already interconnected and functioning as a system. These key neural connections ensure that at birth, a baby is able to breathe, swallow, and move and that other "automatic" processes (such as organ functioning) are up and running. At first, however, most of the remaining billions of neurons are not yet connected to each other, and the infant brain immediately gets to work in a remarkable series of processes that include the migration, sculpting, pruning, and discarding of cells. These processes serve the purpose of forging the neural connections that will govern and influence that child's behavior for life.

For a newborn child, each moment is a moment of profound learning and absorption. Each piece of stimulation, be it a touch, a taste, a smell, a sliver of light hitting the eye, the sensation of hot or cold, or the cooing sound of a mother's voice, ignites unimaginable activity in the infant brain. Triggered by stimulation, the brain whirs with electrical activity as neurons migrate toward one another and begin to form neural connections, laying down the basic circuitry that the baby will have for life. (The infant brain is so profoundly active that babies need to sleep a full 20 hours a day simply to preserve the metabolic energy

needed for this crucial early development.) The newly interconnected neurons grow and are strengthened by ongoing interaction. As the great neurophysiologist Donald Hebb, PhD, put it,
"Neurons that fire together, wire together." As an infant grows,
the neurons and the resulting synapses that are constantly activated are retained and expand, while those that are not activated wither and fall away.

The pace of infant brain development is feverish: Each year,
the brain grows millions of connections between neurons that
are then tied together with axons and dendrites. Over time,
these neural connections, if used, become stronger and heartier,
branch out, and develop further interconnections (there are trillions of these connections in a healthy brain). These connections
govern all functioning of the body and mind. From birth to
adulthood, the brain actually quadruples in size in response to
this remarkable growth.

During early development, the free neurons that aren't used
during the ongoing construction of this complex architecture of
the mind are discarded. The first part of this process is known
as wiring, or sculpting, which is most rigorous in early childhood
(from birth to roughly age 6); it ebbs and flows and finally slows—
but certainly does not stop—throughout adolescence and into the
early twenties. Indeed, scientists are just beginning to understand (and can see on brain scans) that a second wave of sculpting occurs during adolescence. This new awareness will, I hope,
change the way we view—and treat—our older children when it
comes to mood and behavioral problems.

The second part of the process, known as pruning, is also
crucial since it pares away cells that actually overlap or "clog"
the hearty neural connections that are now in place. Pruning
speaks to the fact that where the human brain is concerned,
if you don't use it, you quite literally lose it. This kind of self-
selectivity between brain cells is a very healthy process, just as
the appropriate pruning of an apple tree encourages it to bear

more fruit. The infant brain comes into the world with far more brain cells than it can ever possibly use. But through the processes of migration, then sculpting, and finally pruning, the chaotic overabundance of brain cells that fill an infant brain gives way to the finely tuned circuitry of the maturing child's brain. This, to my mind, is the most glorious and wondrous process of creation and editing that occurs anywhere on the planet, and it's one that we parents need to intensively support.

What, exactly, influences this massive editing that each child's brain engages in? We now know that both the quality of the relationships an infant enjoys and the environmental influences around her can have a profound effect on the shaping of her brain. That's why it's so crucial that babies be not only loved and nurtured but also brought up in a serene, secure, and safe environment so the building of this precious architecture can take place under the most optimal circumstances.

Recently, researchers have begun to understand just how crucial nutritional influence is for healthy brain growth and development. For instance, they now know that DHA is needed for myelination (development of the fatty layers that sheath and protect nerves and help them transmit information more efficiently). Myelin is crucial to a nerve's function since it speeds up transmission between cells. Without adequate DHA and other nutrients, a baby's nervous system may not develop as well as it could or should, and therefore her brain will not function as well as it should. I'll discuss the nutritional needs of the growing brain in much more depth in Chapter 4.

Environmental factors, such as heavy metals, pesticides, inadequate sunlight, lack of sleep, and others can also harm a child's growing brain, as can a chaotic or unsafe physical environment; I'll address these issues in Chapter 5.

The external factor that most affects the ability of the infant/child brain to grow to its healthiest potential is the quality of the relationships the child enjoys with her primary caregivers. I'll explore this topic in Chapter 6, which is devoted to discussing how parental involvement (or lack thereof) influences a child's mental and emotional health.

The process of sculpting is the aspect of brain building that actually sharpens and strengthens key neural connections and is, in the minds of many experts, the most crucial aspect of brain development.

Neuroscientists (such as Jay Giedd, MD, of the National Institute of Mental Health) are now doing brain imaging that suggests that a child's brain undergoes a second major growth spurt during adolescence that continues into early adulthood. During this time, there is a thickening of the gray matter (the cerebral cortex, or "thinking matter" of the brain), followed by another period of rigorous sculpting. This is also the time when the frontal lobe (the area of the brain just behind the forehead) undergoes very crucial development, and the ability to use forethought and reason is sharpened. (The frontal lobe also allows us to regulate our emotions, and this skill, scientists are finding, is largely acquired after puberty.) This research has potentially far-reaching implications, including giving a scientific explanation for why teens are often not well equipped (literally!) to make adult decisions or to act in their own best interests, since the area of the brain that allows for sophisticated judgment is still under construction at this time. It also explains why teenagers are so often emotionally volatile.

Because of this finding, researchers believe that what a teen does with his brain during this time (such as maintaining close, intimate bonds with his parents; studying classical music; mastering a sport; or lying around playing video games) may have a lasting impact on his brain. The quality of the stimulation a teenage brain receives will, we now know, greatly influence how his neural pathways are further set.

This new information makes the thinking that significant brain development takes place only during the early years obsolete.

We now know that what goes into a child's brain at any time—straight into adulthood—has far-reaching implications. As a child psychiatrist, I find this to be crucial information for parents since it reinforces the fact that parental involvement, rather than dropping off as a child gets older, should—at key times—actually increase in order to ensure that the child and his growing brain are well supported during vulnerable periods of development. It is my great hope that this new brain research will remind us all—parents and practitioners—that our older children need our vigilance and guidance just as much as our younger children do.

STIMULATION: THE KEY TO BRAIN GROWTH

Knowing that a baby's brain can grow and develop only through interaction, it's important that parents understand how stimulation affects the brain. With the right kind of stimulation, the human brain, which begins the extraordinary process of self-assembly and self-organization even before birth, grows optimally. Without enough stimulation (or with the wrong kind), brain development suffers.

The stimulation that most enlivens a child's brain is intimate, loving contact with another human being. This may seem like an obvious statement, but I feel it's important to repeat it because parents today are prone to the aggressive, seductive marketing of products—educational videos, flashcards, CDs, and toys—that are touted as being superior forms of stimulation. These claims are just plain wrong—and harmful to our children. The fact remains that constant, loving, nurturing attention by a devoted adult is the most critical factor for proper brain development, and it is far more important than any "product" meant to stimulate brain development.

One need only remember the thousands of Romanian babies

who were neglected in state-run orphanages in the 1980s and 1990s to get a dramatic glimpse of how devastating a lack of human interaction can be to a child's brain. Many of these orphans were left almost entirely alone for the first years of their lives. They were warehoused in dirty cribs in overcrowded and unclean nurseries and were stimulated by adult interaction only when they were fed or changed. They spent the vast majority of their days in isolation. The brains of these infants were so understimulated that as a population, they have suffered from high rates of brain damage (including language delays, learning disabilities, and emotional and behavioral disorders) that is a direct result of not getting enough physical and emotional stimulation from caregivers during the crucial early days and months of babyhood. A long-term Canadian study of these orphans revealed that those who spent the most time in orphanages experienced more severe attention difficulties (43 percent demonstrated clinical or borderline clinical attention and self-regulatory difficulties at approximately age 12) as compared with those who had shorter stays in orphanages (16 percent) or those who were not orphaned (6 percent). What these findings reveal is that it isn't genetics or personality that determines this kind of risk, it is the lack of stimulation and interaction between a child and a caregiver.

If the quality of stimulation is positive and high (meaning that it's consistent, nurturing, rich, and varied), the neural connections that are formed will be forged in a context of peaceful rigor and will be optimal. If the stimulation is neutral and low (neglectful, inconsistent, or bland), the infant brain will respond just as sluggishly, and the neural connections will be weaker and less abundant than they ought to be. If the stimulation is negative and high (due to outright abuse, severe neglect, severe stress, or trauma), the neural pathways that develop will be tuned and poised to respond to the world as a dangerous place.

In a child who is exposed to unhealthy stimuli, the brain is used to being flooded with stress hormones (such as cortisol) and is constantly on high alert, which makes it much less able to properly absorb and process information and stimulation. The emotional and behavioral paths of children raised in an environment of chronic high stress will be quite fraught—unless there is active, intensive, and early intervention.

REVERSING A BAD START: THE POWER OF PLASTICITY

By now you're beginning to understand how incredibly receptive and also how incredibly vulnerable your child's brain is. The good news is that it is also so malleable—or plastic—that great damage can be undone, and a poor developmental start can be reversed or significantly improved with the right kind of love and stimulation. Researchers are just beginning to gain a full appreciation for this and can now track, by using high-tech imaging, what kind of benefit—or damage—life experience has on a young brain. What they are discovering is often quite surprising: A child's brain may bounce back quickly from a single severe traumatic experience (for example, being involved in a car accident), while its circuitry may be wired for a lifetime of sadness because of the damaging, negative stimulation it received during long-term exposure to a mother with untreated depression.

The growing brain of a child is so malleable that it can actually form long-term tendencies for behavioral and emotional problems, just as it can develop a love of music or a talent for tennis. In this regard, a child's brain is quite literally like a sponge that absorbs—and stores—everything that is put into it. But this is also reversible, as with a sponge: What is stored can also be released, modified, or even let go of if we parents intervene swiftly when we know that something less than healthy is going into it.

Appropriate and timely intervention can be powerfully—and

at times miraculously—corrective. Research has shown that a child's IQ can be raised by as much as 30 points if negative or absent stimulation is replaced with positive, nurturing stimulation. Disadvantaged kids who get rigorous help can escape mental retardation and compensate for severe disabilities (which often have a genetic component) such as dyslexia. It all comes down to our acknowledging that the brain thirsts for positive stimulation the way a flower thirsts for rain. With enough good stimulation, a disadvantaged brain can bounce back, while a healthy brain will continue to grow, flourish, and flower.

Nothing illustrates the power of neuroplasticity as impressively as the way a child's brain responds to the physical trauma of being literally taken apart. Take the case of Rachel, a bright, athletic, and intuitive 11-year-old who, due to her parents' extraordinary care, enjoys remarkable mental and emotional health despite having had a large part of her brain removed when she was just a baby.

Rachel

One day when Rachel was just 9 months old, her older brother found her twitching and writhing uncontrollably in her bassinet, where she was napping. Rachel's mother immediately took her to the doctor, who, sensing that something serious was afoot, referred her to a top pediatric neurologist. It was quickly determined that Rachel had a brain tumor. The only course of treatment was to remove the tumor and much of the gray matter surrounding it. The day Rachel's parents delivered her into the arms of a surgeon, they secretly alternated between two worst-case scenarios: that this would be the last time they would see their daughter alive, or that they would take home a baby who would be severely brain damaged for life. Both fears, however, were unfounded. Although the doctor removed a relatively large tumor and a significant portion of healthy brain matter, Rachel's growth and development weren't altered in any significant or lasting ways. Other than some early language delays (like many extremely bright children, rather than babbling through her second year, Rachel remained largely silent until she began to speak in full sentences and paragraphs), she hit every major developmental milestone right on time. Now she is an outgoing, popular sixth grader who recently took up figure skating with such a vengeance that she's already acquired the skill level of kids who have been training for half a dozen years or more. Rachel knows herself so well that she recently told her parents that they should be ready to home school her since she's certain she'll be traveling to compete one day soon.

Rachel's experience dramatically illustrates how incredibly plastic and adaptive the young brain is. Even children who undergo hemispherectomies (procedures that involve removing half of the brain) exhibit the power of brain plasticity: The remaining hemisphere acquires and accommodates all the functions of the missing hemisphere, and these kids go on to lead normal, productive, healthy lives.

Plasticity is a quality that is most pronounced in the young brain. Performing a hemispherectomy or making any other kind of dramatic physical assault on the architecture of the mature brain is unthinkable: An adult brain simply isn't plastic enough to bounce back after this kind of disruption. A child's brain is.

WINDOWS OF LEARNING

Knowing that the brain grows and develops in response to stimulation, one begins to understand that all interaction between the brain and its environment constitutes, in the most profound sense, the process of learning. The world around the infant brain is quite literally teaching that brain what to become. In a remarkable never-ending interplay of stimulus and response, the brain begins to build itself. Electrical impulses are generated by

Controversial Claims

In the spring of 2006, a children's advocacy group filed a complaint with the Federal Trade Commission (FTC) contending that several of the companies that produce and manufacture "educational" videos are marketing these products without any evidence to support claims that they are beneficial to early brain development. The group wants the FTC to prohibit the companies from making false claims and to include language on the packaging and in the marketing of these products that states the recommendation of the American Academy of Pediatrics that all kids under age 2 should not watch TV or videos.

what the baby takes in via the senses of sight, smell, touch, hearing, and taste, and this electricity activates the neurons and dendrites and sparks the creation of synapses. This is the physical manifestation of learning in the brain.

Although this explosive activity and the connecting of hundreds of thousands of synapses may seem quite disorderly, even chaotic, there is actually rhythm and order to how the young brain acquires information. Because of the way it organizes and processes information, and because of certain peaks in its plasticity, there are critical times during the life span of the human brain when it is more receptive to one kind of learning than another.

Take the development of sight. Doctors used to treat children born with cataracts by waiting until they were a few years old before performing surgery to remove them, believing that it was best to do the procedure when the child was physically more mature. Although the eyes of these youngsters, once free of the clouded lenses, were perfectly normal and healthy, the children remained blind for life. This tragic fact led scientists to understand that early visual stimulation is key to the development of strong neural connections in the visual cortex. They also deduced that there is a clear—and relatively short—window of opportunity during which the brain develops the necessary neural connections for sight. We now know that this takes place most aggressively during the first 2 to 8 months of life.

The brain also has a very clear, albeit much larger, window during which it is most skilled at language acquisition. All children are born with the ability to learn and understand any language on Earth, but we are just now beginning to understand that language acquisition—like all learning for children—is based on social interaction. Babies do have the capacity to effortlessly learn two or more languages at once, but they can learn another language only when it is spoken to them by another person—not when they are plunked down in front of an educational video.

From roughly age 4 to age 10 is the period when children are most receptive to learning a language. (This is also the period when they learn to read music and play an instrument with relative ease, and again, these skills are based on social interaction.)

One indicator of how primed a young brain is to learn a foreign language is the fact that children very rarely have accents when speaking a second or third language. For those of us who don't learn another language until we are well into adolescence or adulthood, however, we are bound to speak it with an accent.

Learning is what drives a child's brain to grow and thrive, and strong emotional connections are crucial for effective learning. A child's brain is so hungry for stimulation and close, attentive interaction that even children who are understimulated during their early years can benefit intensely—and permanently—from even short-term educational intervention. Even relatively serious learning disabilities, when detected early enough, can be overcome with the right kind of restorative, emotionally grounded stimulation.

OPTIMAL WINDOWS OF LEARNING

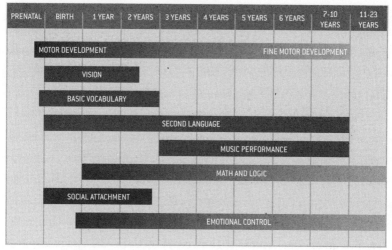

PRENATAL	BIRTH	1 YEAR	2 YEARS	3 YEARS	4 YEARS	5 YEARS	6 YEARS	7-10 YEARS	11-23 YEARS
	MOTOR DEVELOPMENT					FINE MOTOR DEVELOPMENT			
	VISION								
	BASIC VOCABULARY								
	SECOND LANGUAGE								
		MUSIC PERFORMANCE							
	MATH AND LOGIC								
	SOCIAL ATTACHMENT								
	EMOTIONAL CONTROL								

YOUR CHILD'S EMOTIONAL BRAIN

Your child's cognitive brain isn't the only part that is rapidly growing and changing in response to the stimulation it receives; concurrently, his emotional brain is growing and developing as well.

Like learning, emotional development is hardwired into the architecture of the young brain and is the result of a child's interaction with the world around him. Emotions are not (as was previously believed) free-floating aspects of personality or temperament; they are actually biologically based circuits located throughout the brain but largely in the limbic cortex, the brainstem, the amygdala, and the hypothalamus. As the neural circuitry of emotional experience is wired into the young brain, children begin to show a range of emotional expressiveness and experience and begin to develop what we think of as emotional intelligence and maturity.

Researchers used to believe that every newborn starts life with the brain's neural circuitry preset to feel emotional well-being.

Now they are finding that even prenatal stress can have a deleterious effect on a child's emotional wellness. Women who smoke, use drugs, drink, or otherwise ingest toxins during pregnancy stress their babies in ways that undoubtedly affect their emotional (as well as cognitive) brain development. A mother-to-be who is under inordinate emotional stress (a woman in a physically abusive relationship, for example) will give birth to a baby whose largely unformed brain is already drenched in the stress hormone cortisol. And a newborn whose primary caregiver is chronically and seriously depressed (and therefore unable to interact with a child on an appropriately attentive and emotionally intimate basis) will suffer developmentally from this relational stress. The areas of that child's brain that regulate joy, happiness, and curiosity often remain underdeveloped.

A child's brain is most stimulated by healthy close contact and interaction with a loving adult or adults. This social stimulation is especially important to the healthy development of the emotional brain. A child's most powerful emotional experiences take place when she is in contact with another human being (such as while being fed, held, or comforted, or when a toddler is being read to or heartily played with). Because of this, we can think of the emotional brain as also being the social brain.

The emotional experiences of infants are far richer and more sophisticated than we previously thought. Scientists and child psychiatrists once believed that babies came into this world essentially as emotional "clean slates." We are just beginning to understand (thanks in large part to the burgeoning field of pediatric neurobiology) that newborns are capable of experiencing intense feelings, such as sadness (including depression), grief, anxiety, jealousy, and anger, as well as joy, happiness, and empathy. Infants also have a very acute and unique visual capacity; babies as young as 3 months old can identify even scrambled photos of their mothers. They also have relatively sophisticated powers of deduction, the ability to process patterns, and a much larger capacity for memory than we've previously given them credit for.

We often have difficulty understanding an infant's emotional brain because babies have such limited ability to convey their emotional experiences to us. An infant's cry can mean many things—she could be hungry, tired, wet, or just uncomfortable. She may convey positive emotions when she appears serene, such as when she is being held, sung to, or fed. Otherwise, it's up to us caregivers to pay close attention to our infants (to their body language, the quality of their cries, the expressions on their faces) in order to understand the rich and complex emotional lives of even newborns.

During infancy, babies are simply incapable of modulating the expression of their feelings, and they have very limited ability to control their emotions. Babies are already learning important associations between how their caregivers do (or do not) respond to their emotional needs. This interaction strongly influences how each baby's emotional and social brain will develop.

The emotional brains of toddlers and preschoolers are much more sophisticated and complex than those of infants. Young children begin to have the capacity to interpret their personal experiences in relation to how others respond to them. The wiring, sculpting, and pruning—the refinement—of the emotional brain builds on the foundations established during infancy. As a child matures, the range and sophistication of the emotions he experiences and can express increases dramatically. Toddlers and preschoolers also begin to learn the skills of managing their feelings, which all parents know is one of the most challenging tasks of early childhood.

As a child leaves preschool and enters the elementary school years, she has a strong emotional foundation in place, and her emotional brain is well developed and defined. Children of this age are capable of anticipating feelings, talking about them, and observing their own feelings as well as those of others. The range of emotions a school-age child experiences broadens dramatically to include such complex feelings as guilt, embarrassment, pride, and shame, all of which we equate with social functioning.

It's no biological accident that a child's emotional brain matures on pace with the development and acquisition of language: As a child matures, she is able, through language, to express her emotional truth with ever-increasing clarity and understanding. This is when we as parents can experience the delight of seeing our children begin to identify, express, and regulate their own emotional experience. Such self-regulation, as it's called, is the ability to identify and appropriately express emotions; it's a learned skill that develops over time as a child's brain matures. The concept of regulating emotions is very important and will be discussed at length in Chapter 9.

I can't stress enough how important this kind of self-regulation is to strong emotional health in kids. When a child has difficulty managing his feelings, his overall thinking becomes impaired. When his thinking is impaired, learning becomes difficult and relationships become fraught. Without the ability to self-regulate emotions, there's a domino effect, and when the ability to learn falls apart, we see other behavioral and emotional symptoms in our kids.

I can't overstate how important it is to understand that emotional and cognitive brain growth are interrelated; as neural circuits are formed, then strengthened, the interplay between the emotional and cognitive brains becomes quite dynamic, and one fortifies and influences the developing circuitry of the other. For example, an infant who is in a room with his mother exhibits a sense of emotional serenity that allows him to play with others or even learn a new skill. If his mother abruptly leaves the room, the child erupts with upset (because he doesn't yet understand object permanence), his emotions become disregulated, and any play or learning stops. As the child matures, he'll begin to understand that his mother's departure isn't permanent and that whether she is physically present or not, he can enjoy the emotional safety of the relationship and is free to learn away from her. As a child

What a Child Needs for Optimal Brain Development

- **A safe and secure home life.** We all need to feel safe and secure on every level, or we don't learn well. Stress (and trauma) is known to retard brain growth. Children need peaceful, serene, safe homes.

- **Love and touch.** Without touch, love, and connection, children can literally wither and die. Children who are not touched, nurtured, and loved can suffer severe brain disabilities that can cripple them for life. The good news is that these disabilities can be overcome with the right kind of corrective love and nurturing.

- **Proper nutrition.** Research shows that proper nutrition—especially prenatally and during early childhood—is crucial for a growing brain. Feed yourself and your child well, and you will reap the rewards with a child whose brain is well fed and high functioning.

- **A clean environment.** Environmental toxins and pollutants (including noise and light) can really damage a child's brain. Do what you can to eliminate these stressors from your child's life.

- **Stimulation.** Multisensory human contact that's filled with novelty is best for a child. Playing, laughing, and reading with your child is far more effective than plunking him down in front of a video. A child's brain is best activated by interaction with another human being.

- **Strong, stable relationships.** Strong, healthy relationships with parents, siblings, friends, teachers, relatives, and neighbors are the key to mental and emotional health.

grows, his emotional brain becomes ever more connected with his cognitive brain, especially as the place where reasoned decision-making (the frontal cortex) grows and develops.

These are dynamic, exciting times in terms of how rapidly we're gaining awareness of the sophistication and complexity of a child's emotional brain. Pediatricians, neurobiologists, and child psychiatrists are finally beginning to realize that tracking the healthy development of the emotional brain from birth is just as crucial as tracking the development of the cognitive brain. We now see that the emotional brain develops in tandem with the cognitive brain and that the emotional brain also enjoys the benefits of plasticity. We know that early corrective intervention for emotional brain development can have a profoundly positive effect on ensuring a child's emotional health for life.

CHAPTER 3

Relationships and the Young Brain

We humans are intensely social creatures: We need regular, meaningful interaction with others in order to thrive—even survive. This is especially true for the most vulnerable among us, our infants and children, and the relationship that has the most profound impact on any child's development is the one between parent and child.

As I discussed in the preceding chapter, a child's brain grows and develops in response to the quality of stimulation it receives from the world around it. The most potent and influential brain stimulation comes from our relationships, and the relationship between mother and child (or infant and primary caregiver) is the most influential.

MOTHER-CHILD BONDING: THE KEY TO BRAIN DEVELOPMENT

In recent years, visionaries such as Allan Schore, PhD, professor of psychiatry and neurobiology at UCLA Medical Center, have been synthesizing neuroscience, psychology, and biology to create a fuller, more comprehensive model for understanding how relationships affect the developing brain. Dr. Schore points out that the brain undergoes a tremendous growth spurt that starts during the third trimester (in utero) and continues for another 18 to 24 months. This is when the right brain (limbic brain), which is involved in social cognition, attachment, and regulating bodily and affective states, develops the most rapidly. "The human cerebral cortex adds about 70 percent of its final DNA content after birth," he reports, "and this expanding brain is directly influenced by early environmental enrichment and social experiences." Recent PET scans have confirmed Dr. Schore's belief, as we now know that the right brain (the seat of the emotions and social skills) is predominant during infancy and through the third year of life.

This means that a baby comes into the world with a brain that's literally bursting with potential but is largely unformed. A child is also born with only the most tenuous kind of attachment to other humans. When she leaves the womb, she is compelled to seek out the attention of the one person who has thus far cared for her—her mother. This primal urge is hardwired into the brain of a newborn, since she must immediately bond with a caretaker in order to survive. Not only does bonding with her mother or another loving caregiver ensure the infant's physical survival, but it's essential for emotional, psychological, cognitive, and neurological development as well.

New parents hear a lot of buzzwords, such as *bonding, mirroring,* and *attachment.* But what do these words really mean? How crucial are they to the emotional and mental health of our children? Great theorists, such as John Bowlby, MD; Heinz Kohut, MD; and others, have always intuitively understood that a close, connected relationship with a primary caregiver is crucial to psychological health. Now researchers and scientists are validating these theorists in ways that will change the way we think about parenting forever by demonstrating that our earliest relationships—especially the primary one—directly influence the wiring and development of the brain.

Bonding, mirroring, attachment, and other words that are used to describe the quality of interaction between parent and child all reflect one crucial factor: the quality of *attunement* between the two.

Attunement

I like to use the word *attunement* to describe the engaged inter-play that takes place between parent and child because it con-veys a singularity of focus and an *active awareness* on the part of the participants that other words just don't convey. Being in attunement means being present, being open, and being fully in the moment. It's the opposite of being distracted, worried, stressed, or "tuned out." Being attuned with your child means being in harmony with him. It's the state of being gracefully in sync with each other.

When there is healthy attunement between a parent and an infant, then mirroring (the reflecting back of experience from one person to another) and bonding (the formation of relation-ship) can take place. When a parent and a child begin to bond, they are also forming an attachment. None of this healthy relat-ing, however, can take place without authentic attunement between them. Without this quality, true mirroring can't hap-pen, and bonding and attachment will be, to varying degrees, weak. When there is weak attachment, a child often grows up with an impaired ability to express or control his emotions or form healthy attachments to others. Many of the kids I treat on a day-to-day basis have problems that reflect impaired attach-ment of one kind or another.

The Mirroring-Bonding-Attachment Continuum

When a baby is born, his brain is in many ways like a vast, complex jigsaw puzzle that's waiting to be put together. The infant brain begins to organize when it's in relationship with an attuned, attentive caregiver, someone who is able to accurately mirror back to the infant his nascent human experience. Mirroring is quite literally a parent reflecting back to a child that child's experience. When a child cries, a parent mirrors awareness of the upset by mimicking his grimace. An attuned parent picks him up and employs all available senses in an effort to "read" the baby's signals and fulfill his needs (feed him, cuddle him, speak to him, hear him—*understand and validate* him). Daniel Siegel, MD, medical director of infant and preschool services at UCLA, describes attunement as taking place when "the infant feels felt." In other words, his current state must be constantly validated by someone else in order for his brain to organize and formulate healthy neuronal connections.

In a very profound sense, the mother (or primary caregiver) actually serves as an auxiliary, external brain for her infant in that she mirrors back what the child is experiencing. In a very concrete way, the maternal brain feeds vital information about the "self" to the infant brain.

The concept of mirroring recently took on more-tangible meaning when researchers discovered that children with autism, who have a profound lack of social attunement, actually have abnormal "mirror" neurons in their right brains. This means that no matter how attuned a mother may be, the mirroring capability of a child with autism is actually distorted, and his brain can't engage in the mirroring exchange in a functioning way.

Most children, fortunately, don't have the genetic weaknesses (such as abnormal mirror neurons) that lead to conditions such as autism, but their brains are adversely affected when there is a lack of proper bonding and mirroring—when there is a lack of attunement from a primary caregiver.

Researchers have even been able to "see" the physical impact a lack of attunement has on an infant brain by using EEG (brain wave) scans on adolescents who have experienced some form of abuse. (Seventy-two percent who had been subjected to serious physical/sexual abuse had abnormal EEGs, compared with only 27 percent of those with no known abuse.)

Depressed Moms

The quality of the maternal-child bond has enormous influence on a child's mental health. If a mom is emotionally unavailable because of depression, her child suffers enormously. A recent study headed by Myrna Weissman, MD, at Columbia University documented the essential nature of this connection.

In this study, the children of depressed mothers were monitored throughout the mothers' treatment. The first notable observation from Dr. Weissman was that "children of depressed parents have high rates of anxiety and disruptive and depressive disorders that begin early, often continue into adulthood, and are impairing." In short, children who are deprived of the maternal connection often become symptomatic themselves and are given psychiatric labels.

Researchers also found that kids of moms with improved depression showed marked reductions in their symptoms. A full third of the labeled kids lost their labels when their moms got better. On the other hand, if their moms didn't get better, almost a fifth of these kids gained labels during the course of the study. This relational connection between depression and other labels indicates clearly that this isn't a genetic issue but rather a social one. Indeed, in my practice, the majority of kids I see with severe behavioral problems have depressed mothers.

Other studies show that infants who have depressed mothers also have abnormal EEG results that indicate asymmetry in the right frontal lobe. (At 3 months, 12 out of 17 infants showed this right-brain asymmetry, compared with only 2 out of 15 infants with nondepressed mothers.) This concerns researchers such as Dr. Siegel, who understand that "repeated experiences of certain states can result in their becoming traits." In other words, an infant who is mirrored by a depressed mother will absorb faulty information about himself since the maternal depression colors her perceptions of the world around her. This child's limbic brain will absorb what the "depressed" mirror reflects back to him.

This research helps us to understand that mirroring works both ways: Not only do we mirror back to our children what we see in them, but they also absorb and "wire in" what they see in us. If a parent is joyful or depressed, angry or forgiving, relaxed or tense, this information will be wired into a young child's brain.

It's important to keep in mind that no parent can be perfectly attuned with a child 100 percent of the time. In fact, brief periods of misattunement, which end when a caregiver steps in and responds appropriately, can actually foster the development of trust, self-regulation, and resilience in the child, since she will learn that times of intermittent stress can be overcome and that these cycles are natural. In fact, researchers now believe healthy cycling of misattunement/reattunement may be crucial to building a foundation of empathy in a child.

WHY HEALTHY ATTACHMENT IS CRUCIAL FOR EMOTIONAL AND MENTAL HEALTH

No word is more bandied about than *attachment* when it comes to parenting, and it's often hard for parents to get a grasp on exactly what it means, since it means different things to different people, including experts.

In its most basic sense, attachment is the capacity to form and maintain healthy relationships. From a behavioral standpoint, attachment protects a child from fear and harm, allowing him to safely explore the world around him. From an emotional perspective, attachment is the creation of a mutually loving bond. All of us are born with the need to attach to and bond with others, and we learn this skill in our first primary relationship (typically, mother-child). Newborn babies are, once the umbilical cord is cut, essentially "unattached." They are dependent on the adults around them for their very survival. A newborn's primal need to be cared for is what establishes and drives the core relational bond that will serve as a template of attachment for life. A baby's sense of attachment develops on many levels as she is fed, bathed, played with, smiled at, cooed to, and so forth. Every moment of engagement with another sparks her brain to develop specific neural connections, so while she is becoming attached socially and emotionally, her brain is becoming more solidly wired and formed, too.

One of the reasons mirroring, bonding, and the resulting attachment are so important is that an infant who is well nurtured is also relatively free of stress. Healthy attachment means not just a healthy baby but also a happy one. Researchers know that the attuned gaze of a loving mother does more than just soothe an infant's distress; it activates the release of brain-nourishing chemicals (neurotrophins), which are necessary for synaptogenesis (the creation of brain synapses, needed for the transmission of information between neurons). A happily attached baby's brain is busily wiring for health, whereas the brain of a poorly attached child is flooded with stress hormones (and deprived of neurotrophins), and his brain development is invariably impaired.

When a baby breaks into a smile, it's pretty nearly impossible to resist smiling back. Researchers can now monitor the effect that loving, joyful, and even playful bonding experiences have on a baby. Just as brain scans show that babies with depressed mothers tend to "absorb" maternal depression, research also shows that babies' brains are "sparked up" by shared laughter, shared smiles, and shared play. The parts of the brain associated with pleasure are closely connected to those associated with relationships; where there are strong emotional bonds, there is greater potential for joy and pleasure. When healthy attachment is being forged, mother and child are in step with each other, and the good feelings of this harmonious relationship show: A delighted, well-attached baby develops a robust brain that is primed to learn, share, explore, and enjoy life.

When Attachment Goes Awry

Just as our height and weight are expressions of the interplay of our genes with our environment, our ability to attach with others exists on a continuum and is not static. Our ability to form attachment bonds also matures as our brains do, and if we enjoy healthy attachments early in life, we are likely to enjoy a wide variety of sophisticated and varied emotional relationships throughout a lifetime.

Healthy attachment is built over time as one positive bonding experience is layered onto the next. When there are disruptions in this building process, an infant's biological and emotional foundation often becomes fragile or weak. This weakness leads to problems in establishing healthy relationships in the future. The window of opportunity during which bonding and the formation of a strong attachment is most crucial is during the first 2 years of life, when the growth and development of the brain is greatest. Given that a child's brain reaches 90 percent of its adult size by age 3, many experts contend that the earliest bonding experiences (especially those during the first year of life) are the most crucial. Children who suffer severe neglect during this first year may be unable to establish close, meaningful relationships for the rest of their lives.

No one knows for sure if remedial attachment experiences can make up for this kind of neglect, but we do know that repairing this severe damage can be a long, difficult, and frustrating experience for caregivers and children. Here's an example of how difficult it can be for a child to recover from poor attachment.

Kip

Kip was mandated into a full-time residential treatment facility when he was just 5 years old, after he nearly killed a kitten by dropping it out of a second-story window. Kip, who had exhibited very violent and antisocial behavior from a young age, had a severe form of attachment disorder. He was born to a 15-year-old, Lisa, who had run away from home to live with her older drug-dealer boyfriend, who was Kip's father. The father was stoned much of the time and was physically abusive. When Kip was 3, Lisa fled with him to a homeless shelter. A year later, they were living in a halfway house, where Lisa was successfully treated for her drug problem. Next, they moved into their own apartment, and Lisa, then 18, worked full-time during the day at a discount store and studied at night for her GED.

Kip had been attending a kindergarten for special needs kids (his conduct and behavioral issues were extreme and had been identified immediately), but he was unable to be in a group of children without constantly harassing them and even harming them. The school authorities had told Lisa that Kip would not be able to stay, and then he hurt the kitten. Lisa did the right thing and called social services, and Kip was removed from her care and brought to our center.

Treating a child like Kip is a long-term proposition that takes a tremendous amount of skill, patience, and commitment. Fortunately for us, Lisa—despite how violent her life with Kip had been—was utterly committed to learning how to parent him better and to do the hard work to help us repair the terrible damage done during those crucial early years.

Kip's early life was riddled with neglect (he was often left in a dirty diaper for hours when Lisa was on a drug binge or out selling drugs with her boyfriend) and abuse (his father slapped him when he cried, even as an infant). These earliest traumatic experiences wired Kip's brain to believe that his needs would not be met, that the world was unsafe, and that there was no one he could count on to care for him. With children who are this severely abused, it isn't uncommon to see violent antisocial behavior. In a perverse way, it makes sense: These kids excel at keeping warmth, compassion, and tenderness at bay in order to feel and experience at least a degree of control in their lives. In essence, they re-create the trauma of neglect by engaging in actions that will ensure that others will continue to steer clear of them.

For Kip to begin to heal, it was essential that we provide him with a safe, predictable, and therapeutic environment. We worked on his nutrition, made sure that he got adequate rest (which was a huge struggle because he had never had a set bedtime), and provided highly structured days that were full of therapeutic and educational programs. The heart of our treatment plan was addressing the severe trauma he had endured, so we employed a number of noninvasive techniques to address this, including EMDR (eye movement desensitization and reprocessing) therapy, play therapy, and art therapy. Slowly, Kip's brain began to show signs of moving past a state of high alert and trauma, and his terribly fragile personality began to emerge. We also worked closely with Lisa to educate her about how the years of neglect and abuse had damaged Kip (she was also involved in her own intensive trauma recovery work at our center) and to teach her the basic parenting skills she needed in order to continue to parent Kip toward recovery once he left our center.

Kip was with us for a full year. When he left, he was no longer an out-of-control, violent boy, though he still had many deficits in terms of being able to regulate his behavior appropriately. But he was able to go home with Lisa, who now had a good job as an office assistant with regular 9-to-5 hours. They both continued several aftercare programs at our center and would stay in treatment indefinitely. Kip was also able to begin school again. He entered a kindergarten program at an alternative school that specialized in treating badly abused kids, where he could continue to repair his attachment issues in an environment that was sensitive to his needs.

Kip has a long road ahead of him, and chances are that he'll have some degree of difficulty in establishing and maintaining healthy relationships, given how damaging his earliest attachment experiences were. But with appropriate ongoing treatment, he has the potential to live a life of peace rather than violence and to find a meaningful place for himself in the world.

Reversing Insecure Attachment

There are, in the most basic terms, two types of attachments: those that are secure and those that are insecure. In very recent years, experts have even identified an extremely rare "non-attached" bond, which afflicts children who lacked any consistent caregiving at all. The majority of kids (generally estimated to be 55 percent) in this country enjoy secure attachment bonds. The remaining kids (roughly 45 percent) have varying levels of emotional and behavioral problems, depending on the severity of their attachment impairment. I see children with mild attachment issues who suffer from low-grade social anxiety and a tendency to be loners. I also treat children with significantly insecure attachments who have aggressive, even violent tendencies due to a deficit in empathy. The following table contains a quick snapshot of the differences between securely and insecurely attached kids.

Securely Attached Children	Insecurely Attached Children
Have a strong sense of self	Feel unsure of self and insecure in many settings
Have a strong sense of safety and security	Feel apprehensive and frequently ill at ease
Are able to take advantage of life opportunities	Often feel victimized by life and are passive
Are better liked by their peers	Are often disliked because of hostile, aggressive behavior or insensitivity to others
Have superior leadership and social skills	Are followers
Are more confident	Are insecure and lack self-esteem
Have strong conflict management skills	Are more prone to blaming or moving to physical or verbal aggression
Cope with stress better	Often "melt down" or withdraw when stressed
Have higher levels of empathy, compassion, and social conscience	Are more likely to be selfish, disconnected, and antisocial
Are far less likely to be labeled and medicated	Are frequently labeled and medicated

Groundbreaking research underscores how attachment bonds affect long-term emotional and mental health. One longitudinal study (which follows participants over a period of time) conducted at the University of Minnesota shows that a child's early attachment history has a greater influence on school performance, psychopathology, and conduct and behavioral problems than factors such as temperament or later family and peer relationships. In a stunning illustration of the strength of this influence, researchers were able to identify kids who would later drop out of high school with 77 percent accuracy, based solely on their attachment histories up to age 3. Interestingly, this research also indicates that the child-father attachment history tends to predict social (external) behaviors, while the child-mother attachment history predicts internal (self-identity) behaviors.

Despite a child's type of attachment history, all attachment bonds are dynamic, so a poor attachment history doesn't necessarily mean that a child will always be incapable of making strong bonds later in life. The trick—as with all factors that influence brain growth and wiring—is to intervene as early and intensively as possible. Here are some ways you can ensure a secure attachment (or repair a tenuous one) with your baby or older child.

The Harvard Mastery of Stress Study

This fascinating and valuable study followed a group of Harvard students for more than 35 years. What the researchers found surprised everyone: The best predictor of health in middle age was not smoking, age, marital status, or family history. Instead, it related to how the students rated their parent-child relationships. Of those who rated these relationships as cold and distant, 87 percent had severe chronic illnesses such as heart disease, ulcers, or alcoholism. On the other hand, only 25 percent of students who rated their parent-child relationships as close and caring developed significant illnesses.

The relationship between mother and child was only slightly more significant than the father-child connection. If one parent-child relationship was close and one was distant, the results were midway between the two extremes above. Nothing is more important to our emotional and mental health and overall well-being than experiencing a close, loving, supportive relationship with our parents during childhood.

- Hold, cuddle, and caress your child often.

- Make frequent direct eye contact.

- Indicate your delight in your child's presence; smile often.

- Be consistently sensitive and responsive to his needs and feelings.

- Provide a safe, secure, and predictable environment.

- Don't judge, negate, or minimize your child's emotional experience; don't say things like "You don't have to cry about that" or "That didn't hurt."

- Speak in warm, respectful tones at all times.

- Seek help if you or another caregiver is unavailable (depressed, anxious, addicted).

Remember, children who enjoy secure attachments with their primary caregiver(s) feel loved, safe, and happy.

Establishing healthy attachment is a mutual process. In order to understand this dynamic, it's helpful to understand what inherent traits a child has that may influence this relationship. Key among them is temperament. You may be surprised by how strongly this characteristic influences the quality of the parent-child bond.

TEMPERAMENT: SAME GENES, DIFFERENT PERSON

Once a child is conceived, long before she is even born, she is blessed with a unique temperament, personality, and budding point of view that are absolutely different from anyone else's. Many parents, though, are unaware of this or deny it, and they make the mistake of thinking that a child's innate temperament can be either shaped or changed. I would argue that one of the core jobs parents have is to nurture and support this unique individual—even if it means that we have to put aside our own expectations about who she is. In other words, the hardest—and truly most important—job we parents have is to resist the urge to label our children and instead see and accept them for who they are.

I've often heard parents say that the person they just sent off to college is basically the same person they met on the day of birth (or adoption or assuming custodial rights). Whenever I hear this, I relax, knowing these people have been blessed with "clear parental sight." If I were to sit down with these happy parents (and their happy college-bound child), I would probably hear that the level of intimacy and mutual acceptance that they now enjoy was hard-won, that over the years, the parents had to work to maintain a clear sense of who their child was. They constantly had to check their own biases, expectations, and issues at the door and stay aware of their child's individuality. In order to do this well, a parent must first and foremost identify and accept a child's innate temperament.

The word *temperament* refers to the cluster of inborn traits and coping skills with which we all come into the world. Because I know that temperament is a biological trait, like hair or eye color, I find it fascinating that the word *temperamental* is so badly misused (and misunderstood) in our culture. This term should be free of any specific connotation, but instead it has become a negative, judgmental label that's often affixed to kids who are spirited, sensitive, or simply blessed with a wide array of emotional and stylistic responses to life. This outlook is a shame, and it makes my work more challenging than it should be. The truth is, we are all temperamental; that's what makes us human, and it's what makes each one of us so valuable and unique.

In the 1950s, two researchers, Stella Chess, MD, and Alexander Thomas, MD, identified nine basic, broad traits of temperament in order to provide a meaningful framework around which we could develop a compassionate understanding of childhood temperament. While there are many variations, these are the nine basic traits.

Activity level: A child's basic "speed" (sluggish and supercharged are extremes)

Distractibility: How easily a child turns away from an uninteresting activity (such as listening to Mom instead of the TV)

Intensity: The quality (positive or negative) of the response to any new situation (is there a slight frown or a full-blown reaction with tears?)

Regularity: How regular a child is in regard to biological functions, such as eating and sleeping

Sensory threshold: How sensitive a child is (or isn't) to physical stimuli

Approach/withdrawal: How a child handles new situations

Adaptability: How a child handles change (even switching from one activity to another)

Persistence: How long a child will stay engaged in an activity despite obstacles

Mood: Whether a child tends to react generally to the world in a positive or negative way

Each child has a particular style in regard to each of these basic traits. You may find that your baby is so energetic (high activity level) that you are run ragged just trying to keep up. You may find yourself with a child who is quite sensitive to loud noises or strong smells (low sensory threshold) in ways that throw you. You may find that you think of your child as being "shy" simply because she's quite sensitive to change (sensitive to approach/withdrawal). Whatever the case, this is your child's temperament, and it has been genetically determined and is basically "set" for life. What isn't fixed, however, is how you (and others) relate to these traits. By parenting in attunement with the true temperamental style of your child, you will be much more likely to develop a secure attachment, and you'll also help "quiet" certain traits that may make it difficult for her to form other strong bonds in life. When you're in sync with your child's temperament, she will flourish.

Much debate centers on how much an infant's temperament influences the quality of the attachment he forms with his parents. Many experts have speculated that a child with a "difficult" temperament is more prone to establishing an insecure attachment with a parent than a child with an "easy" temperament. Compelling new evidence, however, contradicts this viewpoint and indicates that the quality of the *parental* temperament determines the type of attachment (secure or insecure), and the child's temperament plays a secondary role. Knowing that parental temperament can make or break an attachment is huge news and should, once and for all, end the absurd notion that our children (and their brains) are somehow "to blame" when healthy attachment isn't attained. I know from my own experience that when children have attachment issues, I need only look to the primary caregiving relationship to understand why.

Knowing that temperament is biological and not caused by mood or choice, it's important to remind yourself that your child isn't the only one in this relationship who has a temperament— you have one, too. I find that parents who are unaware of their own temperaments and their own unmet needs have difficulty being available for optimal bonding and attachment with their children. These parents tend to blame their babies and children for any and all difficulties in the relationship, which puts the children in a terrible double bind, since they are now labeled and also in the care of someone who cannot provide unconditional nurturance and support.

Temperamental Compassion and Good "Fit"

When we have a realistic (and nonjudgmental) understanding of our own temperaments and those of our children, we can work to establish secure parent-child attachments. Once this attachment is in place, we are available to work on a more superficial but no less important aspect of the relationship—the quality of "fit."

Fit is the dynamic interplay of temperament, environment, and other factors that influence and challenge the parent-child bond. Good fit occurs when two people with two different styles and personalities interact with each other with compassion, understanding, respect, and love and so enjoy a mutually satisfying relationship. When there is unconditional love and acceptance in the parent-child relationship, there is usually healthy alignment and good fit. When unmet parental needs and expectations or other issues (such as family stress and maternal depression) get in the way, fit can be compromised. I treat many, many children, such as Stephanie, whose emotional and behavioral problems are due to poor fit.

Stephanie

After all my colleagues and I had heard about Stephanie, we were prepared for the worst. She and her mother argued constantly, and recently their conflicts had escalated in frightening ways. One night Stephanie even grabbed a butcher knife and held it aloft while she screamed at her mother in a threatening manner. The police were called, and Stephanie was soon enrolled in our day treatment program.

Stephanie was a stocky, tough 15-year-old who preferred to hang out with guys rather than girls. She played sports and did stats for the boys' football team and was an average student whose grades had recently begun to slip. Stephanie is also adopted.

Over the previous 3 years, Steph (as her mother, Marsha, calls her) had been in outpatient therapy since being diagnosed by a social worker as having an attachment disorder related to her adoption. The talk therapy seemed to help her at first, but then things at home got worse. Her mother took her to a psychiatrist, who diagnosed a mood disorder and put her on medication. Steph quickly gained 20 pounds, and her behavior continued to deteriorate. Within months of starting the medication, she had the episode that brought her to our center.

After I got to know Steph a bit, it became clear to me that she was willful and somewhat stubborn, but she was also energetic, playful, and very social. I got the sense that her recent antisocial, nearly violent behavior was anomalous and that she was not really suffering from an attachment disorder. I knew that I'd get a better sense of what was truly going on when I had the chance to get to know her mother and father.

Marsha was a well-spoken woman who knew what she wanted. She was a high school English teacher, and I felt that I would have struggled in her class, given how demanding she seemed. I had a very strong stress reaction to Marsha, and this gave me insight as to what Steph might be experiencing at home.

When I spoke on the phone with Tom, Steph's dad, he struck me as having a very different style and demeanor than Marsha. "Steph is a great kid. She's a handful for sure, but she's also a lot of fun. I don't know why she and Marsha have always struggled. I do pretty well with her myself; though she does give me some resistance from time to time, we always seem to be able to work it out. Marsha and Steph, on the other hand, . . ." He paused. "Their relationship is like fire and gasoline: When Steph doesn't toe the line, Marsha cracks down pretty hard, and this sends Steph through the roof."

After this conversation, I invited Marsha and Tom to join me and Stephanie for family therapy. We began to meet three times a week, and our sessions were often volatile. I got to see how Marsha and Steph were pulled into a dance that brought out their worst qualities and over which neither seemed to have much control.

Parent-Child Fit: A New Kind of Pressure

When I track the trends I've seen over my 25 years in practice, one is particularly notable, and that's an increase in problems related to fit in families. I've given a lot of thought to this issue, and it seems to me that families have become smaller and more isolated, and members are more disconnected from one another. Kids often don't know their grandparents, uncles, aunts, cousins, or other relatives, and this puts even more pressure on the already central issue of parent-child fit.

In the past, a child who didn't have a good fit with a parent often enjoyed good fit in relationships with other adult relatives. (Think of the child who could go to his grandmother and say, "Mom just doesn't understand," and Grandmother would listen respectfully and attentively.) In today's world, we expect the parent-child fit to be flawless, and this puts a great burden on both child and parent. When there is a larger familial network of relationships available to the parent and child who have issues with fit, these secondary relationships often provide the kind of attachment and support needed, as well as some necessary "breathing room" between parent and child.

Over the years, I've seen the issue of fit take on such high significance that it causes a lot of stress and suffering. The truth is, living in a small, isolated nuclear family is tough, and it puts an incredible (and often unrealistic) burden on both parent and child to get along well, even when they may be really different in terms of style and temperament. Where fit is concerned, having access to other strong relationships benefits both parent and child and can provide the "glue" needed to make fit possible.

Steph began to make progress at our center, but at home on the evenings and weekends, her issues with Marsha continued. Finally, Marsha grew so frustrated that she decided to visit her sister in Oklahoma for 2 weeks. With Marsha gone—even for this brief time—Steph became a different person. She relaxed and became less irritable, and for the first time, a soft side of her emerged. I finally understood why Tom enjoyed his daughter so much. I also understood that Steph did not have an attachment disorder; instead, she had a terrible fit with her mother. Once we had identified the problem, I felt it would be interesting to see how things went with Marsha when she returned.

Over the next 2 weeks, we worked to help Steph understand that she and her mother were just radically different people with very different temperaments and styles. We didn't blame or point any fingers; instead we helped Steph to own (without judgment) her own tendencies to be willful, stubborn, and resistant. When Marsha returned, we worked to help her get a better handle on who Steph was and to understand and manage her own temperament. (We knew we were making good progress when Marsha was able to laugh at her own perfectionism.) Both mother and daughter began to see how they unconsciously pushed each other's buttons and brought out the worst in each other simply because they were not aware of their own—or each other's—temperament.

We used role playing to help them detach from this unconscious "dance" and work on alternative ways of relating to each other. We also helped them to understand and better cope with each other's style. We worked with them to develop more "temperamental" compassion and understanding and to strive to be more patient and less reactive with each other. By the time Steph left our program after 8 weeks, she and her mother were enjoying a much better fit, and Steph was off all medication. Even better, she was no longer being labeled as the defiant child. Now she was just Steph.

I saw Steph and Marsha one last time 3 years later, just before Steph was to start college. They wanted me to know how well they had been doing over the past several years, how much they had grown to enjoy each other, and how close they had become. They were even able to joke about the past in ways that assured me that they were now truly enjoying a good fit.

Establishing a secure attachment and working to have a relatively good fit are big, important parenting goals. Attaining them can enhance a parent-child relationship immeasurably and establish a lifetime of emotional and mental health for your child.

CHAPTER 4

Feeding Your Child's Brain for Emotional and Mental Health

In order to ensure that your child's brain is able to function well, optimally process stimulation, and grow, you must first ensure that it is being properly nourished. A sound diet can make the difference between having a child who thrives and one who is erroneously labeled and medicated.

Poor diet is without a doubt one of the major reasons we're seeing such an incredible spike in the number of kids diagnosed with and medicated for mental and emotional disorders. Even drugs can't help our kids when they are quite literally being starved of their mental and emotional health. This is especially ironic today, given that our kids are encouraged to overeat in this age of "super-size" portions. Unfortunately, much of their diet is nutritionally bankrupt, unhealthy processed food.

It's time we took a good hard look at their diets, even if our children don't show outward signs of poor nutrition, such as obesity. Given that there are fast-food restaurants on every street corner and soda machines in the hallways of our schools, it takes a lot of work to successfully monitor what goes into our children's mouths, but the effort will pay off in ways that most parents aren't fully aware of. If we believe that we are what we eat (and I do), then it makes sense that the food we take in might affect our moods or behaviors. Thankfully, I'm not alone in this belief; more and more medical researchers, child psychiatrists, pediatricians, and general health practitioners now examine in earnest how food and nutrition affect a child's mental and emotional health.

When a child comes to me labeled with a disorder such as ADHD, depression, or any other kind of mood or behavioral "illness," I immediately assess his diet for key nutritional deficiencies. If the child is being overfed, I look to see if his diet is overstocked with foods that are nutrient poor.

What exactly is the right kind of diet for the growing American child? The USDA periodically updates its Food Pyramid, which many of us rely on (though only 1 percent of the US population actually meets these criteria) as a rudimentary guideline for feeding our kids. But I've found that even following the USDA recommendations religiously doesn't provide enough vital nutrition for the growing brain of a child. It's all well and good to advocate that our children be given a certain number of servings of vegetables, fruit, protein, or fat per day, but how successful are we in actually achieving this? Or, more important, if we were to achieve this, would it truly be enough? Through my practice, I've learned that the answer to the second question is no. The USDA recommendations for adequate daily food allowances are too broad and too weak. Our children need and deserve diets that are more aggressively focused on meeting their basic nutritional needs—especially the nutritional needs of their growing brains.

FEEDING THE BRAIN: THE VERY BEGINNING

The human brain is an extraordinary organ, particularly because it is so undeveloped at birth. The brain grows so rapidly and dramatically that it makes sense that it has particular nutritional needs. The rudimentary wiring of the nervous system and brain is laid down very early in the gestation of an embryo, and during the third trimester of pregnancy, the fetal brain experiences explosive growth. That's why it's important that expectant mothers get adequate nutrition: What the mother provides the growing fetus lays the foundation for brain health for life. But this prenatal commitment to nutritional parenting is only the beginning. Parents also have to be committed throughout the years of childhood, which, as brain researchers are just now discovering, extends well beyond adolescence and into the early twenties.

The Six Key Nutrients for Brain Growth

When we refer to nutrients, we're talking basically about six things: water, protein, energy (fat and carbohydrates), vitamins (fat- and water-soluble), minerals, and trace elements (which also happen to be minerals but which are needed in very tiny amounts). The first three—water, protein and energy—are considered macronutrients because we need them in large quantities. The last three—vitamins, minerals, and trace elements—are considered micronutrients because, although they're vital, we need them in much smaller amounts.

We know that certain nutrients are crucial to the building of the nervous system and the development of a healthy brain. We know that all nutrients are needed for neuronal cell growth and development. That's why expectant mothers are encouraged to take prenatal vitamins. Deficiencies of certain nutrients during pregnancy may have more profound and easily identifiable effects on brain development and function than deficiencies of others, but many of these conditions can be improved with the right kind of supplementation.

■ A deficiency of protein may affect IQ, verbal ability, and spatial ability.

■ A lack of iron may reduce the transport of blood and oxygen to the brain and muscles and may contribute to low birth weight. Low iron is also implicated in cognitive impairments in children. Also, a recent study found a link between iron deficiency and symptoms of ADHD.

■ A deficiency of folate (folic acid) can cause serious neural tube defects, such as spina bifida.

■ A lack of vitamin A may cause blindness or visual impairment.

■ A lack of iodine (necessary for thyroid function) may cause mental, neurological, and physical retardation.

■ A lack of manganese can cause fetal malformations, such as neural tube defects.

Water

We, like Earth, are largely made up of this nutrient. In fact, the human body is roughly 60 to 70 percent water. Without water, we simply cannot exist. In fact, we can live a lot longer without food than we can without water (indeed, much of the food we eat has high water content). Our blood is mostly water, and we need water to regulate body temperature and to serve as a conduit by which nutrients can flow through our bodies, including into our brains. Water also transports oxygen, removes wastes, and cushions our joints and organs.

Protein

This nutrient is essential to the structure and function of all living cells. Protein is one of the nutrients that provide calories (energy) for the body. It's essential in the diet of all animals for the growth and repair of tissue and in the construction of many parts of the body, including muscle, bone, skin, and blood. Protein can be most readily obtained from meat, fish, poultry, eggs, dairy products, legumes (beans), nuts, and tofu (soy).

- A deficiency of vitamin B_6 may contribute to seizures and, new evidence suggests, to depression.

- A shortage of zinc can disrupt proper fetal growth and has been linked to low birth weight. In a young child, zinc is crucial for proper brain development. In adults, low zinc status has been linked to mental problems such as depression, nervousness, and anorexia nervosa.

Knowing that poor nutritional support for a growing fetus can have a very serious impact on brain development helps expectant mothers understand why getting adequate daily doses of these nutrients is so vital. But good prenatal nutritional support is just the beginning of establishing and ensuring your child's brain health. This is especially true given that the brain does most of its growing after birth.

For Brain Health, Think Healthy Fats

We know that the brain is made up of 60 percent fat, so it makes sense that nutritionally, we need to take in a fair amount of fat in order to nourish our brains. In fact, one can argue that fats are the most crucial nutrient for brain health.

(continued on page 74)

Energy (Fats and Carbohydrates)

I prefer to group fats and carbohydrates together under the banner of the nutrient energy because both are so completely misunderstood by today's consumer. Today's American diet—especially that of our kids—is a mess when it comes to fats and carbohydrates. We're all eating way too many of the wrong kinds of both nutrients. The fact of the matter is that we need both in our diets. The trick is to get them in the right form and, in particular, to take in those that we need for optimal brain health.

Essential Fats

We need fat because it makes up our primary fuel reserve, it's part of every cell membrane in the body, and it cushions our organs. But most fats found in food (especially highly processed and "refined" foods) are not essential, and we can banish most of them from our diets because they either are a source of empty calories or are downright harmful.

The fats we can't live without are the EFAs, or essential fatty acids—the key fats that the body can't produce on its own. These are the polyunsaturated fats, which fall into three main categories: omega-3s, omega-6s, and omega-9s. (The other three kinds of dietary fat, which are nonessential, are saturated fat, monounsaturated fat, and trans fat.)

The EFAs are the most important to us because they are involved in the proper functioning of every cell, tissue, and organ in the body. We need adequate amounts of each of these fats to lower our blood pressure, raise our body temperature, allow our bronchial passages to open and close, stimulate hormone production, and sensitize nerve fibers, among many other things. Above all, we need adequate EFAs for brain health.

Carbohydrates

An important source of energy for the body, particularly the brain and nervous system, carbohydrates are found in foods that are derived from plants; they include sugars and starches. The two main types of carbohydrates are simple (those that are broken down and converted into energy quickly) and complex (those that are broken down more slowly and provide a more "timed-release" and consistent form of energy).

Complex carbohydrates should make up the bulk of our daily carbohydrate intake since they are broken down in a way that is most beneficial to our systems. These carbohydrates include pasta, whole grain breads and cereals, legumes, and starchy vegetables.

Simple carbohydrates should be consumed in moderation and include fruits, milk and milk products, and nonstarchy vegetables. Some simple carbohydrates should be avoided altogether, including those made from refined sugars, such as candy, table sugar, syrups (not including natural syrups like maple), and sugary carbonated beverages. These refined, simple carbohydrates are often referred to as empty calories because they provide energy without any nutritional benefit. They are largely responsible for the epidemic of obesity in this country.

The key building blocks a growing brain needs are the essential fatty acids (EFAs), so called because we need them for healthy cell growth, but the body doesn't produce them on its own. The only way to get EFAs is through diet. All EFAs (especially the omega fatty acids) are needed for proper neuron development and function. We know that when the firing of neurons in the brain is impaired, various emotional and mental disturbances may result. This is why it's so crucial that our children get enough of the right EFAs, beginning from the moment they are conceived.

There are literally hundreds of EFAs, but the most important by far for the developing brain of a child is DHA (docosahexaenoic acid). DHA is as important to brain development as calcium is to bone development, and low levels have been linked to an array of behavioral and neurological conditions, including ADHD, dementia, depression, memory loss, and vision problems. (Researchers have also suggested that the depletion of DHA in a

Vitamins

There are 13 vitamins essential for health: vitamins A, C, D, E, and K and the B vitamins (thiamin, riboflavin, niacin, pantothenic acid, biotin, vitamin B_6, vitamin B_{12}, and folate). They can all be obtained from foods, and vitamins D and K can also be synthesized by the body. Vitamins work together with enzymes, co-factors (substances that assist enzymes), and other key substances in the body necessary for health.

Each vitamin has a specific function. If optimal levels of a particular vitamin aren't met, a deficiency disease will result. The damage to brain health caused by certain vitamin deficiencies is well known, and researchers are learning more and more about this.

Minerals

Minerals are chemical elements that are required by all living organisms in order to exist. Primarily, minerals help enzymes to function, and enzymes are crucial since they are molecules that act on other molecules and are the catalysts for all metabolic change. Some minerals, such as calcium, magnesium, potassium, and sodium (salt), are vital to our health in relatively large amounts, and they can be found in many foods. Most people, however, don't realize that they must be taken in adequate doses and appropriate combinations to work as effectively as possible.

woman's blood following childbirth may be a contributing factor to postpartum depression.)

DHA is crucial for brain and eye development. In the infant brain, which grows at such a rapid rate during the late stages of fetal development, DHA content increases three- to fivefold during the final trimester. After birth, the amount of DHA in a baby's brain triples during the first 12 weeks of life!

The foundational growth of the brain certainly doesn't stop at birth, nor does the brain stop needing nutritional support. We know that the process of rapid brain development continues throughout babyhood (and beyond), and EFAs remain quite crucial for brain growth and development well into early adulthood. This is particularly true during the first 12 to 18 months of life, when the brain is forming the foundational circuitry that will support both cognitive and emotional function for life.

Without a doubt, the best source of key EFAs, including DHA, for the population at large, including pregnant women, is fresh fish. But there is a caveat: Pregnant women are often warned about the dangers of eating fish that may have high

Trace Elements

These chemical elements are required by all living organisms—including humans—in very small but crucial amounts. For example, consuming too much zinc isn't inherently harmful, but it will lead to a deficiency of copper and problems associated with the deficiency. In human nutrition, the most important trace minerals include (in alphabetical order) chromium, copper, iodine, iron, magnesium, manganese, potassium, selenium, and zinc.

mercury content (and rightly so), but they tend to err too far on the side of caution and eat much less fish than they ought to while pregnant.

Once a baby is born, the best source of DHA is, without a doubt, human breast milk. (Breast milk also contains more than 150 other EFAs that are not available in manufactured infant formula.) Another important EFA is EPA (eicosapentaenoic acid), which has been found to be helpful in treating mood or depressive disorders. Research also indicates that DHA is beneficial in treating developmental, coordination, and learning issues.

Mother's milk is rich in these fundamentals, and in the past couple of years, DHA has been added to baby formulas sold in this country. Numerous studies show that compared with babies who are fed formula without DHA, those fed breast milk have IQ levels that are on average eight points higher. Taking all of the variables (IQ, social class, and so forth) into account, research also shows that children who were breastfed are 38 percent more likely to graduate from high school than those who were fed DHA-free formula. Infants fed formula supplemented with DHA also show significantly better development at 18 months than those fed formula with no DHA.

DIETARY GUIDELINES FOR A CHILD'S GROWING BRAIN: THE BASICS

Once a child moves beyond breastfeeding, it's up to us parents to take on the awesome responsibility of navigating our way through a pretty lousy American diet and nourishing our kids in ways that help—not hinder—their growing bodies and brains.

This is more challenging than it ought to be, because the American diet—especially for kids—is so skewed toward empty calories. Too many of the foods favored by kids have too much carbohydrate and sugar but not enough protein and far too few good fats (especially EFAs) and micronutrients.

It's our job, then, to make sure that our kids aren't poisoned or sickened by diets that are aggressively high in sugar and high in saturated fat but low in protein, vitamins, minerals, and essential trace elements. We need to resist the urge to let marketing efforts (especially those of the fast-food industry) lure us into giving our kids the wrong kind of nutrition. Instead, we have to dedicate ourselves to feeding them adequate amounts of the six key nutrients.

Over the years, parents have asked me to provide a quick overview of the basic dietary guidelines they should follow with their children in order to promote optimal brain health and development, which also means optimal overall growth and development.

Dr. Shannon's Basic Dietary Guidelines for All Children

If you have the desire to enrich your child's diet in order to safeguard healthy brain growth and development, here are a few simple guidelines that may help. I encourage you to consider these suggestions, but please disregard those that don't apply to your child. For example, if you already know that your child has a peanut allergy, of course she shouldn't eat nuts. If your toddler seems to tolerate dairy well, there's no need to switch him to rice or soy products. Feeding our children well requires effort, but it isn't complicated. The results will be well worth the effort. Here are the basics.

1. Ensure that your child is well hydrated and drinks plenty of water every day. This may seem like a no-brainer, but even slight dehydration makes the effective absorption of all other nutrients impossible.

2. Make sure that your child gets enough protein. Unlike carbohydrates, protein is a steady, slow-release form of energy. I recommend eating two servings a day of chicken, fish, tofu, eggs, or meat.

3. Emphasize good oils. Monounsaturated and polyunsaturated oils such as olive oil and canola oil are good choices. Use butter instead of margarine, though in moderation. Reduce your use of corn oil and safflower oil if possible.

4. Feature cold-water fish, such as salmon, cod, and herring. Ideally, every child should have a minimum of two or three servings a week of fresh fish.

5. Include nuts and seeds. A rich assortment of raw nuts and seeds is best. Put them in salads, cereals, and casseroles. They're also great as snacks.

6. Emphasize a changing variety of cooked and raw vegetables.

7. Include plenty of fresh fruits, particularly those currently in season.

8. Favor whole grains. Whole grain breads, pastas, rice, and cereals are the way to go.

9. Serve a wide array of foods that are fresh, locally grown, and full of color (which indicates the presence of nutrients). Serve fruits and vegetables seasonally to ensure that your child gets the greatest possible range of nutrients.

10. Watch out for "monochromatic" eating patterns. If your child eats only white foods, such as rice, bananas, bread, and macaroni and cheese, she's missing out on nutrients.

11. Supplement your child's diet with an adequate variety of brain-building vitamins, minerals, and other essential nutrients.

Things to Limit or Eliminate from Your Child's Diet

Just as there are foods that you should promote in abundance, there are other foods that you should work to keep out of your child's diet.

Refined sugar. This means candy, cakes, and even juices. Occasional treats are okay, but they shouldn't be part of a child's daily diet. Watch out for drinks (including fruit juices labeled 100% natural), as they often contain enormous amounts of sugar.

Caffeine. Caffeine has no nutritional value. It's a stimulant that may affect your child's behavior, especially his ability to sleep well. In addition, caffeine is a diuretic and may contribute to dehydration.

Trans fats. These fats are found in hydrogenated oils. Most commercial baked goods are loaded with these terrible fats. Buy whole wheat, whole grain, and minimally processed cereal products instead. Avoid fried foods, which are usually cooked in hydrogenated oils (and which, in the Netherlands, have been outlawed as a public health hazard).

Dairy products. Limit dairy intake to three to five servings per week, especially in small children. I recommend this because dairy-based foods are the number one cause of food allergies in children, and kids with food allergies often exhibit behavioral problems. If your child tolerates milk, I recommend buying only organic milk to avoid the hormones routinely fed to cows. If you

Food Allergies

Food allergies can cause our children serious upset and can be a challenge for parents to manage. But it's important that we address any food sensitivities our children may have, since their side effects often mimic the symptoms of conditions such as ADHD.

Does your child have headaches, abdominal pain, long bone pain, bad breath, foot odor, skin rashes such as eczema, chronic sore throats, runny noses, sinus infections, persistent insomnia, frequent sneezing, a chronic cough, dark rings under the eyes ("allergic shiners"), or excessive gas? Also, was your child colicky or intolerant of milk as a baby? Is there a strong family history of allergies? If you can answer yes to any of these questions, your child may have food allergies.

What do you do if you suspect your child has food allergies or sensitivities? I recommend trying an elimination diet, in which you remove a suspicious food from your child's diet for a month and see what happens to the symptoms. (In my experience, this works better than having your child's blood tested for allergies, as these blood tests often miss sensitivities that may still cause serious side effects.) Dairy products (especially milk), wheat, corn, eggs, chocolate, and citrus are the most common causes of food allergies in kids.

feel that your child would benefit from an alternative, try rice or soy milk, both of which also provide calcium.

Soda. Avoid it altogether, as it has no nutritional value whatsoever. The caffeine it contains leaches vital nutrients out of a child's system, and the sugar only wreaks havoc on the metabolic system. Also, a diet high in soda is likely to be low in more nutritional beverages such as milk or fruit juice.

Excessive carbohydrates. If there is a history in your family of mood disorders, alcoholism, or depressive symptoms, your child may need a high-protein diet. Along with being a better, more stable energy source, a high-protein diet will also help a child who struggles with obesity. And it will feed his brain.

Travis

When I met Travis, he was an unhappy 6-year-old who had no control over his moods or behavior. He seemed to live in a chronic state of agitation, and his parents, Cindy and Joe, simply could not control him. He was angry, hyperactive, aggressive, and destructive. He had been kicked out of three preschools, and Cindy and Joe had even given up on ever being able to keep a babysitter. In short, Travis's problems were ruining not just his life but his parents' lives as well.

Travis had already been labeled as having ADHD by his pediatrician and had been put on Adderall (amphetamine-dextroamphetamine), a stimulant. This medication made him only worse, and it exacerbated a sleep problem, cutting his inadequate 6 hours of sleep a night down to only 3 hours. The pediatrician wisely stopped the medication and referred Travis to me for an evaluation. He suspected Travis had bipolar disorder, but he wanted my opinion since he knew that the diagnosis and treatment for this disorder are quite serious, especially in a child so young.

Travis's parents were leery of meeting me, especially Cindy. She was skeptical about a "holistic" approach to treating Travis, and she wanted me to work with his pediatrician to find the "real medication" that would help her son as quickly as possible. I understood that she was panicked about Travis's situation, and I reassured her that my job was to work with her belief system to help her son. We made an agreement that we would try the conventional psychiatric approach for 6 months. If this approach failed to significantly help Travis, we would move to a more holistic approach. So I put my usual protocol of looking first at the quality of Travis's nutrition status on hold, and over the next 6 months, we instead tried a total of four very powerful psychiatric drugs. All of them failed to alleviate his terrible symptoms in any meaningful way. (Although some of these drugs helped temper some of his behavioral symptoms, the side effects they brought on far outweighed any benefits.)

Over the course of this trial, Travis's behavior steadily deteriorated and became downright dangerous. He eventually became violent, and his erratic behavior was a real threat to himself and others. At this point, Cindy and Joe decided that we should stop drug therapy, so we sat down together, and I outlined for them how I suspected that Travis's brain just wasn't getting the dietary and nutritional support it needed to function well enough to allow him to behave normally.

If I had chosen to label Travis, I also would have reached for the bipolar label, as he certainly met most of the *DSM*-IV criteria for this disorder. But his history told me that this wasn't the bedrock issue for him. Cindy and Joe adopted Travis when he was just a few days old. His biological family was devastated by severe problems with alcoholism, depression, drug abuse, and violence, and he was given up because his biological parents were unfit to care for him.

Because Cindy and Joe were able to provide this crucial information about Travis's family history, I understood that he had inherited a brain that didn't operate very well on a conventional diet and that he probably needed aggressive nutritional supplementation in order to overcome the genetic weaknesses he had inherited. I knew that turbocharging Travis's brain with the right kind of nutritional building blocks would mitigate much of the structural weakness he was born with, and his brain would be better able to develop and grow.

I started Travis on a nutritional supplement program that was more than double what I normally recommend for the kids I see, watching him closely for any signs of toxicity. I did this while I also began to taper him off the last of the psychiatric medications we had tried in vain.

What Travis needed was not the usual FDA-approved diet but rather a high-protein diet to provide the crucial building materials he needed. Since he was so young and not likely to eat more chicken, fish, meat, or eggs, I suggested his parents use protein powder in smoothies, on cereal, and anywhere else they could add it in a way that was palatable for him. We also talked about "easy" sources of protein, such as nuts and cheese, that they could offer him.

Because of Travis's severe symptoms, I also asked Cindy and Joe to educate themselves about the dangerous effects artificial dyes and food additives can have on children. A large study completed in England in 2004 demonstrated that young children given large amounts of dyes and food additives fared badly on tests of focus and attention. These were huge issues for Travis, so we worked to reduce dyes and additives in his diet by steering clear of most processed foods and replacing them with healthy whole grain, additive-free cereals and snacks.

Next, we had to work to cut sugar from Travis's diet—a challenge with any 6-year-old. When I met him, Travis was a junky for sugary, colorful cereals; soda; desserts; and candy. In order to keep his blood sugar level from spiking, which only exacerbated his mood swings, we had to wean him off sugar, or his brain wouldn't have a fighting chance. To do this, we had to work gradually. I recommended that Joe and Cindy use honey or maple syrup whenever Travis carped about being deprived of sweets, as both are slower acting than more refined sugars. They did this with the idea that even these sweets would eventually be eliminated entirely.

Travis also began to take two multivitamins a day, and I added more vitamin C, B vitamins, vitamin E, and omega-3s.

Six weeks after we started him on the supplements and put him on a high-protein diet, Travis was much less volatile, his attention span was better, and he was happier than he had been in ages. He smiled at me for the first time ever. His mother said that he was now sleeping 8 hours a night and even seemed to get tired before bedtime.

Now that Travis's moods and overall metabolism were stabilizing, and he was able to focus, Cindy and Joe were able to work on his specific behavioral issues, and Travis started to respond to their discipline and to become more social.

Eighteen months later, Travis was off all psychiatric medications, and his parents were continuing to provide needed social and emotional support as well as a highly nutritious diet. Although Travis may have begun life with some inherited genetic weakness, with the right kind of nutritional intervention, his brain is becoming stronger, healthier, and better able to function. His story dramatically illustrates that nutrition is powerful medicine.

Dr. Shannon's Basic Supplement Plan for Kids

I'm a firm believer that every child who eats solid foods would benefit from taking nutritional supplements. This is, of course, especially true for any child who's exhibiting mood or behavioral problems.

Along with getting adequate water, protein, carbohydrates, and fats, children need to get the right vitamins and minerals. It's essential for their overall health and growth—and for brain health. Here are my general recommendations.

> **Ages 2 to 6:** A high-quality chewable multivitamin, plus 100 milligrams of vitamin C, 100 IU of vitamin E (be sure to buy a brand that contains several types of E), and 250 to 500 milligrams of EFAs

> **Ages 6 to 12:** An adult multivitamin, along with 250 to 500 milligrams of vitamin C, 200 IU of vitamin E, 50

milligrams of B-complex vitamins, 250 milligrams of calcium/magnesium (in chewable tablets), and 1,000 milligrams of EFAs

Age 12 to adult: A multivitamin, plus 500 to 1,000 milligrams of vitamin C, 400 IU of vitamin E, 100 milligrams of B-complex vitamins, 500 milligrams of calcium/magnesium (tablets), and two 1,000-milligram doses of EFAs a day

I believe every child needs to start with the recommended daily amount of all vitamins and minerals that are provided in a standard multivitamin. I augment this with specific supplements because I'm convinced that they will only help a child's mood, behavior, and overall good health.

Vitamin C. This is a known immune system booster, stress reducer, and overall wonder nutrient. It's virtually impossible to take in too much vitamin C, and our children, who are notoriously reluctant to eat the fresh fruits and vegetables that contain C, need it the most.

Vitamin E. The king of all antioxidants, vitamin E protects our cells from free radicals. But it is preventive—it can't undo damage that has already been done. That's why it's important that our children get enough. Vitamin E is key in protecting the health and function of the nervous system and brain. Decreased vitamin E levels are associated with major depression.

B-complex vitamins. I think of the B vitamins (including folic acid) as being crucial components in fighting mood and behavioral problems. These vitamins (which exist together in nature) are essential to energy production in the body, since they extract fuel from the carbs, proteins, and fats found in food. They are also important in the production of neurotransmitters such as serotonin, which affect mood. Aggressive and addictive behaviors, as well as other personality and mental disorders, have been linked to vitamin B deficiencies.

Is Bipolar Disorder a
Nutritional Deficiency Syndrome?

A nutritional supplement called EMPower has been available in Canada for years, and it's been remarkably effective in treating bipolar disorder in adults and children. This supplement contains mainly B vitamins, minerals, and trace elements. There are currently five published studies in peer-reviewed psychiatric journals that document the benefits of this treatment. More than 32,000 people worldwide have been treated using this approach. A large, randomized, controlled trial (the gold standard in clinical science) is currently under way in Canada.

I have been using this supplement in my practice for 5 years and have found it to be nothing short of miraculous in eliminating symptoms in patients with a bipolar label. I'm not alone in my support of this treatment. Charles Popper, MD, a respected professor of child psychiatry at Harvard, also reported positive results with EMPower in an article published in the *Journal of Clinical Psychiatry* in 2001.

The fact that a nutritional supplement can be so effective in treating a serious psychiatric disorder in children brings up some complex issues related to labeling and medicating. If a supplement can eradicate the symptoms of bipolar disorder in a 10-year-old child within 5 days, does the child in fact have bipolar disorder, or is it a nutritional deficiency syndrome? This question merits a serious and sound answer from the medical community.

There is another, more disturbing aspect to this question: I and some of my colleagues who champion the use of supplements such as EMPower are dismayed to observe that patients who have never had treatment with psychiatric drugs respond better to the supplement. This prompts the question of whether psychiatric medications actually impair the natural healing powers of the brain.

Calcium/magnesium. I give these supplements in tandem since, as with many other minerals, they work better when they're in our system at the same time. Magnesium (like its mineral cousin lithium) is a great mood stabilizer, but it's no longer as easily available, since farming practices have significantly reduced the amount of magnesium (and other crucial trace metals) from the soil in which foods are grown. Also, the increased stress our children experience leaches magnesium from their bodies. Along with building bones and teeth, calcium is a great sleep aid, and it complements and bolsters the calming effects of magnesium.

I've already discussed the role of EFAs in brain health at length, so I don't need to stress the importance of making sure that every child gets supplements of these vital nutrients.

All children, regardless of what kind of diet they currently enjoy, benefit from nutritional supplements. The beauty of augmenting any child's diet with brain-nourishing vitamins, minerals, and EFAs is that there is no downside to this approach. Research has shown that if the body doesn't need a nutrient, by and large, it will expel it. Of course, you should monitor the supplementation of children closely with the help and guidance of your pediatrician. But there are very few risks of negative side effects in children given the right kind of nutritional supplementation.

Josh

I met Josh when he was an unhappy, overweight 12-year-old who was failing in school and struggling socially. At that time, he was being treated with an antidepressant and individual psychotherapy. His parents called me because despite this rigorous treatment, Josh was not getting better. In fact, he was getting worse. He had even said he wanted to die.

I'll never forget the day Josh shuffled into my office behind his mother, Mary. When he sat on the couch, he seemed to sink deeper and deeper into the pillows, almost as though he were a balloon deflating. Each time I spoke to him, the bill of his Colorado Rockies cap lifted just enough so I could glimpse his eyes. His halting, quiet voice told me that even making everyday conversation was a challenge for him. When he talked about his life, everything was colored by an attitude of despair. On school: "It's just so hard. I don't think I'll ever pass math." On friends: "Other kids tease me because I am big and fat, and nobody likes me." Most heartbreakingly, on himself: "I am fat, ugly, and stupid."

Josh was indeed quite overweight, but he hadn't always been. He started school as a happy, outgoing 6-year-old, but then he ran into a problem learning to read, and his slowness at mastering this basic skill had the cascading effect of causing difficulty in learning to write. The end result was that he had difficulty doing his assignments and did poorly on tests.

Because of this, he was labeled a problem student. In fourth grade, Josh was moved onto the special ed track. The stress caused by the difficulties he was having in school prompted him to compensate in unhealthy ways, and that's when he turned to food. He would come home from school and gorge himself on ice cream, soda, and chips in order to stuff his frustrations and numb his feelings. His parents, knowing how difficult school was for him, not only allowed this but literally fed into it, buying and offering him the nutrition-poor foods he craved. As Josh's diet spiraled out of control, his weight ballooned, and his mental acuity weakened further. It wasn't long before true, intractable depression set in.

I didn't dispute the diagnosis of major depression, but I didn't think medication and talk therapy (which doesn't always work with children, especially boys) were the best—or only—treatment options available to him. In my view, they were treating only the symptoms and not the underlying problem. Before we could even begin to address Josh's academic or social problems, I knew we had to tackle his terrible diet.

Although both of Josh's parents were slightly overweight, they had the discipline and strategic thinking skills to keep their weight relatively in check. Josh's young brain wasn't yet capable of making such choices. Step one, then, was to educate him and his parents about what he needed to take in food-wise in order to support—not subvert—his growing brain and body. I made it clear to all of them that this wasn't going to be easy and that the eating plan I would recommend was not negotiable—not if they truly wanted Josh to regain his health.

Beginning when Josh was around age 6, his diet had been lacking in protein, EFAs, vitamins, and minerals, and these deficiencies had interfered with his ability to learn well and to develop strong social skills. In addition, the high-sugar, high-carbohydrate diet he followed had made him obese. In a nutshell, Josh needed to be on a diet that would keep his blood sugar levels stable, nourish his still-growing brain, and improve his mood and energy levels.

The nutritional treatment plan for Josh focused on these key areas.

- Addressing a severe protein deficiency
- Increasing his intake of healthy fats
- Reducing his intake of refined carbohydrates
- Upping his intake of vegetables
- Weaning him from sugar

As with that of many American children, Josh's diet was seriously protein deficient. For the young brain, adequate amounts of protein are needed for proper function. Protein provides the material (amino acids) needed to create strong neural connections and neurotransmitters, such as serotonin. Also, protein has a leveling effect on blood sugar, which means that eating a diet high in protein would help stabilize Josh's moods by stabilizing his insulin production. Another benefit of putting him on a high-protein diet was that it would help him immediately begin to lose weight.

Josh also needed to boost his fat intake but *not* with the kinds of fats found in the overprocessed junk food that was the mainstay of his diet. He needed to trade in these fats for more-healthful ones like those that contain omega-3 oils, which are crucial for proper brain and neuron development. Josh's family needed to purge their pantry of bad fats and bring good fats into their diet. I encouraged them to use canola or olive oil whenever possible. I also recommended that they introduce Josh to fresh fish (also a good source of protein), especially types high in omega-3s, such as salmon.

Given his weight issue, I recommended that Josh limit his intake of complex carbohydrates to those found in whole grain products and even then to eat them in limited quantities. Since starches and sweets were Josh's downfall, I had to be very specific about what he could have. Until now, his diet had been mostly refined carbs, and he ate them all day long on an "as needed" basis for emotional comfort. To start, I recommended he eat only whole grain cereal or whole grain rice or bread with meals, just twice a day.

I then taught Josh and his family the basics of the glycemic index (GI), which is a system that rates foods depending on how quickly they convert to sugar in the bloodstream. Foods with a high GI, such as white bread, sugar, and most desserts, cause blood sugar levels to surge and spike, which in turn prompts the production of insulin, which signals the body to store fat. A child prone to chronic insulin production is much more prone to obesity, hypoglycemia, and even diabetes. I recommended that Josh eat foods with a low GI, such as beans, oatmeal, and whole grains, in order to keep his blood sugar levels steady, and to eat a variety of protein-rich foods that would release their energy to his system steadily over time.

To round out Josh's diet and to ensure that he got the other key nutrients he needed, such as vitamins and minerals, I recommended that he eat lots of vegetables (which provide many of the same nutrients as fruit but without the high sugar content)

The Glycemic Index

The glycemic index (GI) is a numerical ranking system for carbohydrate-rich foods, based on the average increase in blood glucose levels that occur after a certain food is eaten. The scale goes from 0 to 100, with a rating of 100 given to the foods that turn into sugar the most quickly, thereby causing blood sugar levels to rise the most rapidly. Foods that have low GI ratings convert to sugar more slowly and thereby help stabilize mood. A rating of 55 or under is given to foods that qualify as having a low GI.

American children tend to eat foods that rank high on the index, and the correlation between sugar and mood is undeniable. Here are some examples of how foods that kids like rank on the GI.

High-GI Foods (70–100)	Medium-GI Foods (56–69)	Low-GI Foods (55 or less)
Baked potato	Bananas	Apples
Cheerios	Brown rice	Fat-free milk
Cornflakes	Popcorn	Lentils
French fries	Raisins	Oatmeal
Ice cream	Whole wheat bread	Plain yogurt
Table sugar		Pumpernickel bread
Watermelon		Sweet potato
White bread		

Eating at regular intervals as well as eating foods with a low GI ranking will keep blood sugar stable and will help kids feel less hungry.

and nuts. By focusing on eating whole and fresh foods, he would benefit from the regular, slow release of nutrients into his bloodstream instead of suffering the ill effects brought on by the bursts of energy he was getting from junk food. This would help him feel sated between meals and help stabilize his mood.

Ideally, I would have recommended that Josh include two daily snacks along with his three meals, but because he was a chronic snacker, I eliminated them entirely at the start. I also banned all desserts from his diet, at least for the short term, as Josh had to break his addiction to sugar and sweets. Otherwise, he would stay locked in a vicious cycle of eating sugar, his blood sugar spiking, and then his mood crashing. After a couple of months, when Josh was feeling better—and more in control—we slowly began to reintroduce appropriate treats at appropriate times (such as birthday cake at a party or a cool soft drink after a ball game).

The hardest thing for Josh to give up was soda. I simply asked him to try it for 30 days and told him that if he couldn't live without it, we would talk about adding it back in. For one month, he was to drink only water or milk. He agreed to give it a try.

I also put Josh on my standard supplement plan, knowing that his brain would benefit from getting strong doses of the vitamins, minerals, trace elements, and EFAs that his diet alone might not provide.

In addition, I put him on a fairly rigorous regimen of natural supplements, the first of which, SAMe (a proven natural mood booster), I hoped would replace his antidepressant, Paxil (paroxetine). The second was the herb ginkgo biloba, which would energize him. (To learn more about the natural supplements I most often recommend, see Appendix 3.) The total cost to Josh's parents for this comprehensive supplement program was roughly equivalent to what they were spending on the Paxil prescription each month.

I planned to keep Josh on the SAMe and ginkgo until his

depression had been gone for a full 6 months. At that point, I would slowly taper him off both supplements. But I recommended that he continue the basic vitamin and mineral supplement program indefinitely since his growing brain and body would benefit from this nutritional support over the long term.

The diet Josh was beginning would, I hoped, become his diet for life.

Once we had addressed Josh's nutritional needs, I urged his parents to get him to watch less television and to exercise more. They found that simply by limiting his combined computer and television time to 60 minutes a day, Josh began to naturally become more active.

Within 2 weeks, Josh felt and looked remarkably different. He sat up, talked more, and obviously had more energy. In 6 weeks, we had him off the Paxil, and at this point, his weight loss accelerated. Before we got him off the drug, he had lost just 4 pounds, which didn't surprise me, given that weight gain is often a side effect of antidepressants. In just another 6 weeks, he lost another 10 pounds. Josh liked this. The more weight he lost, the more he moved and the better he felt. His mood continued to improve, as did his self-image and self-esteem. He told me that he felt much better than he ever had while on medication and much better than he had in years. Josh was on his way.

FEEDING THE TEENAGE BRAIN

Puberty places extra demands on the metabolic machinery of the brain and body as maturation and sexual development accelerate. This is on top of the fact that the brain is only 2 percent of our total body weight but consumes 20 percent of our energy! Sometimes I just sit back and marvel at the amount of food my 19-year-old son eats, and I have to remind myself that his rapidly growing body and brain drive this massive appetite. My greatest responsibility is to see to it that he loads up on all the foods and nutrients that will most effectively and efficiently fuel this growth.

Sadly, as parents, we often assume that our teens are more adults than children, especially when it comes to their ability to make good decisions about feeding themselves. Recently, neuroscientists have been able to show that a teen's brain is more underdeveloped than previously thought. Though our teens may look and sound like adults, their brains are not yet fully formed, especially the areas of the brain that deal with problem-solving and decision-making. This becomes evident when we look at how a teenager manages her diet. Allison, a recent patient of mine, beautifully illustrates this point.

Allison

Allison came to see me a couple of years ago, just after her 17th birthday. The 3 preceding years had been terrible for her, beginning with a Tylenol overdose and psychiatric hospitalization at age 14. In the years since then, she had been in therapy constantly but with three different therapists. She had also been prescribed seven different psychiatric medications by two different psychiatrists. When she was 15, she started drinking heavily and smoking pot.

The first psychiatrist she saw (during her hospital stay) diagnosed bipolar disorder. Her first outpatient therapist, a child psychologist, thought she was depressed, with borderline traits. The most recent psychiatrist she saw diagnosed schizoaffective disorder after learning that she heard voices in her head. Allison and her mother, Jane, were very confused by these heavy-duty psychiatric labels. They came to me in part to help them understand which was accurate and to understand what to do once the "right" label was identified.

Allison was rail thin. She strictly limited her intake of calories and fat, and I found out she had been starving her body this way since she was 13. To my surprise, her performance in school had always been fairly good. "Allison has an IQ of 145 and a full scholarship to UC Santa Barbara to study creative writing," her mother proudly announced. "But we want her to leave for school feeling much better than she does now."

As well as being so thin, Allison had severe mood swings, insomnia, auditory hallucinations, and periodic bouts of severe depression that included occasional suicidal thoughts. When I met her, she was not on any medication. In fact, she had rebelled against being controlled in this way. Plus, the medications made her gain weight and made her feel drugged, which she hated. When we met, her weight was stabilized at 104 pounds, which was far too low but fortunately not so dangerously low as to require immediate hospitalization.

There was no question that Allison was keenly intelligent. Her manner was frank, and she clearly wanted to understand her own issues.

"I just can't seem to manage my emotions. I often get swept away by strong feelings," she explained. "I can become so angry or sad, and I don't understand why since my life is pretty good. I have a boyfriend, lots of friends, great parents—all the stuff I'm supposed to have. But I can still go ballistic over small things or become so sad that I think about killing myself. I go off at people even when I know they don't deserve it. I am going off to college in August, and I am scared that I will fall apart or have to drop out. The first semester of freshman year can be brutal, and I don't know if I can handle it. I have a scholarship to study creative writing, and I really, really want this.

"I know I might have bipolar disorder, according to other psychiatrists that I have seen. I still hear voices in my head, and I can't make them stop, so maybe what I have is more serious than that. My parents and my shrinks want me to take lithium [a trace mineral that stabilizes mood and has been used with great benefit for 50 years] and Depakote [divalproex sodium, a mood stabilizer and anticonvulsant], but I don't like the way the drugs make me feel. They rob me of my spark, make me feel sort of sick all the time, and make me gain weight. Besides, I researched them on the Internet, and I don't like the side effects they have. What else can I do?"

Despite Allison's very serious symptoms, I went straight for a more simple diagnosis. I told her I thought she was suffering from malnutrition, that her symptoms were the sign of a starved and overstimulated brain. Years of hard dieting had robbed her brain and body of the vital nutrition both needed to grow and function optimally. I felt certain that getting Allison's brain fortified with the right nutrition would reduce or even eliminate all of her symptoms. At the very least, it would bring her brain chemistry up to normal functioning level so that from there, I could reassess her condition. For now, I refused to label her as having any major psychiatric disorder at all.

My nutritional treatment plan for Allison focused on four key areas.

- A severe protein deficit
- A harmful lack of omega-3 fatty acids
- Caffeine consumption that was toxic
- Not enough calorie intake to provide sufficient energy

Like most girls growing up in this country, Allison was bombarded with unrealistic images about how she should look, so she had severely restricted her calorie intake since puberty. She did this by basically cutting all protein and fat from her diet, never suspecting that these were the two nutrients her brain needed most. With so few EFAs in her diet, her brain was being forced to draw on less beneficial fats to continue to build neuronal pathways. Ultimately, her poor diet meant that her brain was full of neurons that were less flexible than they ought to be, and this explained why she had such severe "distortion" in her moods and why, I believe, she had auditory hallucinations as well.

As well as upping her omega-3 intake, I pushed her to dramatically increase her protein consumption (aiming for 40 percent of her diet) within the context of a healthy and reasonable calorie count. Allison made this challenging since she was a vegetarian, but I knew she could do it. Many vegetable sources of protein can deliver the same quality of protein that meat sources provide. Fortunately, Allison ate dairy products and eggs, so we also talked about how she could get protein from them. I asked her to eat some protein at each meal, including breakfast (which could be something as simple as a fruit smoothie made with soy-based protein powder).

I also asked her to include foods rich in omega-3s twice daily. These include walnuts, greens, and certain seeds, such as flaxseed. I asked her to make salad dressing with flaxseed oil, and I suggested she grind flaxseed in a coffee grinder and put it on her morning cereal or yogurt. She could even add some flaxseed oil to her smoothies. (Flaxseed oil may be the best source of omega-3s for those who are opposed to or can't tolerate fish oil.) I also recommended that she eat foods enriched with DHA, such as eggs and spreads.

Allison didn't eat many junk foods or sweets, so our work was all about adding positive elements to her diet. She was highly motivated to make these changes, especially once she understood the science behind them.

Allison did have one serious vice, and that was an addiction to diet soda. ("You won't take that from me, will you, Dr. Shannon?" she asked.) I spent a little time explaining how the phosphoric acid in the soda depleted her body of calcium, a mineral that, much like lithium, helped to calm the body and mind. I showed her the studies about how the artificial sweeteners in diet soda caused neurological problems for some people, and I explained how the caffeine in it put her brain on overdrive, reducing her ability to relax and sleep well. She finally agreed to at least taper off on her soda intake. We replaced the soda with herbal teas and juice spritzers. There were even reasonable alternative choices for her when she met her friends at Starbucks.

Allison was a quick study and eager to get her health back, but the hardest challenge for us was to get her to take in enough calories to sustain her growing body and brain. Still, she was becoming a bit of an armchair physiologist, and she understood that by starving her brain and body, she was keeping her system in a constant state of alarm. In this state, the body releases more stress hormones.

Allison worked hard to eat more calories, since she knew all too well what keeping her system on "red alert" cost her. She was desperate to enjoy a good night's sleep, to stop having auditory hallucinations, and to experience more-balanced moods. In short, the allure of more peace and tranquility outweighed the societal pressure she felt to be so thin.

Besides getting Allison to get more omega-3s from whole food sources, I put her on a double dose of my standard supplement plan (just as I had Travis). I also added the supplement inositol, which is part of the vitamin B complex, to her diet. Inositol is required for proper formation of cell membranes, and it positively affects nerve transmission as well as helping the transport of fats within the body and brain. It's a cell-stabilizing substance that also lowers blood pressure and has been shown to have a mood-boosting and anti-anxiety effect. I also suggested that Allison take melatonin at bedtime, since this natural hormone (known as the darkness hormone) regulates the sleep cycle. "That's cool; I can do all of this." Allison said. She understood that all of these nutritional tools would tune up her brain and help it run smoothly.

Once Allison's new and improved diet was in place, we talked about how she needed to round out her treatment plan with exercise and tools that would help her relax. In order for her brain to work at its optimal capacity, she had to shift her body into a lower gear. She had to start living as though she were running a marathon and not a series of short sprints.

After several months, Allison was like a different person. She came into my office beaming and relaxed. "I don't have the same highs and lows, my concentration is better, and I don't hear voices anymore. I don't feel sluggish or stupid, and I still feel creative. My parents have noticed a huge difference; they say I'm not as irritable and grumpy as I used to be. I still slip up occasionally, especially in the mornings, and get angry. Most of the time I can bring it under control. The best part of all is that I'm starting to finally feel comfortable in my own skin." Six months after this meeting, Allison started college on that scholarship.

Allison is now off and running. She no longer needs me, and she no longer needs any kind of heavy psychiatric label pinning her down. Her high levels of intellectual and emotional intensity created a much higher than average need for certain brain nutrients. She merely had a high-octane brain trying to run on substandard fuel. Now that she's fueling herself well, her brain is working like the exquisite machine it was designed to be.

All of these children, from very young Travis and young teen Josh to virtual adult Allison, were able to shed serious psychiatric labels and get off psychiatric drugs simply by being given the right kind of nutrition. The science, physiology, and safety of this approach makes deep intuitive sense to most of the families I treat, and the results of correcting an improper diet can be nearly miraculous. That's why most parents I know feel that providing proper nutrition is a safe, cost-effective, and relatively easy way to promote emotional and mental health in their children. And most parents would surely prefer to heal their children with food, not drugs. Because of the success of the kids outlined in this chapter and the hundreds of other children I've successfully treated by adjusting their diets, I am firmly convinced that food is the best medicine and that providing strong nutritional support for our children is one of the most important jobs we have as parents. In the next chapter, I'll discuss the environmental factors that can cause your child distress and what you can do about them.

CHAPTER 5

Environmental
Causes of Disharmony
in Our Kids

ust as we need to provide our kids with healthy foods that fortify and nourish their growing brains, we also need to create safe, nurturing, and nourishing environments for them to live and play in. It may seem that I'm stating the obvious, but the impact environmental stressors have on a child's emotional and mental health can be quite profound. The good news is that once a stressor is identified, it can be easily fixed.

When we talk about the environment, most of us think about large issues such as deforestation, pollution, or global warming. These general environmental issues are important and deserve our attention, and thinking about them causes us to experience a fair amount of stress. But the environment that most impacts our children—and the one that frequently goes unexamined—is the private, closed environment of the home. Whether we create a tranquil, secure, and nurturing environment or whether we allow chaos, upheaval, and danger to enter our homes has a profound effect on the mental and emotional health of our children.

Creating a healthy, balanced home environment is one of the essential jobs of parenting. When we create an environment in which a child experiences peace, beauty, rest, and love; where he finds healthy, enlivening stimulation; where he gets proper nutrition; and where he is protected from toxic environmental pollutants, we are well on our way to ensuring that he won't be exposed to environmental stressors that may cause symptoms of mental or emotional upset. You can make changes and adjustments to your child's physical surroundings and his routine that will have a strong influence on safe-guarding his brain health and mood.

SLEEP: THE NEED TO RECHARGE THE GROWING BRAIN

Before your child was born, you probably spent a lot of time preparing the place where she would sleep. You probably bought a bassinet or crib, adorable bedding, and snuggly animals. You also probably read up on serious sleep-related conditions like SIDS (sudden infant death syndrome) so that you could take the right measures to protect your baby from harm.

Although most parents spend a lot of time creating a sleep sanctuary for their children, most of us don't really understand why adequate sleep is so crucial to a child's brain development—from cradle to college.

We all know that children need to sleep, but most of us don't know that even low levels of sleep deprivation or chronic minor sleep disruptions can bring on symptoms that look a lot like those of many of the serious psychiatric disorders that kids are currently being labeled with.

Children who are tired are often cranky and fussy, and we too frequently identify this as plain old moodiness rather than the result of a lack of sleep. Kids who don't get enough sleep often have trouble regulating their moods, and their cognitive abilities are impaired. Lack of sleep can affect appetite, physical coordination, and physical health (sleep deprivation has been linked to weakness of the immune system) as well as inhibit brain function.

Paradoxically, kids who aren't getting enough high-quality sleep often don't appear "sleepy" at all. Instead, they exhibit all the symptoms of ADHD: They're hyperactive and impulsive and can't focus well. This happens because they are (quite unconsciously) working to compensate for their brain's sluggishness by stimulating themselves in other ways. When someone—an educator, a doctor, or a mental health professional—suggests that the symptoms look like ADHD, parents will rarely be asked if the child is getting enough sleep.

How Much Sleep Does Your Child Need?

An estimated 30 percent of all children will experience some kind of sleep disorder at some time. (This may explain why the number of sleep aid prescriptions written for children is skyrocketing.) In some cases, it's relatively easy to get to the root of the problem. For instance, severe snoring in a young child can indicate serious breathing problems. Most of the time, a child may be missing just an hour or so a day of deep sleep, but this can be enough to erode his emotional and mental functioning in significant ways.

Most kids need a lot of sleep—much more than most parents plan for or encourage. That's because we underestimate how crucial sleep is for restoration and growth. Here's a breakdown by age of the amount of sleep a child needs during a 24-hour period.

Infant to 6 months: 16 to 20 hours

6 months to 2 years: roughly 15 hours

2 to 6 years: 10 to 12 hours

Grade school children (7 to 13 years): 9 to 11 hours

High school children (14 to 18 years): roughly 9 to 10
  hours (but this may vary greatly day by day)

New research indicates that even minimal sleep deprivation (losing as little as a half hour a night) can have a serious impact on a child's behavior. In toddlers (2 to 3 years), this shows up as oppositionality, aggression, or noncompliance. But preschools aren't in the business of monitoring whether or not your child is getting enough rest. The result? Toddlers and preschoolers who aren't getting enough sleep have a 25 percent greater chance of being diagnosed with a psychiatric disorder than those who get adequate sleep.

For grade-schoolers, lack of sleep can show up in very concrete ways. It's been determined that the difference between a child who makes A and B grades and one who gets Cs, Ds, or Fs can be as little as the loss of an hour of quality sleep a night.

For teenagers, sleep quantity and quality takes on a whole new meaning as their circadian rhythms shift with puberty, pushing them into a more nocturnal time frame. Unlike their younger selves, teens are wired to stay up later and rise later. In the past, most of us chalked this kind of "night owl" behavior in teens to defiance, mood, or both. In reality, it's a true sign of their biological wiring. In 1976, sleep researchers at Stanford University tested the flexibility of the adolescent sleep pattern. They found that unlike younger children or adults, adolescents had severe difficulty adjusting their sleep start times (a teenager's brain needs to sleep from roughly 11:00 p.m. to 8:00 a.m.) to accommodate an early wakeup time. Since most teenagers have no choice but to rise well before 8:00 a.m., many exhibit signs of severe sleep deprivation (including narcoleptic-like symptoms) during the day, since they can't adjust to falling asleep much earlier than 11:00 p.m.

The Stanford team dubbed the stubbornness of the adolescent circadian clock a "phase delay."

Those research findings are finally beginning to influence school policy, and some school districts are redesigning their programs to more realistically match the biorhythms of their students. Many high schools in the United States have shifted or are contemplating shifting their start times to accommodate the fact that few teens are mentally sharp enough to tackle rigorous coursework early in the morning. In 1997, the Minneapolis public school district became the first major school system in the country to change its start time. Middle schools there began opening at 9:40 a.m. instead of 7:40 a.m. This change (according to research done by the Center for Applied Research and Educational Improvement, or CAREI) has had a positive effect on teen school performance and on teen sleeping habits. Since this scheduling change, Minneapolis teens are getting more hours of sleep per night than students at schools with earlier start times. Attendance rates and academic performance have risen, while reports of misconduct (including falling sleep in class) have fallen. The students themselves reported that their moods—as well as their grades—improved with the new start time.

The High Cost of Teen Sleep Debt

Younger, prepubescent children (between 9 and 12) are wired for sleep in much the same ways adults are. That is, they can bounce back from some sleep disruptions pretty easily. Think of an international traveler who can shrug off jet lag and quickly adapt to a new time zone. Younger children just aren't burdened by the "phase delay" that plagues adolescents and can bounce back if they miss a good night's sleep here or there.

It's a different ball game for teens, who just can't recoup when they don't get enough sleep. Instead, their sleep deficit grows and grows. For each hour of lost sleep, an hour that has been stored in the teen's sleep bank must be withdrawn. This puts teens at very serious risk and explains why sleep research-ers are most concerned about teens who are forced to rise after only 7 or so hours of sleep. Who wants a sleep-deprived teen behind the wheel of a car? Ask many high school students, and you'll hear a horror story about a classmate who seemingly inex-plicably fell asleep at the wheel while driving home from sports practice or a dance. That's the worst-case scenario, but there are other much more common ones. Sleep-deprived teens are more likely to suffer from depression, get poor grades, or be too exhausted to participate in extracurricular activities.

Sleep and Learning

We all know how difficult it is to concentrate when our brains are fogged by lack of sleep, so it seems obvious that when our children are sleep deprived, they aren't at their best in the classroom.

Sleeping—and in particular dreaming—is crucial to the con-solidation of memory, which is a fancy way of saying it's impor-tant to learning. When we sleep deeply and our brains are able to drop into REM sleep, very specific changes occur there, including the activation of specific parts of the brain coupled with identifiable changes in brain chemistry. Researchers believe that during REM sleep, the brain processes recent activity in a way that connects it to longer-term memory storage systems. Robert Stickgold, PhD, assistant professor of psychiatry at Mas-sachusetts Mental Health Center in Boston, explains, "Dreams are the mind watching the brain processing memories." During periods of uninterrupted sleep, when the brain moves in and out of REM/dream sleep, it does this work; and learning, which is the storage of new information, is facilitated and fortified. With-out enough sleep, learning is impaired.

What this means for all kids, but particularly for teens and college-age kids, is that pulling an all-nighter is far from the best

Create a Sleep Sanctuary for Your Child

It doesn't matter if your child is a newborn or a teen on the verge of leaving the nest; it's crucial that he have a place to sleep that will optimize his chances of getting a good night's rest. Your child's bedroom should be:

- **Refreshing.** Be sure that your child's room is well ventilated and that the temperature is moderate (not too hot or too cold).

- **Comfortable.** Provide bedding that is clean and offers adequate support.

- **Simple.** Don't allow a computer, television, or stereo in your child's bedroom. If he must have one for some reason, be strict about limiting its use to daytime.

- **Serene.** Eliminate environmental disruptors such as noise, light, and other pollutants. For example, use a sound machine if you need to mask street sounds with something more soothing, put special curtains on the windows if you live in an area that is drenched in artificial light, and don't smoke in or near your child's room.

- **Quiet.** Make sure the rest of the household respects that a member of the family is at rest; keep the noise down.

way to prepare for an exam. What makes better sense is getting a full night's rest on the day of the original lesson. By getting sufficient sleep on the day the information came in, the child's brain will store that information in the most concrete and truly memorable way possible. It's crucial, therefore, that we parents help our children (especially our teenagers) get an adequate amount of sleep. Consider these suggestions to help your child prepare for sleep.

■ **Steer clear of heated family discussions or arguments before bedtime.** These may cause your child stress, which will inhibit his ability to fall asleep or may even cause nightmares. Instead, talk calmly and lovingly about the day's problems so your child's mind is unburdened before bedtime.

■ **Avoid exposure to overstimulating media content.** Don't let your children watch television shows or movies that are violent, disturbing, loud, or otherwise overstimulating, since they will promote psychological or physical (release of stress hormones) stress. This includes monitoring video games and music. Instead, read together.

■ **Shun physical overstimulation.** Rough play is great during the afternoon, but before bedtime, it can rev your child up in ways that diminish her capacity to fall easily into a restful state of sleep. Instead, do some relaxing stretching together or soak in a hot tub (a Shannon family favorite).

■ **Discourage your child from eating too close to bedtime.** Eating puts the body's need to engage in digestion at odds with the brain's need to rest. A light snack and a drink of water are fine since they may help your child slow down and move toward bedtime.

■ **Keep away from caffeine and sugar.** Don't give your young child sugar, and don't let your teenager grab a can of cola on his way to the bedroom. Both substances trigger the body (and brain) to perk up, not slow down. Be cautious, too, with over-the-counter medications, since they may overstimulate your child's nervous system. Do suggest a cup of warm chamomile or peppermint tea, which are both relaxing and healthful.

SUNLIGHT: BRIGHTEN THE BRAIN

While sleep serves as a time for memory and learning consolidation, wakefulness is the state in which the brain actively takes in information, grows, and changes. If the environmental conditions of our waking life aren't optimal, our ability to learn is also impaired, since our brains simply can't function at full capacity.

Just as a child needs the benefit of nighttime darkness and stillness to recharge her growing brain, she also needs sunlight to stimulate her brain to perform at its peak. Researchers are even beginning to explore whether a child's brain growth is compromised before birth when an expectant mother does not get adequate sun exposure. Experts are exploring this link, because exposure to sunlight prompts the body to produce vitamin D, a key nutrient that's vital to strong brain development. In testing on rats, researchers have discovered that a vitamin D deficiency leads to larger brain mass but less brain activity. Some researchers are even exploring the link between vitamin D deficiency (lack of sunlight) and schizophrenia.

Adequate exposure to sunlight is also crucial for newborns. This is especially true for those who have jaundice, a relatively common condition in which there is too much bilirubin (a bile pigment) in the bloodstream. Jaundice is easily treated by exposing an infant to sunlight (or artificial lights that provide the same nutrient benefits as sunlight), because bilirubin is photosensitive and is broken down when exposed to UV light. But severe jaundice in a newborn, if left untreated, can damage normal brain development since it interferes with neural cell signaling. Although rare, severe jaundice can cause mental retardation and blindness and hamper normal physical development.

Getting enough sunlight is also crucial for establishing the inner mechanism that controls a child's wake/sleep cycle. We're programmed to respond to the light/dark cycles of a 24-hour day. When we fall out of step with the body's natural inclination to work and play during full sunlight hours and to rest once the sun has gone down, our health—including our brain health—becomes imbalanced. This is most pronounced in children who spend their days and nights under artificial lighting instead of enjoying more balanced exposure to natural daylight and true nighttime darkness.

This problem (light/sleep deprivation) is a relatively new one that is just now becoming understood as a major source of health problems for all of us—especially our kids. Kids who don't get enough sunlight may suffer from physical problems such as weakened bones and inhibited growth. Vitamin D is crucial for the absorption of calcium and for cell growth, and getting adequate amounts also reduces the risk of developing disorders such as diabetes, cancer, heart disease, obesity, and autoimmune diseases. Vitamin D is needed to help "set" the body's circadian rhythm and helps stabilize mood and blood pressure. Without adequate natural light, our bodies (and brains) simply don't work as well as they should.

Daylighting: Bringing Sunshine Inside

The fact that our kids need adequate exposure to natural sunlight has not been lost on the designers of new school buildings across the globe—and even in the United States. This movement is called daylighting. The Duran Middle School in North Carolina, for example, was designed to bring as much daylight as possible into the building. The new design lowered energy costs for the building by more than 50 percent, and the effect on the students and their performance has been nothing less than astonishing. The school is experiencing record high attendance in the daylighting classrooms, and school officials report improved academic performance in them as well. The kids who are taught in these classrooms report that they are sleeping better at night.

I can't stress enough how important getting adequate daylight is to a child's mental and emotional health (it's also important to note that cloudy days provide the same benefit as sunny days). Children, like adults, are susceptible to a certain kind of depression that's triggered by inadequate daylight and usually comes on during the winter months, when days are shorter and nights are longer. It's called seasonal affective disorder, or SAD.

Researchers suspect that SAD occurs because a lack of daylight exposure causes the brain to "power down," or go into a form of hibernation. The symptoms of SAD are the same as those of general depression.

- Change of mood
- Lack of enjoyment in activities
- Low energy
- Changes in sleep patterns
- Changes in eating habits
- Difficulty concentrating
- A tendency to be more isolated

What sets SAD apart from general depression is that the symptoms recur like clockwork at the same time each year, when daylight hours are on the decline. Light therapy, which usually consists of sitting in front of a light box, is absolutely the best way to treat SAD (though the use of antidepressant medication may by helpful at the start of treatment if symptoms are severe). Talk therapy that focuses on adjusting lifestyle to the change in daylight hours is also very helpful. I used one of those forms of treatment to help a young woman named Wendy.

Wendy

Wendy was a junior in high school when she came to see me a couple of years ago. It was just before the Christmas break, and her mother, Pam, had called me out of desperation. "Wendy has always been sensitive and has tended to be a bit melancholy," she explained, "but at times she plunges into a true depression, and we're worried about her." I asked Pam to bring Wendy in the following week.

The next afternoon, Wendy, tall and fair, with dark hair and expressive brown eyes, slipped silently into my office and sat down. I asked her to describe her mood. She told me that she felt empty, flat; that she couldn't seem to muster any energy or enthusiasm. No matter what activity she was engaged in, she just couldn't seem to shift out of this awful mood. She also said that for the past couple of months, she had taken to sleeping 15 hours a day, but even this didn't seem to be enough. She also couldn't seem to get enough sweets and chips. "I hate myself for it, Dr. Shannon, but I can't seem to resist junk food, and I've put on 10 pounds that I just don't need," she shared miserably. I knew that craving carbohydrates was another telltale symptom of SAD, which prompts the body to behave as if it's going into hibernation: Our brains tell us to store energy for the long, dark winter. I didn't even need to check my calendar to know that Wendy's symptoms came on just as the country was switching over from daylight saving time. During the summer months, when it stayed light well into the evening, Wendy felt fine. Come fall, however, when darkness descended at about the same time school ended, her mood began to slip. Now, just weeks before Christmas, she was miserable.

Pam asked me if there was an antidepressant that might help Wendy. "I believe there is," I replied, "but I'd like to prescribe something else." I took my prescription pad and wrote down the name and phone number of a company that creates light boxes specifically to treat people with SAD. Although these lights are relatively expensive (roughly $100 to $150), they may be covered by insurance and, at the least, may be tax deductible. In the long run, they are also cheaper than drug therapy. I also prescribed my basic nutritional supplement plan so that Wendy's brain would get a nutritional boost while we addressed what I believed to be the cause of her low mood.

Pam ordered the light box immediately, and Wendy began to spend 30 to 60 minutes each morning sitting in front of it. Within just a couple of weeks, she was feeling remarkably better. She had stopped craving carbohydrates, was sleeping 10 hours a night (a good amount for an active teen), and was waking up feeling refreshed and optimistic. She felt like "her old self" and was enjoying her life again, too.

TECHNOLOGY AND YOUR CHILD'S MIND

Probably nothing has caused more dramatic and significant changes in the past few generations than the introduction of technology into our lives. Just over 50 years ago, there were no televisions, no computers, no iPods, no BlackBerries, and no cell phones. There were no video games, no music videos, no DVDs, no Xboxes. Who among us gets through the day without using one or more of these electronic devices?

The days of thinking about television or the computer as an appliance or just a diversion are long over. Our kids are spending most of their time in front of one kind of screen or another. Literally, the average child now spends more time watching TV than attending school. This kind of electronic engagement has had a profound effect on kids' behavior and the development of their brains.

Television

For many of us, television is quite literally our window onto the world. Nowadays, there are hundreds of channels that broadcast around the clock. We can tune into 24-hour news networks that strive to give us "real time" access to the most sensational events of the day, regardless of where on the globe the events are unfolding. We're thrust into the middle of war, feel the impact of natural disasters, and watch crimes in progress with high anxiety. Or we tune into a sitcom and lose ourselves in the fictional life of another family. Or we watch a gruesome murder being solved in record time by brilliant, albeit fictional, forensic specialists. The

What's On?

Did you know:

- In the typical American home, the television is on for more than 7 hours a day.

- The average American kid spends more time watching TV than being in school.

- The average American child spends more time (more than 20 hours per week) watching television than engaging in any other activity except sleeping.

- By the time a child is 70, he will have spent 7 to 10 years of his life in front of the TV.

- The average American kid sees roughly 200,000 acts of violence on TV—including 40,000 murders—by the age of 18.

content is limitless, but the goal of the medium is always the same: to take our attention away from ourselves and shift our focus to the plights, stories, or issues of others.

From a child psychiatrist's point of view, there's a big problem with this. Television and other new technologies demand that we engage in a one-sided relationship. In other words, we watch, but we don't participate. We form a strange kind of bond by becoming familiar with others (fictional or not) without ever having the chance to establish a real relationship with them. It's a one-dimensional kind of stimulation that certainly distracts our kids but doesn't necessarily nourish them.

This is not to say that television is entirely bad. With the right kind of guidance and selection, kids can reap great benefits from appropriate TV viewing. They can learn about other cultures, about nature, about science and life. They can watch programs that will foster their creativity or model for them how to be good citizens of the world—but these programs typically aren't the ones that are hyped and heavily promoted. Instead, they are buried under mountains of mediocre—or worse, violent, sexually explicit, inappropriate, or otherwise overstimulating—fare.

As with everything else in life—especially where our children are concerned—we need to make firm decisions about which kind of television is acceptable and which is not. I recommend that children spend a very limited amount of time in front of the television, because it's known that watching too much can lead to a host of problems in children, including obesity, social isolation, antisocial or risky behavior, and dulled cognitive function.

A recent study published in the journal *Pediatrics* indicated that television viewing actually "rewires" the brains of very small children and that the rapid-fire images a child sees on television or in videos cause her neural pathways to develop in ways that may lead to ADHD later on. This damage typically shows up by the age of 7, when the child has difficulty focusing on routine tasks and schoolwork. The study even managed to quantify this: For roughly each hour a day of television that an infant or toddler watches, there is a 10 percent higher chance that she will be diagnosed with ADHD by age 7. Because of this study, the American Academy of Pediatrics urges parents to severely limit the amount of TV young children watch and to not expose children to television at all before the age of 2. I prefer that, if possible, children watch no television before age 4.

Violence on TV

It's not just the electronic stimulation of the TV screen that has medical experts worried; it's also the content. Recently six powerful medical groups in this country (the American Academy of Pediatrics, the American Academy of Child and Adolescent Psychiatry, the American Psychological Association, the American Medical Association, the American Academy of Family Physicians, and the American Psychiatric Association) banded together to issue the warning that a diet of media violence tends to foster antisocial and aggressive behavior in children. It also makes children fearful, desensitizes them to violence and the victims of violence, and, most frightening, gives them the erroneous message that violence is a normal part of life. Consider this example of a child who was severely affected by watching the wrong kind of television programming.

Megan

When I met Megan, she had just turned 9. She was fidgety, restless, and very distractible. Her teachers found it hard to keep her in her seat, and her school performance lagged significantly behind that of her classmates. Though Megan's parents were divorced, they co-parented well and had remained friends. Megan alternated weeks with each parent, who lived very close to each another so that she could remain in her school. Karen, Megan's mom, worked for the local power company. Her dad, Ken, was a construction worker and a volunteer EMT.

Karen was concerned that the divorce (which had taken place several years earlier and had gone smoothly) was the cause of Megan's restlessness. In talking to Megan and her parents, however, I learned that she was a sensitive child prone to fearfulness. As a toddler, she had a run-in with a big dog, and though she was not harmed physically, she had nightmares about the experience for months afterward.

Karen and Ken had taken Megan to a child psychologist during the divorce in order to make the transition as smooth as possible for her. The therapist worked with Megan for several months and then told Karen and Ken that she thought Megan was handling the change well and no longer needed treatment. Then Megan's school performance began to fall apart. Ken and Karen decided to consult their pediatrician. Ken told me he was stunned by the diagnosis: She scored above the cutoff on the

Conners Scale (one of several rating scales used by physicians) and was diagnosed with ADHD. The pediatrician prescribed Adderall (amphetamine-dextroamphetamine).

Initially, Megan's academic performance improved, but within a couple of months, she began to have severe trouble sleeping and lost some weight. At that point, her parents decided to stop the medication, and they called me.

It took a few sessions for me to see beyond all the agitation and see Megan. It became quite clear to me that underneath all of the nervous energy was a little girl who was somewhat shy and fearful. During our third session, Megan confided in me that she became so anxious at night that she couldn't fall asleep. When she finally did fall asleep in the early morning, she had terrible, violent dreams. Now Megan's agitation made sense to me: She was getting only a few ragged hours of sleep a night, not the restful 10 or 12 hours her growing brain needed. I asked Megan if she had any idea what might be causing these nightmares, and she said no. She also told me that she hadn't told her parents about the nightmares because she didn't want to worry them.

After our meeting, I phoned both Karen and Ken and asked if they knew of anything that might cause such severe anxiety in Megan that she wasn't able to rest at night. Both of them said they'd think about it and call me back. The next day, Ken called. "Dr. Shannon, I don't know if this would cause Megan's problem or not, but as part of our bedtime routine, we watch my favorite shows together." I asked what shows they were. "*Cops* and *America's Most Wanted*," Ken replied, then quickly added, "I thought they were okay because there is no sex and no graphic violence."

What Megan was experiencing was a mild variation of post-traumatic stress disorder (PTSD), which was brought on by the content of these shows. I asked Ken to engage in a more appropriate evening activity with his daughter, such as reading to her or playing a board game. Almost immediately, she began to relax, and her sleep improved. Because she had had such severe sleep deprivation for so long, I gave her the supplement 5-HTP to further help her relax at bedtime. I also put her on my standard nutritional supplement regimen to ensure that her overtired brain was getting enough nutritional support.

I also spoke to Karen and Ken about how crucial it was for them to closely monitor all of the media Megan was exposed to, whether it was television, movies, or the Internet. They both made a commitment to be more vigilant and more mindful of how sensitive Megan was to violence and stress.

After just a few weeks, Megan was much less anxious, she was sleeping through the night, and her school performance began to improve significantly.

Computers, Games, Music, and More

Just as we need to manage the television our kids watch, we also have to monitor their use of computers, games, and even music and phones. It's important for us to know what Web sites our kids are visiting, what kinds of games they play, and what kind of music they are listening to. The quality of the electronic or digital content will have a great impact on the wiring of their young brains, so it's important for us to know what kind of entertainment our kids are enjoying. Here are a few guidelines to help you teach your kids to use electronic media in the right measure.

- Establish strict rules about when and what your children may watch on TV or the computer and what kind of music they can listen to. (I recommend no TV viewing at all for children 4 and under, 1 hour or less per day for kids ages 4 to 6, and no more than 1 to 2 hours per day for children over 6.)

- Watch TV or play video games with your children so they become interactive activities, not forms of social isolation.

- Do not use TV, computer, or game time as a reward.

- Make mealtime TV-free time.

- Keep your child's bedroom an "electronics-free" zone. Put TVs and computers in other rooms.

- Whenever you can, suggest alternative activities, such as reading, playing outdoors, or doing art projects.

- Be a good role model: Use good judgment and self-discipline when selecting what, when, and how much television you watch and how much time you spend online.

THE HEALING EFFECT OF NATURE

Our brains evolved over millions of years in an outdoor, natural environment. After spending lots of time outdoors in the Rocky Mountains, I can tell you that it is not always pleasant or comfortable. Bone-chilling cold, mouth-parching heat, drenching rains, and biting wind make it no picnic to be outdoors at times. Throw in the ants, gnats, and mosquitoes, and the great indoors can become quite appealing.

But one reason that I make regular pilgrimages to the high country is that it offers me deep solace and a kind of comfort that is unlike anything I find in a manmade environment. I'm not alone in this. Research is beginning to show that nature is beneficial to a wide range of health problems, including mental health issues.

Biophilia is a term that was coined by Harvard biologist Edward O. Wilson, PhD, in 1984. It describes the innate bond we share with all creatures and plants in the natural world. Dr. Wilson defined biophilia as "the connections that human beings subconsciously seek with the rest of life." Several formal studies show that patients recover faster when they are exposed to nature or greenery—even if only in a photograph. Our blood pressure falls when we sit and watch a tank of tropical fish. Many people feel a bond with their pets unlike anything they experience with other humans.

One study found that people who swam with bottlenose dolphins for 1 hour a day for 2 weeks had significantly reduced rates of depression as compared with people who swam alone. This randomized, controlled study of patients with moderate depression found that 9 out of 10 patients who swam with the dolphins experienced lasting relief, even many months later. Many other studies have found it beneficial to mental health to own a dog or cat. Therapy dogs are now commonplace in nursing homes and hospitals.

Children also benefit significantly from exposure to nature. A large study conducted in 2004 found that 452 kids diagnosed with ADHD improved significantly when given access to natural outdoor settings. (The benefit is greater when the setting is "wild" as opposed to highly groomed or manmade.) The symptoms of ADHD melted away for the kids immersed in nature.

The writer Richard Louv has even coined the expression "nature-deficit disorder" to describe the symptoms experienced by modern kids who have become too disconnected from nature. In his book *Last Child in the Woods: Saving Our Children from Nature-Deficit Disorder,* he offers anecdotal information from parents and kids across the country and cites scientific research that indicates that children who are exposed to nature early and often thrive intellectually, spiritually, and physically in ways that their "shut-in" peers don't. "Nature play," Louv writes, has become a successful therapy for conditions ranging from ADHD to anxiety disorders in children.

Our children now spend so much time in artificially lit classrooms, in front of computer monitors, or plunked down on the couch in front of the television set that they are largely cut off from the natural world. In the cloistered, technologically driven world we live in, we've forgotten how restorative the right kind of environment can be—especially for our kids. And the best kind of environment is one that has been relatively untouched by man. Parents who make efforts to keep their children connected to nature are helping them to stay balanced in ways that will strengthen their emotional and mental health. Here are some quick tips to help you reconnect your child with nature.

- Make sure your child gets plenty of outdoor time all year round. Being in tune with the change of seasons will keep your child in sync with the rhythm of nature.

- When possible, visit beautiful natural settings, including local parks and gardens.

- For your next vacation, bypass the theme park and head to a national park.

- Watch the Discovery Channel with your child so he can partake of the wonder of nature on a regular basis.

- Encourage your child to play outdoor sports.

- Take the time to stop and notice the natural beauty that surrounds you and your child, whether it's in the middle of a large urban area or in the country.

ENVIRONMENTAL TOXINS: HIDDEN AND HARMFUL

Where do you live? You may live in a big city or in the country. When it comes to heavy metal poisons, pesticides, and other environmental toxins, it no longer matters. We live in a global environment that has become saturated with more than a century's worth of residues from manmade toxins. No matter where you live, these toxins show up in the air, water, and food.

Children are at the greatest risk from these environmental pollutants because their immune and nervous systems are still fragile and developing; they breathe more air per pound of body weight than adults do, they tend to pick things up and put them in their mouths, and they eat more food per pound of body weight than adults do.

Most of us know that intense exposure to heavy metals (lead, mercury, arsenic, aluminum, and cadmium, for example) can have a very damaging impact on our health, including our neurological and brain health. But most of us don't know that even low-level exposure to these toxins can be harmful. Children are at highest risk from this kind of exposure because their bodies absorb toxins quickly but release them slowly.

The two most common heavy metals, mercury and lead, pose a great risk to our children's brain health.

Lead

Although it has been taken out of gasoline and is no longer an ingredient in paint products, the EPA estimates that 1.7 million children are affected by lead toxicity today. The majority of those children (roughly 900,000) are under the age of 6. Lead poisoning causes symptoms in children that mimic those of some very serious psychiatric diseases, which, not coincidentally, are on the rise in the United States. Children with lead overload can have lower IQ scores, struggle with learning disabilities, and be labeled hyperactive. These kids may also exhibit aggressive or disruptive behaviors and have difficulty maintaining focus and concentration.

The symptoms of lead overload mimic the symptoms of many behavioral and cognitive problems we see in kids. Behavioral symptoms of lead toxicity may include:

- Poor memory
- Inability to concentrate
- Attention deficit
- Aberrant behavior
- Irritability

- Temper tantrums
- Fearfulness
- Insomnia
- Lowered IQ
- Difficulty with reading, writing, language, visual, or motor skills

People ask me if I routinely test for lead toxicity in kids who come to me diagnosed with ADHD or other behavioral problems. I do test for lead poisoning if I suspect that a child may be at risk for this kind of exposure, especially because the test is inexpensive and easy. This testing can do only so much, however, because

How to Protect Your Child from Lead Poisoning

- Have your child tested for lead poisoning, especially if he has any of the symptoms listed on pages 122 and 123.
- Clean floors, window frames, windowsills, and other surfaces weekly.
- Use lead-free paints.
- Don't try to remove lead paint yourself.
- Don't bring lead dust into your home from work or a hobby.
- Have your water supply tested.
- Eat whole foods (organic, if possible) and don't store food in leaded pottery.
- Filter your water or at least let it run for 20 or 30 seconds before taking a drink.
- Wash fruits and vegetables carefully.

(Source: EPA)

once toxic levels of lead are detected, the damage has already been done. But knowing the true cause of your child's symptoms will allow you to make appropriate treatment choices that will guarantee the best outcome.

Mercury

Mercury is another heavy metal that causes severe neurological problems in kids, and some experts consider it to be more toxic than lead. The National Academy of Sciences estimates that up to 60,000 children born in the United States each year may be affected by mercury toxicity.

In this country, nearly one in six children born each year is at risk for exposure to mercury levels that are known to cause learning disabilities, motor skill impairment, and memory loss. Couple that with this astounding estimate, released by the EPA in 2004: Nearly 630,000 children are born each year at risk for lowered intelligence and learning problems because they were exposed to high levels of mercury prenatally. Symptoms of mercury toxicity include:

- Insomnia
- Nervousness
- Hallucinations
- Memory loss
- Headaches
- Dizziness
- Anxiety
- Irritability
- Drowsiness
- Emotional instability

▣ Depression

▣ Poor cognitive function

These symptoms are serious and can even be life-threatening; severe mercury toxicity can be fatal. Mercury sneaks its way into our bodies in various ways.

Mercury in our mouths. There is a lot of debate these days about whether the mercury in dental fillings is a source of toxicity. Although the jury is still out on this, I advise parents of my patients to err on the side of caution and request that their children get polymer fillings rather than "silver" fillings.

Mercury in childhood vaccines. The controversy that surrounds the use of mercury in vaccines is one of the most explosive and problematic for child psychiatrists, pediatricians, and parents today. This is because thimerosal, a preservative that contains mercury, was added to vaccines in the 1990s, at the same time that the rates of autism and autism spectrum disorders—or at least diagnoses of these disorders—were skyrocketing in this country. The number of children diagnosed with autistic disorders increased tenfold with the introduction of thimerosal into vaccines. Recent studies, however, cast doubt on this association.

Although the debate over the toxicity of mercury in vaccines is far from over, I can't help sympathizing with those parents who have an intuitive, gut feeling about this kind of exposure. I am a firm believer in the overall benefit of vaccinations, but I'm also a proponent of delaying and spacing them in order to give our children's bodies time to grow and develop enough to withstand the negative side effects of vaccines, including being able to handle any toxic fallout from them. The good news is that since 1999, there has been an aggressive drive to have thimerosal removed from routine childhood vaccines.

I recommend, however, that parents take the threat of

mercury poisoning—whether it be from dental fillings, child-hood vaccinations, or tainted fish—as seriously as possible.

A colleague, Keith Berkowitz, MD, founder of the Center for Balanced Health in New York, recently shared the following astonishing case history.

James

In the fall of 2004, a young man of 19 came to my office com-plaining of fatigue, malaise, and depression. He felt that he was running on empty. I asked him how long this had been going on, and he told me that his symptoms started when he was 16 and had gotten progressively worse over the past couple of years. He had such difficulty concentrating that he could not hold a job or complete his classes at college. He had been to see several psy-chiatrists who had concluded that he was indeed clinically depressed, and one had diagnosed him as having schizophrenia since he described some episodes of hallucinating. He was put on a complex regimen of medications when he turned 18, including Wellbutrin (bupropion), Zyprexa (olanzapine), and Risperdal (risperidone), and promptly gained 50 pounds. His parents, fear-ing that the medication was causing more harm than good, called me.

When I met James, I asked him to outline his physical symp-toms for me. He told me that he had carried a low-grade fever around for most of the past 2 years and that he had begun to develop severe allergies. He was also often bloated and consti-pated. Based on these complaints, I suspected that something in James's diet might be the culprit, and I wasn't surprised when he told me that he ate fish three times a day. To confirm my suspi-cions, I ran a full series of blood tests and ordered a urinalysis to screen for toxic metal overload. Sure enough, James's tests came back indicating that he had mercury poisoning. I put him on a rigorous vitamin and nutrient supplementation plan and moni-tored him while we weaned him from all psychiatric drugs.

Once he was medication (and fish) free, James underwent a series of treatments (chelation) to rid his body of mercury. He also had the mercury fillings in his teeth replaced with plastic-based fillings. Once we were able to determine that most (but not all) of the mercury was out of his system, the change was nothing short of dramatic: His mood became stabilized, his brain fog lifted, and he was able to reimmerse himself in his college studies. Today, he's an A student who has chosen to pursue a career in nutrition.

Mercury and ADHD: Is There a Link?

Just as there is no definitive link between mercury toxicity and autism, there is no body of research that makes the rock-solid case that mercury toxicity causes ADHD or other behavioral problems in kids. But the fact that the symptoms of mercury poisoning (and other heavy metal toxicity) mimic those of ADHD should give those parents whose kids have been diagnosed with ADHD pause. Certainly—as with any serious condition that warrants the use of potent prescription drugs—you will want to rule out any underlying condition that may present as ADHD in your child. This, of course, includes mercury poisoning.

PESTICIDES

The poisons that are used by farmers are exceedingly dangerous to a young child's brain. Pesticides have a direct impact on the central nervous system, including inhibiting neurotransmitter synthesis and brain development. Even low-dose exposure to common pesticides can impair learning, disrupt thyroid function, and induce the symptoms of ADHD.

Recent studies suggest that 90 percent of kids tested have detectable levels of pesticide metabolites in their urine. What is so disconcerting about this is how little understanding we have of the impact pesticides have on the developing brain. Of the more than 2,800 chemicals commonly used in pesticides and herbicides in this country, only 12 have been tested for developmental toxicity. These toxins, which are on our food, in our air, and in our water supply, become concentrated in fatty tissue. Dioxin, one of the most dangerous of the 12 known toxins, is found in the highest concentrations in human breast milk. It has been proven to disrupt hormone function and severely impair neurological development.

CULTIVATING PEACE OF MIND

The environment surrounding us is in a constant state of change and flux. Trying to control all of the environmental factors that influence our children's brain growth and development is impossible—and unrealistic. We are part of our environment, not separate from it, and learning to live in harmony with it is key to our health, including our brain health. But how do we parents navigate a world that is so environmentally comprised? We do it by bearing in mind that knowledge is power and that awareness can bring change. Although we can't single-handedly clean the air we breathe or the water we drink, we can take actions that will minimize the harm some key environmental factors can visit on our children. This is one of the best ways to protect our children from labels and drugs. Here are some things you can do to improve your child's environment.

1. Buy organic food and natural meats. This is especially important with fruits and vegetables that don't have a removable skin or peel.

2. Wash all nonorganic fruits and vegetables with a product designed to remove contaminants.

3. Buy and eat wild fish harvested in a sustainable manner.

4. Use glass containers instead of plastic ones to store and heat food.

5. Recycle.

6. Grow a garden.

7. Join a local food co-op that supports local organic growers, or shop at farmers' markets.

8. Eliminate all pesticide and herbicide use in and around your home.

9. Use toxin-free, sustainable cleaning products in your home.

10. Consider getting a HEPA air filter for your home.

11. Install a water filter in your home.

12. Exercise and play in clean, safe places (avoid decks and play structures that have been treated with arsenic, a known toxin).

13. Avoid traveling with your child through heavily congested traffic whenever possible.

14. Lobby politicians to strengthen environmental rules and regulations.

Whenever you take even a small step to improve your child's environment, you are actively protecting her brain growth and health. You are also modeling for her how to be proactive—a noble quality that you will want your child to develop, too. There is so much in our environment that we simply cannot control or change, but by changing or improving what we can, we can cultivate a sense of peace and well-being that will improve the lives of everyone around us, especially those of our kids. In the next chapter, I'll discuss the relationships a child has within the home and how they significantly affect emotional and mental health.

CHAPTER 6

The Family System and Fit: School, Intelligence, and Learning Style

F amily relationships, probably more than any other single factor, have the greatest influence on neuron growth and the quality of evolving neural connections in a child's growing brain. We are social creatures, and our brains quite literally reflect this fact. We learn, love, and live in a web of relationships that determine to a large degree how our brains grow and develop. Our earliest relationships inform the quality of the other relationships we have throughout our lives.

The *experiences* a child has in her relationships literally become imprinted on her brain. The interactions she has with others serve as the sparks that ignite development in her emotional brain, and these experiences profoundly influence how her brain will ultimately be wired. These relational experiences also become the bedrock of her personal history, since her brain records the facts of her relationships and interactions in minute detail. This is why, when we begin to search for the root of emotional or mental problems in children, we need to look closely at their relationships, particularly those with family members.

THE FAMILY SYSTEM

Until the 1960s, my profession was based on the assumption that the psychology of human behavior was rooted in the individual, so treatment was focused almost exclusively on the individual. This notion was turned upside down in 1966 when Murray Bowen, MD, a psychiatrist at Georgetown University, offered a new theory, which proposed that in order to understand an individual's emotional and mental state, one must look at the relationships that person has with others, particularly relationships with family. Dr. Bowen stressed that just as other organisms in nature are interdependent, humans are born interrelated, and this fact must be brought to bear when treating the individual. He and some of his contemporaries understood that families are living, ever-changing, dynamic natural systems built upon interdependence.

Family systems, which can be looked at as small, intimate communities that foster both independence and dependence, are highly sensitive: What affects one member ripples through the system and eventually affects all members. When change occurs, the configuration—and health—of a family shifts and adjusts. But family systems are not by nature chaotic. In fact, like all other natural systems, families tend to move toward a state of homeostasis, or balance, and the members of the system become used to this steady state.

Over time, the family (or system) becomes, to varying degrees, resistant to change, whether good or bad. This makes looking at stress within the family difficult. Also, family systems tend to be fairly closed, operating out of the view of the community at large. This also makes it difficult to identify any problems that may be challenging the system.

Understanding that this tendency to resist change is part of the organic makeup of families may help explain why we as a culture tend to be a bit reluctant to look at the whole family and its dynamics whenever a child is in distress. Although I've been treating children for many years, I see that it's still our first impulse to label a child's symptoms rather than dig in and work to root out the true source of stress in that child's life. This is particularly true when the stress comes from the family itself. We (parents, practitioners, educators, all of us) need to work hard to accept the notion that none of us exists in a vacuum. When we can do this, we begin to see that whenever a child is suffering, it's highly likely that at least one other family member—if not more—is suffering, too.

As I mentioned earlier, I rarely meet a child who has a true, organic mental or emotional disorder. Most of the symptoms I see in kids are reflections of a problem or problems that are plaguing the entire family. What happens, however, is that the child who outwardly expresses the family problem—through falling grades, aggressive behavior, isolation, or pronounced, unusual social problems—becomes the "canary in the coalmine," or what medical professionals call the identified patient. In other words, as the child begins to manifest the greater stress plaguing the entire family, his emotional or behavioral health begins to falter.

Too often, in our label-happy culture, the suffering child is mistakenly viewed as the cause of the stress ("If only Oona would stop skipping school, everything would get back to normal"), and the true cause goes even further underground.

I see many children who have been labeled as the main source of family stress, even by their own parents and caregivers! But the truth is, kids are simply the most vulnerable members of the family system, and when the system is stressed, they are the first to show the signs and symptoms of that stress.

When a child comes to me already labeled as the source of the family problem, treating him (never mind getting appropriate treatment for other family members) becomes quite a challenge. When the problems of the family have been transferred onto the child or children, developing or even sustaining mental and emotional health is nearly impossible for these kids, and the chances that they'll receive appropriate treatment are slim. Let me give you a vivid example of what happens to a child who has been labeled as the source of family stress.

Danny

Not long ago, a bubbly, energetic 8-year-old bounced into my office. "Hi, Dr. Shannon! I'm Danny," he announced with a big smile as he shot right past me and started rifling through the things on my desk. His mother, Julia, sighed and gave me an apologetic smile. His father, Mark, silently followed them into my office.

When the three of them settled down, Julia outlined why they had come. Danny was their second child. He had a much older sister (by 8 years) who had always been an easy, quiet child and an excellent student. Danny, on the other hand, had "come out running" and hadn't stopped since. His energy was exhausting, and recently his third-grade teacher had suggested that he might have ADHD and need to be on medication. Julia and Mark, in an effort to resist this label, decided to seek the advice of a specialist, so they called me.

Although Danny did have many symptoms of ADHD (he had trouble following directions, settling down to work, and staying in his seat), I felt these were treatable behavioral issues more typical of an exuberant child who might be experiencing some kind of unidentified family stress. In short, I had a gut feeling that something was amiss in the family system, and I asked Julia and Mark if they would mind if I withheld my diagnosis until I had a chance to meet with them separately. They agreed, and we set up a meeting.

Julia arrived first, and I noticed that without Danny there to manage, she seemed much more relaxed. I asked her how she was coping, given the problems Danny was having, and she told me that she had recently started taking an antidepressant on the recommendation of her ob-gyn. Julia said she was exhausted by Danny and that she had great difficulty sleeping at night. I made a note of this. Then we both looked at the clock: Mark was a full 15 minutes late. I decided to keep the conversation going, and Julia, clearly agitated because Mark was so late, bit her lip and said, "You know, he's always late . . . if he shows up at all." Then she blurted out, "He's either buried at the office, holed up alone at home, or away on business." She also confided that she felt Mark drank too much. The sorrow and resignation in her voice were unmistakable.

Finally, Mark arrived. A large middle-aged man, who was probably close to 50 pounds overweight, he wore a suit that seemed to barely contain him or his obvious agitation. Even before he sat down, he announced that he would have to leave promptly, as he had another meeting right after this one. It became evident that Mark was highly defensive and unwilling to talk about himself except to provide what seemed like well-rehearsed answers to my questions. I told him that I thought making it home for family suppers would be very helpful for Danny as well as Julia, who would benefit from an extra pair of hands during the busy evening hours. He replied that his job was demanding and that he did the best he could. He made it clear that he already felt quite burdened by family responsibility, and I noticed that he barely made eye contact with Julia during our session. I got the sense that she was overwhelmed and depressed because she had become a de facto single parent who had no emotional support from her spouse. Mark was also operating in isolation, and he managed his own stress and unhappiness by staying away from the home and family and by eating and drinking too much. Sitting before me were two adults who were living separate—but equally miserable—lives. Unfortunately, the person who was showing the worst symptoms of this troubled relationship was their son.

With just a few minutes left in our meeting, I brought the conversation back to Danny and told Mark and Julia that I was grateful for this meeting because it had confirmed my belief that Danny did not have ADHD. I then outlined what I thought needed to happen for Danny to settle down and for the life of the family to improve. The first recommendation I made was that they consider going into couples counseling so they could learn to be more united in their work as a family. I also suggested that Danny would benefit from counseling. I told them I believed that if they could work on strengthening their family system (which always begins with the marriage, if parents are still together), Danny's behavioral problems would probably resolve themselves.

Before either of them had the chance to respond, Mark looked at his watch, announced that the hour was up, shook my hand, and moved toward the door. Julia rose more slowly and looked me deeply in the eyes. "Thank you, Dr. Shannon, we appreciate your advice." Before they left, I managed to schedule another appointment in 2 weeks. I told them that at that meeting, I would put together a nutritional plan for Danny, and I would have the opportunity to really assess his behavioral issues and get to know him better.

Two weeks later, just an hour before our appointment, Julia called. "Hi, Dr. Shannon. I'm sorry to give you such short notice, but we're canceling our appointment for today." I asked why. "After we saw you, we took Danny to our pediatrician for a second opinion," she explained, "and he confirmed Danny's teacher's diagnosis of ADHD. We started Danny on Concerta (methylphenidate) right away at 36 milligrams a day, and he already seems to be doing much better. We do appreciate everything you told us. Mark is going to try to make it home more often in the evenings, and he said he would try to curb his drinking." With that, she said goodbye, and that's the last I heard about Danny.

What is so heartbreaking—and frustrating—about Danny's story is how difficult it was for his parents to acknowledge that they might be having problems that were taxing the family system in ways that caused their son real distress. Instead, it was easier for them to label their child, attach a serious medical diagnosis to him, and subject him to very powerful medication—all in the name of keeping up an illusion of family peace, of resisting changing a family system in peril.

STRESS AND THE FAMILY

Stress is a part of life. It's also widely misunderstood. Without stress, we wouldn't be motivated to meet life's challenges. Think of a child who practices his violin intensively in order to be relaxed and prepared for an upcoming recital, or one who hits tennis balls against the garage door in anticipation of trying out for the school team. Imagine the thrill a small child feels when taking those first, tentative steps. Stress is inherent in any challenge, and the act of rising to the occasion (and taking advantage of the adrenaline that stress releases) activates and broadens our sense of what we can accomplish, what we can achieve.

Too much stress, however—especially over a prolonged period of time—can have a harmful impact on the emotional and mental health of all family members, especially the young.

Stress is often difficult to define. Clinically, it is any real or perceived threat (physical and/or psychological) that tends to disturb an individual's homeostasis. In simpler terms, stress (as defined at www.stress-counselling.co.uk) is "the uncomfortable gap between how we would like our lives to be and how they actually are." Stress is all the stimulation that flutters around us and within us and keeps us from feeling at peace. Stress (like death and taxes) is a given in life, and we often fall prey to the belief that we should somehow be able to rid our lives of it entirely. Even contemplating this impossible challenge causes us to feel more stress! Instead of thinking about escaping, eliminating, or even reducing stress, those who have strong emotional and mental health know that the trick is to learn to live well with stress and take advantage of it to learn, change, and grow.

No family is immune to stress. In fact, by their very makeup, family systems constantly generate and process tremendous amounts of stress. The challenge for a family—and each of its members—is not to try to avoid the stress (this will certainly cause emotional and mental upset, especially for children) but instead to learn to cope with and address it in healthy ways. Family stressors include the mundane (juggling different schedules, getting the chores done, keeping the noise level down) to the profound (job loss, divorce, a death or illness in the family). Every day, almost every minute, every family—and every family member—is managing a variety of stressors of one kind or another. Each of these little tests serves to make the family stronger (like an inoculation) or weaken it, depending on how that family copes with stress. Here are some common causes of major stress in families.

- Arrival of a new member (birth or adoption)
- A change in family configuration (due to divorce or remarriage)
- Financial difficulties
- Unresolved marital discord
- Job stress or loss
- A move or relocation
- Untreated addiction

- Illness (including mental illness) of a family member
- Death of a family member
- Domestic violence

These sources of stress are often the primary cause of major emotional and mental upset for family members across all age ranges. For a number of reasons, though, the impact each of these has on emotional health is invariably greater for children than it is for adults. For starters, children are often powerless, having no control over these events, and on top of that, their brains aren't developed well enough to cope with high-level stress without adult support.

A Word on Divorce

In my experience, one of the most damaging (yet least often addressed) causes of major stress for children is divorce. This may surprise some readers: How can divorce be more damaging than the loss of a parent or worse than a home environment tainted by violence, for example? Since roughly half of all marriages end in divorce these days, we've become numb to (or we simply deny) the tremendous emotional and mental toll divorce exacts on all family members. The lives of children who experience divorce are literally turned upside down and torn in two, as these kids will probably have two homes and two different (and often contentious) realities to deal with.

Of course, many parents work diligently to help their children manage the inevitable stress that divorce brings, and these children are able to reasonably incorporate the experience into their lives. Their overall mental and emotional health, though challenged, isn't severely compromised. There are also certainly times, especially in cases of domestic abuse or violence, when divorce is the best option, the healthy choice, in terms of protecting the welfare of children. Too often, though, divorce is just the final gesture made by adults who have never mastered the mental and emotional skills they need to navigate conflict, stress, or life's inevitable disappointments. In other words, divorce itself is often a maladaptive response to life stress, the seemingly "best option" for parents with poor coping skills. Here's an example from my practice.

Marilyn and Christopher

I had heard variations of this story many times: Dad is a superstar cardiac surgeon, while Mom stays home to raise the kids. At midlife, Dad decides that he's no longer "understood" by his wife of 18 years, so he leaves her for his much younger adoring nurse. A bitter, adversarial divorce follows, with both parents suing for custody of their two children, Marilyn and Christopher. The bloody custody battle rages on for years. By the time the issue is settled, Dad is married to his former nurse and is living with her and his two young stepchildren across town. Mom has a new live-in boyfriend and has devoted herself to spending as much of her ex's money as she can. Completely lost in this mess are their own two children.

I met them when Marilyn had just turned 14 and Christopher was 12. Marilyn had recently been put on an antidepressant and was having trouble with shuttling back and forth between two homes. She was spending more and more time alone and had lost touch with her group of girlfriends. Her brother wasn't faring much better, but rather than shutting down, Christopher was borderline out of control: He had a quick temper and a tendency to get into fights. He treated his mother with obvious contempt and refused to follow her rules. With his father, he wasn't much better. He was also often suspended from school due to his disrespectful attitude and belligerent style. He was on medication for his aggressiveness and had been diagnosed by another psychiatrist as having intermittent explosive disorder.

In the wake of their parents' divorce, Christopher and Marilyn were left to fend for themselves, emotionally and psychologically. When their father left the family, any semblance of a safe, secure environment in which these children could develop and mature was blown to smithereens. Now they were paying the price.

Immediately, I put both kids on my brain-supportive nutritional plan and got each of them into individual therapy. Their therapist and I worked aggressively to restore some order and stability to their lives. In addition to looking at their diets, I worked to ensure that they were getting adequate rest and helped them incorporate exercise and even play into their disordered lives while helping them to stay focused on their schoolwork and extracurricular activities. Concurrently, my colleague worked tirelessly to shore up their damaged psyches and help them develop effective coping skills. In short, we became surrogate parents to them while we brought both of their parents up to speed on what we were observing in their children.

Fortunately, Dad was very responsive. He and his new wife worked hard to encourage Marilyn and Christopher to talk about their feelings, no matter how "difficult" they might be. They created an open, safe environment in which the challenges of being in a blended family were always up for discussion. Dad even went so far as to agree to let Marilyn live exclusively with her mother so she wasn't always shuttling between two households. The effect was profound: She was able to get out from under a form of chronic stress that severely inhibited her ability to cope and relate. Dad understood that in order for both of his children to heal from the divorce, they had to have the chance to manage some of the outcome themselves and experience a degree of control over their own lives.

A year later, Marilyn was thriving again, and although she lives with her mother full-time, she sees her father often and describes her relationship with him as strong. Christopher was able, once he learned to express his feelings appropriately, to channel some of the adrenaline produced by the stress of his new, more complicated lifestyle into a successful basketball career.

Helping Your Child Cope with Stress

While this example highlights some of the more insidious aspects of divorce, it also illustrates how even children can overcome seismic shifts in their lives and develop the coping skills needed to navigate life's stresses. It also illustrates how fluid and resilient a family system can be when the leaders of that system—the parents—address problems with care.

Most parents, especially those of you who have picked up this book, know instinctively that one of our biggest jobs is to help our kids cope with stress. But few of us are clear about how best to do this. Helping our kids learn to manage stress is an ongoing process, and whenever you practice a new skill, you're bound to make mistakes along the way—we all do. But the "stress points" we bump into as we learn to manage stress are also the best opportunities we have to expand our understanding and skill. These points are the places where children have the chance to build the kind of cognitive "muscle" that will ensure their emotional and mental health. The challenge is to not shy away from the problem or stress but instead to work to face it as directly and appropriately as possible. Here are some tips on how to enhance your child's ability to cope with stress.

Maintain a safe, serene, well-structured environment. When a family is faced with a life crisis, it's important to ensure that a healthy infrastructure doesn't fall away. The home is the safest and most secure environment a child knows. During times of high stress, it's important to maintain a space and rituals that give a child a sense of control and provide healthy respites from the stress. Things that you can do to "stressproof" your environment include keeping your home clean and well stocked with food and supplies, helping your child stay on track with school, and making sure he attends extracurricular activities, continues hobbies, and maintains connections with friends.

Make sure your child gets adequate food and rest. During periods of stress, it's crucial that your child eats well and gets enough sleep. If a parent is ill, for example, and the other parent must spend significant amounts of time at the hospital, make sure there is another adult available to ensure that your kids' needs are being well met. Being fortified nutritionally and with proper rest will help your child roll with the punches that invariably accompany any major life stress. It will also strengthen his brain so he can cope with the stress as efficiently as possible.

Maintain open communication. Sometimes families who visit my office begin the conversation by saying everything is "fine." A red flag goes up immediately whenever I hear this, as it indicates that there is some kind of stress within the family that has been pushed underground. Families who are coping with stress communicate openly and well: They name the stress, talk about how it's affecting them, and strategize—openly—about how best to contend with it.

Provide consistent support and encouragement. When a major stress hits a family (for example, the death of a beloved grandparent), it's critical that the parent whose own parent has died and who is also deeply affected remain available and accessible to the child/children despite his or her own challenges with the stress. During times of duress, parents need to let their children know that they're aware of the stress, that they're there for them, and that they understand what's going on. The tough times are when extra hugs and kisses, pats on the back, and one-on-one time are called for.

Avoid overprotecting your child. This may sound counterintuitive, but we parents must resist the urge to shield our children from life's inevitable stresses. Children learn to cope with stress only by experiencing it, so we must be willing to stand back and let them grapple with some stressful situations on their own. Allowing for this kind of autonomy (while *always* providing appropriate support) will strengthen your child's emotional and mental health.

Work to build your child's sense of self-esteem. Children build self-esteem when they are aware of their own ability to cope and solve problems. Giving your child appropriate responsibilities, such as doing chores—even during times of crisis—will give her a sense of control, capability, and belonging. Let your child make decisions, too—and encourage her to develop interests in areas where she can succeed. Offer appropriate praise and encouragement, and your child's self-esteem will soar.

Model appropriate coping skills. It's important for parents to convey to children that stress is normal (and not "out to get them") and show them by example how to cope with it with skill, grace, and calm. Nothing is a more powerful teacher for a child than seeing his parent using strong coping skills in the face of adversity. Strive to be an optimist in the face of stress to show your child that it is normal, temporary, and manageable.

Nurture problem-solving skills. Start by helping your child clearly identify a problem, then help him generate a list of possible solutions (and refrain from judging them). Walk through the list with her, discussing the pros and cons of each scenario without trying to steer her thinking one way or another. Instead, encourage her to choose what appears to be the best solution. Praise her if the chosen solution works and encourage her if it isn't perfect. Part of developing strong problem-solving skills is having the opportunity to make mistakes and learn from them.

Teach assertiveness. Children who don't feel entitled to stand up for themselves have trouble handling stressful situations, as do those who by nature are passive or shy. Assertiveness is learned, and parents need to help their children develop it. Role-playing stressful situations is a great way to help your child develop this quality and teach him how to stand up for himself in appropriate, nonaggressive ways.

Help your child develop an appropriate sense of humor. Children who can see the humorous side of things and laugh at themselves tend to handle stress better than those who see only the gravity of a situation or are too hard on themselves. Parents should help their children learn to not take themselves or stressful events too seriously. Laughter is a great stress buster.

Encourage your child to participate in enjoyable/relaxing activities. If your family is experiencing stress, encouraging your child to engage in activities he finds enjoyable or relaxing will help him cope with the stress more effectively. Listening to music, reading in a quiet place, making art projects, or playing a game can take a child's mind off his troubles and allow his young brain to recharge. Also, encourage your child to play sports; vigorous exercise is a great stress reducer.

Seek professional help if your child needs additional support. Being stoic in the face of overwhelming stress is not heroic; in fact, it's an indicator of a lack of healthy coping skills. Parents who recognize that a stress is too great—or that their stress management skills aren't strong enough to support their children well—and seek outside help are exhibiting excellent coping skills.

When we help our children learn to cope well with stress, we are helping them learn to cope well with life.

RESILIENCE: THE GREAT STRESS BUSTER

Resilience, or the ability to thrive even in the face of great stress, is probably the single most important trait a child needs in order to manage stress and enjoy a lifetime of strong mental and emotional health. The great news about resiliency is that it is a learned trait, an acquired skill, so every child has the potential to be a resilient child.

Several longitudinal studies that followed people over the course of their lifetimes have consistently shown that between one-half and two-thirds of children who grow up in families plagued by major stress (including those raised in families where there is mental illness, parental addiction, abuse, poverty, and so forth) do overcome the odds, turn a trajectory of risk around, and enjoy success and happiness in life. All children have access to these skills.

The word *resilience* is a catchall for a cluster of traits that one must have in order to adapt, grow, and change despite risk or adversity. These traits include social competence, problem-solving skills, autonomy, a positive mental attitude, critical consciousness (which enables people to have an objective, accurate awareness of the stressors in their lives), and a strong sense of one's inherent value. When these traits are in place, a child also has a strong sense of purpose and of being prepared for life.

The tools needed to develop resilience are quite similar to those needed to ensure strong brain health in general. These include the presence of at least one caring, compassionate adult in a child's life (for high-risk children, this often turns out to be a teacher) who provides support for healthy development and learning; the establishment of high, though not unrealistic, expectations for him; opportunities to problem-solve; and opportunities to make autonomous decisions about his own life.

All children are resilient, but that resilience can easily be eroded by stress if we're not attentive. Whether resilience is nurtured or suppressed is up to us, the parents and caregivers. Fostering resilience is an ongoing endeavor and simply takes awareness on our part, but the rewards of helping a child build resilience are immeasurable and glorious. I'll share with you a story from my practice about a boy whose resilience helped him beat extraordinary odds. He remains an incredible source of inspiration to me to this day.

Sherman

Each session began the same way. Sherman, a 9-year-old who had been mandated into our residential treatment facility, entered my office without making a sound and then sat in stony silence for the entire hour. He was a handsome, lanky boy of African American and Native American descent whose strong features stood in stark contrast to his startlingly soft demeanor.

Sherman's eerily calm presence seemed incompatible with his chaotic history. His mother, a full-blooded Zuni Indian from the pueblo west of Albuquerque, led a nomadic existence, wandering between Phoenix, Flagstaff, and Albuquerque in search of drugs and alcohol. She turned to prostitution to support her habits. Sherman was the product of a one-night stand with an African American soldier. From what history I could piece together, his mother, though loving and attentive, couldn't sustain her relationship with Sherman, so brief, sporadic periods of nurturance and love were bracketed by long periods of outright neglect. When he was a baby, he was taken from his mother by social services after a frustrated bartender called the police when the young mother passed out, with the squalling infant in a stroller by her barstool.

After Sherman was removed from his mother's custody, he spent the next 3 years in an uncle's home south of Albuquerque in only slightly better conditions. Allegations of physical and sexual abuse finally brought this chapter of his life to a close. He then enjoyed a period of relative quiet and stability while living with a foster family in a middle-class suburb of Albuquerque.

Then, at age 7, Sherman exploded.

Seemingly without provocation, he became belligerent and wildly aggressive. He blew through three foster homes in under 2 years, wearing out each well-intentioned family. He was mostly withdrawn but would periodically explode in fits of white-hot rage.

Since Sherman had been at our resident facility, I had been trying for weeks to get him to open up to me, with little success. Then one day, I handed him some paper, a cup of water, a handful of paintbrushes, and some watercolor paints. "I thought you might like these," I said. "They'll give you something to do for the hour."

Sherman just sat there, impassive as usual. After many minutes, I picked up a brush and began to paint. I watched Sherman's demeanor begin to change as he watched me lazily swirl one color into the next. Then he picked up a brush of his own. I stepped back and watched him work. He intently mixed blacks and browns, and soon the striking image of a horse emerged on the paper before him. Just as abruptly as he had started, Sherman put the brush down, looked me square in the eyes, and announced, "This is Runner the horse. He goes on lots of adventures." Then he left for the day.

Over the next 20 weeks, Sherman spent his daily hour with me painting furiously while sharing the saga of Runner, which I dutifully transcribed. At first, Runner's adventures were short and simple, like Sherman's drawings. Over time, however, the stories became more complex and sophisticated, and this was reflected in his paintings, which became richer and more complex, too. One story was about Runner flying in a plane that crashed, and in another, he was caught in a tornado. Runner was a horse who survived terrible odds, traveled long distances, and lost some friends along the way but made others. He persevered regardless of how tough the going got. In short, Runner was a survivor.

As Runner's identity and history emerged, so did Sherman's. His sullenness began to be replaced by an inherent brightness and an appetite for life and connection. His rages subsided, too, and eventually they became just another part of his history. He even began to exhibit a keen, kind sense of humor. Sherman was beginning to heal. His resilience was beginning to take hold. He had spent a year with us, surrounded by adults who believed in his ability to heal; who believed in his right to a happy, healthy, stable emotional life; and who worked tirelessly to foster his innate resilience. When Sherman was finally well enough to leave us and find his place in the stressful world beyond the protective walls of our center, he promised me that we would keep in touch.

He kept his promise, and we are still in touch. Many years have passed since I met the silent, hurt boy who has become a successful young man who wins awards for his beautiful Native American–inspired paintings. Sherman, his wife, and their young daughter live a simple, happy life in his hometown of Albuquerque. He isn't enslaved by depression or drug abuse as his mother was. He has never been on any psychiatric medications. Recently, I went to Albuquerque on business and had the chance to spend some time with him and his family. They took me to lunch in Old Town and then to a nearby art gallery, where his work was on display. I felt as proud as any parent would as I stood before Sherman's work, reveling in the bounty of his talent, health, and glorious resilience.

THE GIFT OF STRESS

When children are allowed to grapple with life's challenges, they are given the opportunity to connect with their own strengths in ways that will enhance the development of their inner resources. Children who are allowed to struggle and engage with stress get in touch with what experts call their innate "self-righting" tendencies, and they come to recognize, trust, and believe in their ability to appropriately adjust and adapt to the changing circumstances of their lives. Having the opportunity to learn to cope

Qualities of Kids Who Manage Stress Well

- High self-esteem

- A feeling of having control over their lives

- A safe, consistent family system

- A supportive social network

- Open communication with family members

- A loving, supportive relationship with parents or caregivers

- Recognition and support of their resilience

- A sense of humor

- Optimism and faith in the future

with stress in a healthy way isn't only for gifted or "super" kids; it's the birthright of all kids.

The family is the most basic and essential unit of society. It's within the systems of our families that we learn to play, to share, and to love. All families encounter stress; it's inevitable, but those who handle stress best become the healthiest. Strong, resilient families share many of the same characteristics.

Commitment. Every member of a resilient family is recognized and valued. Each is committed to supporting the well-being of the others.

Appreciation. Resilient families celebrate diversity and autonomy and don't expect unreasonable conformity among members. Strong families look for the good in each other and express appreciation and gratitude for the strengths each brings to the larger system.

Spiritual awareness. Resilient families live a life of spiritual awareness, and they respect and cultivate this in each other and as a family. Resilient families know that spiritual health is key to emotional health.

Resourcefulness in crisis. Resilient families enjoy a collective "adaptiveness," wherein the commitment of its members and the appreciation they have for one another's skills make them particularly resourceful in times of stress, conflict, or crisis.

Steadiness and predictability. Resilient families enjoy rituals and routines that give them an identifiable rhythm. They function in attunement with one another.

Closeness. Resilient families like to spend time together: They eat together, play together, and work together. This shared time provides them with memories and experiences that fortify and unite them.

The family is the foundation for social learning, and kids take these lessons with them into the rest of their lives. Among external social settings, school has perhaps the greatest impact, and that's the subject of the next chapter.

CHAPTER 7

School, Learning, and the Young Brain

O utside of the home, no environment is more important to a child's overall social and mental development than school. School is the place where kids build on the relational and learning foundations that have been established at home and where they broaden and hone the skills they need for succeeding in life.

Going off to school is a momentous occasion. School is usually the first environment children inhabit where they are unsupervised by parents; starting school signals a profound step toward autonomy and independence. If we've done a good enough job of parenting up to this point, delivering our children to school evokes feelings of pride and happy expectation, perhaps somewhat flavored by the bittersweet realization that they are truly beginning to separate from us (in healthy, necessary ways). For children who have been well parented, beginning school feels like an exciting adventure, perhaps tinged with some healthy fear of the unknown. All of these feelings are to be expected, given the magnitude of the changes school brings on for our children—and for us.

I view the school environment as the next "ring" in an ever-broadening pool of dynamic social and intellectual communities that embrace and support a child throughout his lifetime. The primary ring, family, always remains the most influential. The next ring, school, ideally moves fluidly around the child, in rhythm with his family life and with both environments nurturing and supporting his learning brain with flexibility and appropriateness. That's the ideal, anyway. In the real world, the interplay of family life and school life is rarely a perfect fit, and the friction that arises between the two often ignites a spark that may trigger symptoms of emotional or mental distress in a child. This is often when I come into the picture.

Over my years of practice, I've seen that there's often a fair degree of disharmony between the home life and school life of a child in distress. The environmental synchronization between home and school doesn't happen automatically. These two very powerful areas of influence are concentric, but they don't overlap, and consequently, parents—and school personnel—sometimes fail to see the deep connections between them. There is in essence a vibrational relationship between home and school, and if there's upset in one realm, it will be felt—and expressed—in the other. In other words, the success of a child at school absolutely depends on her success at home—and vice versa.

If a child is thriving at home and is developing solid emotional and mental health, she is likely to thrive in school, as long as the school environment is accepting, flexible, and accommodating of her basic needs and learning style. She will thrive in school if there is a good enough "fit," just as she will at home when there is good familial fit.

THE BENEFITS OF SCHOOL

For most kids, school serves as a rich microcosm of the larger world, reflecting its diversity, challenges, and complexity.

Regardless of its size or philosophical orientation, school is where a child learns to interact with authoritative adults who are not his parents and to live in harmony with his peers. It's also here that a child hones the basic skills of reading, writing, and arithmetic and may also develop a taste for music, art, organized sports, and other extracurricular activities. In short, school has the potential to provide many of the tools, resources, and opportunities—including important nonfamilial relationships—that a child's brain needs for growing and maturing optimally. Fortunately, most schools offer a healthy variety of stimuli, and most children do well enough. But I believe our children can do better, especially in the areas of social and emotional growth, if parents and teachers work harder to understand each child's needs, especially the needs of his growing, learning brain.

THE LIMITATIONS OF SCHOOL

Schools today have a difficult mandate: They are meant to provide a safe, nurturing, enriching environment and experience for every student. As parents, we expect our schools to provide state-of-the-art teaching and dynamic curricula while also replicating and building on the nurturing aspects of home life. Unfortunately, these expectations are simply too high (though not unreasonable in many respects), given the government's mandate to "leave no child behind." This program forces schools to adhere to a "middle of the curve" mentality and to set standards and goals that are meant to educate the greatest number of children as adequately as possible. This approach (which, ironically, was designed to be broadly inclusive) tends to exclude not only children who have learning disabilities or other obvious weaknesses that may hinder their ability to learn but often those who are the brightest and most potentially gifted as well. The "one size fits all" approach to education that most schools must follow today directly feeds into our cultural orientation toward a very limited definition of "normal," which in turn leads to more labeling (and diagnosing and medicating) as more and more children can't fit into the narrow band of "normal."

INTELLIGENCE: A MULTIFACETED TRAIT

Part of the reason schools today value conformity over individuality is the emphasis that has been put on certain kinds of intelligence, which Harvard psychologist Howard Gardner, PhD, calls traditional intelligences. The most highly regarded of these (though certainly not those that will ultimately predict meaningful success in life) are logical (math) and linguistic (verbal) skills. These are the two types of intelligence that are roughly measured by IQ tests. Standardized tests also measure for these, but many experts—myself included—question the benefits of such tests, since they don't reveal anything of interest about a child's learning style or true potential. Instead, relying solely on standardized tests to judge children's learning potential only serves to further label and divide them.

Dr. Gardner is a true visionary. He's helped us to understand that children possess an array of intelligences and has identified eight core types: logical, linguistic, musical, physical (kinesthetic), spatial, interpersonal (understanding others), intrapersonal (understanding oneself), and naturalist (the science of nature, plants, and animals). He believes—and I agree—that an individual rarely possesses only one style. Instead, all of us fall along a continuum in each of these areas of intelligence; we simply exhibit more strength in one (or several) than in the others. But all intelligences need to be present and activated in each of us—especially our children—to live life well and to learn as optimally as possible.

Many schools, however, still operate on the misguided model that says there are really only two types of intelligence (logical and linguistic) and that these are best evaluated by tests. This limited view is finally starting to change, thanks in large part to the work of Dr. Gardner and other educational visionaries such as Melvin Levine, MD; Joseph Renzulli, EdD; and Eric Larsen, among others.

Another limitation of most schools today is methodology. It may be just a function of large class size and less than optimal student/teacher ratios, but most schools employ only didactic methods (lectures, handouts, for example) at the expense of interactive methods (small groups, student-initiated projects, discussion-based lessons, and so forth) in order to maximize the dissemination of information. We know, however, that a didactic approach isn't necessarily the best one, because learning is about process and is driven by relationships.

LEARNING VERSUS PERFORMANCE

Schools today are also focused on rewarding performance rather than on promoting learning, much to the detriment of a child's growing brain. For a young child, learning is a dynamic, interactive process that engages and activates many parts of the brain. It is also a process of trial and error, so an optimal school environment would be one that allows for mistakes, false starts, and even dissent.

Optimal learning takes place when a child engages in something willingly and freely and is able to bring to a task a high degree of motivation, self-direction, and passionate effort. When a child is fully engaged and learning, her brain is activated on every level (sensory, cognitive, emotional, physical), and it buzzes with electrical activity that elicits positive feelings, including satisfaction, engagement, curiosity, and capability. The *experience* of learning encourages brain growth on all levels and fosters the ongoing intellectual, social, and emotional development of the child.

When a school is forced to measure a child's success by tallying up grades, test scores, class rank, and other quantifiable measures of perceived success, the child's true potential often goes unrecognized. Schools tend to measure student success by the ability to memorize and repeat material (test taking is nothing if not a static, one-sided endeavor) rather than by measuring the success of each child by his joy and immersion in the active process of learning. Emphasizing results rather than process can actually inhibit a child's ability to learn for a number of reasons, not the least of which is the stress this kind of "performance" pressure puts on our kids.

Stress and Learning

A little bit of stress can sharpen us up, get us to focus, and prepare us to learn or take on a new challenge. Too much stress, however, can inhibit our ability to take in and retain information. The line between motivating levels of stress and toxic levels of stress is a fine one, and if left unmanaged, any amount of stress can tip into overload. We've all had the experience of being so stressed out that we've found it difficult to even hear what someone else is saying to us, let alone absorb anything complicated that's being said. This is because the physiological changes that occur in the brain when we're stressed override virtually every other brain function. When the brain is drenched in cortisol or other stress-related hormones, it is quite literally diluted and unable to function well.

Perhaps a child goes to school bearing the stress of his family's financial problems, or he goes to class sick with worry over the inevitable daily run-in with the school bully. Perhaps he dreads facing a page full of blank ovals on yet another standardized test. Whether the stress comes from within school or without, any child burdened by such stress will struggle to function in the classroom. Kids who are experiencing ongoing stress simply can't adhere to the "middle of the road." They may also begin to exhibit emotional and behavioral symptoms that pull them further from the center, and this is when labeling and medicating usually occur. The types of school stress are:

■ Academic pressure

■ Peer pressure

■ Bullying

■ Poor fit with teacher(s)

■ Lack of support for learning style

■ Unacknowledged learning disabilities

■ Environmental issues (such as overcrowding, lack of light)

■ Poor diet

■ Lack of sleep

■ Family stress

The symptoms of school stress look like the symptoms of every other major source of stress. They include:

■ Depression

■ Irritability

■ Impulsive and hyperactive behavior

■ Excessive fear

■ Worry or anxiety

■ Nervousness

■ Social withdrawal

■ Exhaustion and/or agitation (both indicators of sleep problems)

■ Inability to concentrate

■ Moodiness

One could easily take this list and assign a serious psychiatric diagnosis to any of these symptoms. If a child exhibits several—

watch out! A label (and entry into the doctor-diagnosis-drug cycle) is often not far behind.

Being in school often exacerbates these types of symptoms, which is why so many behavioral problems are related to school performance. When symptoms arise while a child is attending school, I find it particularly important to resist labeling and being overly aggressive about trying to alleviate the symptoms (by turning to drug therapy, for instance) until the true root cause of the stress has been identified and addressed. If the stress comes from home, parents or caregivers may actually find the school to be a great source of support and an ally while the stress is being addressed.

If, on the other hand, the stress seems to come from school, it's important that both parents and educators take a close, hard look at how well the school's teaching style matches the child's learning style. This is when knowing—and honoring—your child's learning style becomes paramount.

YOUR CHILD'S LEARNING STYLE: THE KEY TO SUCCESS AT SCHOOL—AND IN LIFE

Understanding and honoring your child's learning style is key to having her thrive in the school environment. I find it helps parents to focus on the following four broad styles of learning (which encompass many types of intelligence, including the eight proposed by Dr. Gardner) when working to identify their child's style.

Visual/verbal learners: Learn best with verbal visual aids, such as outlines, textbooks, written lessons (on chalkboards or overhead projectors). Visual/verbal learners are often bookworms and enjoy reading on their own. They are good note takers, use verbal clues (such as notes or outlines) to help them retain information, and often enjoy writing.

Visual/nonverbal learners: Learn best with pictorial visual aids such as film, video, maps, and charts. When committing something to memory, visual/nonverbal learners "picture" it. They often thrive in art classes and with multimedia assignments. Both nonverbal and verbal visual learners take cues from the facial expressions of those who are engaged in the learning activity with them, particularly their parents and teachers.

Auditory learners: Learn when hearing (not seeing) new information. These learners enjoy lectures and group discussions. When committing something to memory, they "hear" the way the information is delivered and often repeat it out loud to themselves. These kids learn best when there is a listener/speaker exchange. They also absorb difficult or complex information by rephrasing and repeating it. Auditory learners take cues from the tone and volume of the voice delivering the information. They also tend to love music and often need to listen to it while studying.

Kinesthetic learners: Learn best when engaged "hands-on" and in a relaxed environment where movement is permitted. If kinesthetic learners must stay seated, sitting up front where there is a lot of activity on the part of the teacher will help keep them engaged. They retain information most effectively when they can relate it to something tangible, such as building a model, doing a lab experiment, or spending time in the field. In order to absorb information, these students have to move while taking it in, so they're often up and away from their desks or work standing up while others may be sitting quietly. Kinesthetic learners need to be physically engaged in order to learn and so take cues from the physical environment around them. If the environment is open and active, they thrive. If it's shut down, they suffer.

Understanding your child's learning style will allow you to select a school setting that best supports that style. We know, based on how the brain works and how learning occurs, that strength begets strength, and the more we play to a child's strengths, the stronger his development will be across the board. Here's just one example from my practice.

Kyle

I met Kyle just after his 10th birthday, which coincided with him starting fourth grade. His mother, Maggie, called me in late September, exasperated and sounding a bit scared. Here it was, just weeks into the school year, and already Kyle had been flagged as a "problem." His teacher was considering assigning him to a special ed track because he refused to complete assignments and had received only Ds on the few quizzes and tests he had taken so far.

Maggie and her husband, Rob, had been told since Kyle was in preschool that he probably had ADD (attention deficit disorder without the hyperactivity) because he always had great difficulty following instructions, was diffident and stubborn, and generally had trouble "toeing the line" in school. Maggie and Rob knew that Kyle was difficult (he had been a very colicky baby and was quite sensitive), but they also knew him to be quite bright. What they didn't know—or hadn't yet figured out—was what his learning style was. I asked them to bring Kyle in to see me.

Kyle came in shuffling his feet and clearly unhappy about being in my office. I understood from my phone conversation with his mother that he had been evaluated not only by his pediatrician (who had, over the years, offered to medicate him) but also by several school-recommended psychologists. Kyle was indeed bright, and he came away from these appointments with the understanding that the adults in his life were trying to figure out what was wrong with him. It made sense, then, that he was wary of meeting me.

I asked Kyle some general questions about his health (he was a bit overweight but not unusually so for a boy of his age), his sleep patterns (he said he slept "like a bear"), and his diet (which seemed to be terrific, given his mother's skill in the kitchen). When I broached the subject of school, he said that he never felt at ease in school, that he often felt bored there, and that he absolutely hated doing homework. He told me sitting down to write a book report was like torture for him. Then he looked up at me, laughed nervously, and said, "I guess I'm just lazy. That's what my teachers have always said."

Then I asked Kyle what he enjoyed doing in his free time. He told me that he was enrolled in soccer but didn't like it too much. He was also learning to swim, which he enjoyed a bit more. Both of these activities felt like school to him because he was supposed to follow pretty rigid instructions. I asked if there was anything he liked to do that didn't feel like work, and there was one: playing the piano. I asked him to elaborate.

Although he admitted that he hated his lessons ("My teacher is always on me for slumping over the keys") and that practicing felt like homework, Kyle told me that he loved to sit at the piano and make up songs and sing aloud, especially when no one else was around. Rob told me that given the chance, Kyle would spend hours at a time tinkering away at the keys and that he had an uncanny ability to play songs from memory.

I thanked Kyle for sharing so much about his life with me and then asked him to wait while I spoke to his parents. Once alone with Maggie and Rob, I praised them for resisting the urge to label and medicate Kyle, particularly when the going had gotten tough. I then said something that stunned but didn't surprise them. "I think music is going to be the key to Kyle's success," I said. "I may be wrong, but I suspect that Kyle is an auditory learner who has been excluded by a school system that's geared more toward visual learners. Encourage his love of music, and let's see how the rest of this year shapes up for him." Maggie and Rob seemed somewhat amused by the idea that music might be the "medicine" that Kyle needed, but they also seemed encouraged. Before they left, we agreed that they would check in with me by phone as needed.

Just before Christmas, Maggie called me with some exciting news. "Kyle is going to sing in the church Christmas pageant! We had no idea he was interested in this kind of thing. He came home one day and told us he was going to try out and then asked if one of us would take him to the audition. He got the part of the first Wise Man." I was thrilled with this news, especially hearing how self-motivated Kyle was in pursuing this. I asked Maggie to share my enthusiasm with Kyle and to keep me posted.

In early February, she called back to say that Kyle, who had sung his heart out during the holiday season, had asked if he could stop swimming and try out instead for the all-city choir. His parents didn't hesitate. Slowly, Kyle's grades had begun to inch up, and now, instead of dreading his homework, he raced through it so that he could get back to the piano and practicing singing. Over the next couple of years, I learned that Kyle's interest—and skill—in music continued to grow and flourish. At about age 12, he asked for and received an electric guitar for Christmas. He made friends who were also interested in music, and they would get together to "jam." He also continued to sing in the all-city choir and perform in school musicals.

It's been 4 years since I first met Kyle, and this year he began high school. Maggie checked in with me just before the start of the year. "This is it, Dr. Shannon. It's do-or-die time for Kyle and school." I asked her what she meant. Although Kyle had become immersed in a world of music and musical accomplishment, his school performance still lagged; instead of getting Ds, he now routinely got Cs. Maggie and Rob feared that Kyle's options for college would be severely limited if he couldn't get his grades up. He still hated taking tests, and his parents feared that he'd do poorly on the SATs (the tests required by most colleges to be considered for admission). For Maggie and Rob, both graduates of prestigious private colleges, the idea of Kyle's education ending with high school was unimaginable. I encouraged them to relax. To her credit, Maggie acknowledged that her disappointment had nothing to do with who Kyle was and that it was her issue, and I congratulated them on allowing their son's love of music to flourish despite his less-than-stellar academic performance. I had a hunch that the success and accomplishment that Kyle enjoyed with his music would eventually spill over into other areas of his life.

In early November, I got the call I'd been hoping for. "Dr. Shannon!" Maggie gushed. "You won't believe this. First, Kyle's choral group has been selected to travel to New York to perform at Carnegie Hall next spring." Wow! I could feel Maggie's pride oozing through the phone line. "And here's the shocker. Kyle just came home with his first high school report card: he got four A's and two Bs! Rob thinks Kyle has just finally grown into accepting the way school works and that he's not fighting it anymore. But I know it's because we let Kyle blast music while he's studying," Maggie said with a laugh. "Whatever it is, we're just so relieved—and so grateful. It's been a long haul for us—and for Kyle. He's finally found his way." I laughed and told Maggie that blasting rock and roll very well may have been the reason for Kyle's success, as he had indeed turned out to be an auditory learner. Before we hung up, I praised Maggie for how patient she and Rob had been while Kyle discovered and developed his natural learning style. Now that he's grounded in his strengths, Kyle will be able to meet any challenge school—or life—throws his way.

Kyle's parents offered their son access to a variety of activities and experiences (soccer, swimming, music lessons) and then stepped aside and allowed him to select the ones that truly appealed to him. By doing this, they didn't impose their expectations and plans on their son, and they didn't give in to the pressure to overpack his schedule with activities. They had faith that he was not inherently lazy—or worse, suffering from ADD. They knew that he had his own learning style and simply needed to find it. By giving Kyle the room he needed to follow his own pace and make his own choices about how to spend his free time, they let his own very competent and interesting style of learning emerge.

WELL-ROUNDED OR OVERWHELMED?

I don't want to minimize how impressive it was that Rob and Maggie resisted the tremendous pressure parents feel today to enroll their children in a ridiculously wide array of activities. The pressure to excel academically as well as at sports and to engage in extracurricular activities puts incredible demands on children, and if we parents aren't mindful of the effect this kind of overload has on our kids, we may watch our best intentions backfire. Here's the story of one of my patients, a remarkable young woman named Katie who was crumbling under this kind of stress.

Katie

"Katie does not have any psychological problems," announced her mother, Monica. These were the first words I heard after I introduced myself to 14-year-old Katie and her parents. "All right," I said. "Why don't you tell me why you're here?" I listened patiently while Katie's parents took turns relaying her medical history and an overview of her academic life. All the while, Katie sat silently between them on the couch in my office. They were here, Monica finally said, because about a month before our meeting, Katie had developed such severe stomachaches that she was missing school. They took her to the pediatrician, who found nothing physiologically wrong with her, so he recommended that they see me. I took a few notes, smiled at Monica, and asked few questions.

I learned that Monica is an attorney who works 12-hour days

and travels a great deal. Her husband, Bill, is a high school social studies teacher who plays the flute in an Irish band on weekends. Katie is an only child. Both parents, especially Monica, put a high premium on academic achievement. I sensed that Monica was a bit angry with Katie for having missed so much school over the past several weeks.

Once I had a general sense of the overall family, I asked Monica and Bill to wait outside while I had a chat with Katie. As it turned out, Katie was an excellent student who received mostly A's and was enrolled in the "accelerated" academic program at her school. She also took part in a number of extracurricular activities and especially enjoyed being on the staff of the school newspaper (she not only edited the paper but also took pictures for it). I asked her what she did when she wasn't involved in school activities, and she looked at me blankly. "What do you do when you're just hanging around with your friends?" I pressed gently. "I don't hang around with anyone, Dr. Shannon," she answered. "I just don't have time."

I asked Katie to describe a typical day. She had to be up by 6:00 or 6:30 a.m. at the latest in order to be ready for the start of school at 7:30. Three days a week, she spent hours working on the school newspaper. On the other days, she volunteered as a reading tutor at her old elementary school. (When she mentioned this, it was the first time I saw the glimmer of a smile.) By the time she got home, she was exhausted, but she had to spend several hours each night doing homework. It was rare for her to get to bed before 11:00 p.m., which meant that she was logging only 7 hours of sleep per night—and that was on a good night. She told me that on the night before a test, she could barely sleep at all. On top of this, her diet was lousy: The whole family ate on the run. Katie also told me that she didn't play any sports.

I asked her what she enjoyed about her life and what she found lacking. She told me how much she loved working on the newspaper and that the deadlines were exhilarating. She loved the camaraderie and the creativity this activity offered. She also enjoyed volunteering with the younger kids and said she felt "relaxed" around them. What she hated, and what caused her to worry to the point of debilitating stomachaches, was the pressure to be a straight-A student and have to take the toughest courses her school had to offer. "I just don't understand, Dr. Shannon, why an A in regular math isn't good enough. I don't understand why it has to be an A in the IB program." This was an excellent question and one that would, I was certain, lead us to the source of Katie's stress.

I asked Katie to tell me why she felt that she had to excel in the toughest academic track. "It's just not okay to be good enough, Dr. Shannon. You have to be great." She sighed and went on. "But sometimes I wish I could just be good enough."

I had no doubt that Katie was more than good enough. She clearly had high intelligence on many fronts, and she was among the top handful of students in her class. The problem was that the stress of performing was making Katie sick to her stomach. It was also causing her to have insomnia and terrible bouts of crying and depression. With each passing day, the fragile self-esteem, along with the mental health, of this very capable 14-year-old was eroding.

I took a deep breath and asked Katie a question. "What would happen if you switched off the IB track and just took regular classes?" Katie looked at me, shocked. "My mother would freak out! She thinks I'm smart enough to do the IB work, and she'll be disappointed if I don't finish at the top of my class." I nodded my understanding, but I thought to myself that Monica might be disappointed, but only temporarily. Although she was clearly an overachiever herself, Monica struck me as a caring and sensitive mother. I couldn't imagine that she'd demand academic perfection over her daughter's mental health. I told Katie that I wanted to bring her parents back into my office so we could all talk about her and school together.

When Monica and Bill were reseated, I cut right to the chase. "It seems clear to me that Katie is suffering from too much pressure, too much stress to excel academically. I'd like to recommend that she be moved into a regular academic curriculum so there is less pressure on her." Monica opened her mouth to speak, but Bill placed a hand on her arm, so I continued. "It's all about rebalancing Katie's life. She needs to be able to rest at night, and right now she's getting only 7 hours of sleep when she should be getting at least 9. She's also not nourishing her body and brain the way they need to be, and she needs to make time to slow down and eat properly. She also needs to have time to exercise and see friends; both of these crucial activities are almost nonexistent for her." I paused and looked from Bill to Monica to Katie. Bill actually spoke first. "Are you telling us, Dr. Shannon, that school is making Katie sick?"

I explained that it wasn't school that was making her sick at all but that the extreme pressure of the current track she was on had thrown her life way out of balance. As a child psychiatrist, I couldn't emphasize enough how important downtime, play, and social interaction were to Katie's development. I tried to assure Bill and Monica that I had no interest in "dumbing down" their daughter. On the contrary, I believed that she'd perform better and, most crucially, feel better if she were able to strive for A's in a regular curriculum and fill in the rest of her time with rest, exercise, and some fun.

I then talked through what, ideally, I'd like Katie's day to look like. I understood that she had never enjoyed team sports, so I suggested that she take up yoga or a martial art that would help her focus and relax while also toning her up. I pointed out that she was drinking far too much caffeine (in a futile effort to stay awake) and that she needed to learn the fundamentals of proper nutrition and eat three well-balanced meals a day (she often skipped lunch at school so she could cram for tests). She also needed to be able to goof off once in a while by doing things like seeing a movie with her friends or going to a game at school. Bill and Monica looked at each other knowingly and told me they would think about everything I had said and call me in the morning. I took this to be a good sign.

The next day, Monica called to say that beginning with the next term, Katie would be enrolled in a regular curriculum. She asked if I would mind if she checked in with me periodically before, during, and after this transition, and I told her I'd be delighted. I heard from her a few weeks later. She told me she had really listened to what I had said and had decided to reduce her own work hours so she could be home early enough to cook and eat dinner with Katie and Bill. She also told me that Katie had begun to take yoga classes on Saturdays and was enjoying it so much that she had talked Monica into joining her! I was thrilled with all this great news and told her to keep up the good work and check in with me again soon.

The next time I heard from her, Katie had begun her new school program. Monica told me that the changes in Katie were nothing short of miraculous: She came home from school energized and happy and spent her evenings reading, developing pictures, or listening to music with friends. She was sleeping better than she had in years, too, and she looked more rested than Monica could remember. The best news? She hadn't had a stomachache in months. I told Monica how thrilled I was and reminded her that she had been right: Her daughter didn't have any psychological problems. In fact, she was on track to have excellent emotional and mental health for life.

THE RIGHT RELATIONSHIPS ARE EVERYTHING— EVEN AT SCHOOL

One of the biggest drawbacks of our current "no child left behind" mindset is the expectation that every child will find his way in the system and will somehow figure out how to "make the grade."

What this expectation does, unfortunately, is negate the very real need for meaningful personal interaction in the learning environment. By emphasizing test results, our system depersonalizes the learning process in ways that can be quite harmful to children. Let me give you an example of how easily a child can slip through the cracks of this system, even when parents are paying close attention.

Chelsea

My office usually gets a surge of calls after the start of the school year, which then taper off in very telling ways. The school year begins here in late August, and by mid-September, I get calls about students who are having serious, dramatic difficulties. By October, these have tapered off, and this is when I start getting the calls about the subdued kids, the ones who seem to be fading into the background. It was late October when I got the call about Chelsea, an 11-year-old who had just entered middle school as a sixth grader.

When I met shy, introverted Chelsea, she struck me as being much younger than 11 emotionally. She was petite, with thick dark hair that hid her tiny face. She literally clung to her mother, Janet, who had brought her in on a crisp autumn morning. Chelsea, her mother explained, had been inexplicably sickly since starting at the new school. In fact, she had already missed more days than she had attended. When she did make it to school, there would be an inevitable call from the school nurse's office, usually just before lunchtime.

Chelsea had been thoroughly checked out by her pediatrician, who had systematically ruled out any physical cause for her symptoms, which included headaches, nausea, and stomach upset. Deducing that Chelsea was suffering from anxiety, he suggested that her mother contact me.

I learned from Janet that Chelsea was the youngest of three children. Her two brothers were 20 and 18 and, besides being much older than Chelsea, were temperamentally very different. The boys were outgoing and rambunctious, whereas she was shy and a bit fearful. Janet told me that the boys had initially challenged her own reserved temperament, but she credited them with "opening her up." She figured that her daughter would eventually emerge from her shell, too.

Chelsea, however, unlike her brothers, preferred to be home and close to her mother. She had never enjoyed playgroups as a baby and, also unlike her brothers, was afraid of school right from the start. Janet and her husband had been sensitive to this and had found a small elementary school for Chelsea where the teachers got to know her and where even the lunch counter ladies in the cafeteria went out of their way to acknowledge and support her. It was a nurturing, loving environment, and in this small setting, she was able to thrive, excelling at school and finding her way.

I asked Chelsea if she would mind spending some time with me alone, and she reluctantly agreed, only because she knew her mother would be waiting for her just beyond my office door. I asked her if she liked to play Connect Four, and she gave me a shy smile and nodded yes. As we played, I asked her about school.

Chelsea had left the warm, intimate confines of the small elementary school (none of her classes had had more than 15 students) and was now in the lowest grade of a gigantic middle school that had more than a thousand kids. Instead of spending most of her day with just one teacher, she now had to shuttle from class to class several times a day. "It's so frightening, Dr. Shannon. I feel surrounded by strangers all day long. I ache for home so badly that I feel sick." She was literally being swallowed up by the sheer size of her school.

When Janet came back into the room, we discussed ways that she could help connect Chelsea to the faculty at her new school to help ensure that her daughter got "plugged in" instead of being left out. We agreed to touch base again in a couple of weeks.

Janet called 2 weeks later with distressing news. Despite great cooperation from the school (which had assigned Chelsea an academic counselor who was available to her all day long), Chelsea still made a beeline for the nurse's office and bailed out of school before lunch: Entering a noisy, packed cafeteria was simply too much for her. At this point, I asked Janet to bring her back in so we could work on her anxiety. I started by prescribing my basic vitamin supplement plan so that Chelsea's brain would be fortified against the stress of her new environment. I also added two natural supplements, valerian and inositol, which are known to reduce anxiety. Next, I recommended a terrific therapist who did biofeedback work with children and adolescents to help them gain a tangible understanding of what happens to their bodies under stress and how they can cope with these physiological changes. Even with this kind of support, however, Chelsea still couldn't integrate herself into the school by the end of the term. I realized that we would have to take treating her to an entirely different level.

Just after the holidays, I met with Janet again and suggested that she seriously consider putting Chelsea into a smaller, more intimate school setting, much like her elementary school. I reminded Janet that Chelsea herself had said, "I do better with less people in all areas of my life." I gave her the names of some of the smaller schools in our area that I admired and recommended that she visit them with Chelsea so she would be a part of this exploration and decision-making process. Less than a week later, I got a call from Janet with some exciting news: "We're moving Chelsea into a home-schooling situation in our neighborhood. It's run by a woman who used to teach at the middle school. Now she's home schooling her own child and five other kids her age. A spot recently opened up, and we're going to take it."

Chelsea took to this intimate learning environment like a duck to water. She immediately settled in and began to thrive. Three years later, having matured and feeling more self-confident, she made the decision on her own to move into a slightly bigger, more formal environment and began high school at a Lutheran school that had a whopping 25 kids in the entire ninth-grade class. She thrived there and even joined the choir.

The last I heard, Chelsea had graduated with a near-perfect attendance record and decided to enroll in a very small private college close to home so she could visit her parents often. She's a great example of how crucial intimate relationships (and school size) can be. In the right environment, every child will thrive.

AFFECTIVE EDUCATION

The greatest wish most parents have for their children doesn't involve wealth or fame. Most parents simply want their children to be happy and satisfied with life. We know that being good in math or science has very little correlation with personal happiness in adulthood. Adults who find true contentment in life always describe their close relationships as the greatest sources of their joy. On our deathbeds, we don't reflect upon our success with algebra or our knowledge of the Krebs Cycle; we think of our loved ones. Even though this is a truth we all agree on, we don't include the teaching of emotional and social skills in our schools today.

Affective education is the term used to describe a curriculum that supports the positive emotional development of children. Eric Larsen, a master educator from Fort Collins, Colorado, has created a very successful affective education program for at-risk teens called the Discovery Program. It has been so successful that it is now being implemented around the United States.

Before teens can enroll in academic classes at Centennial High School in Fort Collins, they must first go through the 6-week

School-Based Mental Health Services

Imagine this scenario: 20 percent of the children in a disadvantaged country suffer from serious mental health issues. Of those kids, only 20 percent ever get treatment of any kind. This would be a travesty in Rwanda, Haiti, or Thailand, but unthinkable as it may be, this is the case in the world's richest country, the United States.

Innovators like Steven Adelsheim, MD, director of New Mexico's school-based mental health care programming, are leading the way. In New Mexico, teachers, principals, and school counselors work side by side with therapists and child psychiatrists to identify kids in need and provide effective on-site services for them. "We have found that school-based programming is the most cost-effective way to reach children in our state," Dr. Adelsheim told me recently. "Every time you involve another location or another professional, the number of children treated drops off."

These clinics offer not just early identification and symptomatic treatment with medications but also skill-building services, therapy, and family support. The rationale behind these creative programs is irrefutable: Kids who have depression, anxiety, rage, or addictions or who live in abusive situations do not learn very well or reach their potential. School-based mental health programs like this one model a way to treat children without automatically turning to labels and medication first.

Discovery Program. They learn crucial skills in anger management, problem-solving, feelings identification, family dynamics, effective communication, mutual support, community building, positive mental attitude, introspection, and substance abuse prevention. Over the years, this program has demonstrated significant benefits in preventing dropouts, increasing attendance, and improving academic performance. Centennial is a small high school that supports the establishment of connected staff-student relationships. Clearly, it's doing a fantastic job of addressing the complex needs of high-risk teens in my community.

If more schools taught emotional and social intelligence, academic performance would naturally rise. Children who are struggling emotionally do not learn well or behave well. Studies demonstrate that children who have these positive life skills are less likely to drop out and are much more likely to be successful on all levels (vocational, academic, social, financial, and so on).

I believe an affective education curriculum should be part of every child's education, beginning with elementary school. This would enhance the emotional growth of all kids long before they would be identified as being at risk. I know some people argue that this kind of education is the purview of parents. I agree that responsibility for teaching core values should fall to parents, but the development of healthy emotional and social skills is one that crosses all areas of life and should be part of our public educational process.

PUTTING IT ALL TOGETHER

I find that most parents—even when they have authentic appreciation for their child's temperament and a basic understanding of her learning style—grossly underestimate how active they must be in order to ensure her success in school. As I mentioned at the outset of this chapter, the worlds of home and school are the most important in every child's life, but they are often too far apart or intersect in stressful ways that cause emotional and mental upset for countless students. It is therefore the job of parents to monitor both worlds and work to bring them into harmony for their child. When they do this, either by eliminating stressors at home that compromise a child's ability to learn or by addressing stressors at school that do the same, they are expanding their child's universe in ways that will ensure that her young brain and mind can grow optimally. In order for the school-home system to work optimally for your family, try to implement the following suggestions.

- Select a school that is a "good fit" for your child.

- Be involved with the school (know and approve of the school's educational philosophy, rules, regulations, and so on).

- Listen to your child's complaints about school openly and attentively; work to look beyond generalities such as "I hate school."

- When a child identifies a school-related problem, work with her to address it proactively and appropriately.

- Manage your own expectations about your child's academic performance.

- Watch for signs that your child is being overburdened or understimulated.

- Understand your child's limitations (learning disabilities, temperamental style, and so on).

- Know (and when possible, choose) your child's teachers.

- Become acquainted with your child's friends.

- Learn and model stress management techniques that your child can use on a daily basis.

- Encourage your child to be involved in activities that strengthen her social support network.

- Make sure that your child is well rested.

- Ensure that your child gets proper nutrition.

- Don't let your child rely on stimulants like caffeine.

- Don't allow your child to take illegal drugs or drink to cope.

- Encourage and teach your child how to relax and recharge.

- Monitor your child's self-esteem (especially negative self-talk).

- Get professional help for yourself or your child if school stress becomes unmanageable.

Above all, remember that learning should be the most enjoyable experience of all for your child. When he loves learning, he'll be building a healthy brain and will have the best chance of living a life marked by strong emotional and mental health.

Monitoring your child's life in school is crucial to ensuring her mental and emotional health. In the next chapter, I'll discuss how trauma—even the everyday, garden-variety social stresses a child faces at school—can make it impossible for her to succeed if it's left unaddressed.

CHAPTER 8

Understanding
Trauma

W hen we think about trauma, horrific events such as the terrorist attacks of 9/11, the devastating Asian tsunami of 2004, and the aftermath of Hurricane Katrina come to mind. The toll these events took on humankind is undeniable. But traumatic events aren't always so dramatic or so obvious: Trauma actually lurks around us every day. Just turn on the nightly news and you'll hear about fires, accidents, and violent crimes right in your own neighborhood. All of these events are traumatic to the people involved (and may even be mildly traumatizing to the young child watching the news alongside you). Other life events are also traumatic, such as car accidents, illness, the inevitable death of loved ones, and so on. Though less catastrophic than a natural disaster or an act of war, these events have a great impact on the emotional and mental health of the people involved.

The spectrum of traumatic experience is a broad one, and there are even forms of social or "daily" trauma that remain particularly well hidden from view—at least for adults. Before I address the subtler forms of trauma that are most likely to affect children, I think it's important to share some startling facts and figures about trauma so you get a full sense of how profoundly traumatic experiences affect the brain.

TRAUMA DEFINED

In broad, basic terms, trauma is any unplanned event or experience that wounds profoundly. Trauma sometimes has a physical component (the injuries sustained in a car accident, for example), but more significantly, it tends to have a profound impact on the brain, the psyche, and the victim's sense of self and safety. Any traumatic event has six main characteristics. The event:

1. Occurs without warning (no one can prepare for it).

2. Is overwhelming (often both physically and psychologically).

3. Is violent in nature (a flood, a physical assault, verbal abuse).

4. Destroys any sense of safety (it's inescapable danger).

5. Renders one powerless (one can't stop a hurricane, a fist, or a bullet).

6. Instills a feeling of terror.

A traumatic event can be either a one-time occurrence (a plane crash, a mugging, or a tsunami) or chronic and pervasive (abuse, poverty, or neglect). What may be stressful for an adult (divorce or a move across the country) can actually be quite traumatic for a child, who simply doesn't yet have the cognitive and emotional skills to effectively process and deal with the event.

The impact of a one-time traumatic event (such as a natural disaster) can certainly cause great psychological stress—especially if the trauma isn't addressed. But this kind of trauma, which is usually overt, can be treated immediately. It's much more challenging to treat chronic and pervasive trauma, especially as it relates to children, since there is often a large degree of secrecy around it, such as with incest or a situation of ongoing domestic abuse or neglect. Aside from the difficulty in actually identifying the trauma, there is, distressingly, often a stigma attached to this kind of traumatic experience. This stigma makes treating the trauma all the more difficult for children and their healers.

Exposure to chronic trauma—especially in children—also profoundly reprograms and reshapes the brain. In my experience, it's very difficult to treat a child who has had to live with chronic trauma, but it's not impossible. This is where the miracle of the brain's plasticity (and the indomitable spirit of most children) truly comes into play.

THE TRAUMATIZED BRAIN

My profession made great strides in understanding the psychological cost of trauma following the Vietnam War of the last century. Hundreds of thousands of soldiers, most of whom had spent many months in combat, returned from the war forever changed. They all seemed to suffer from a similar cluster of psychiatric symptoms, and their condition (which has been identified throughout the ages but never before with as much scientific understanding) was given a name—posttraumatic stress disorder, or PTSD. Following the war, a huge amount of research was done on PTSD, and we gained great knowledge about how trauma affects the adult brain. It wasn't until the end of the last century, however, that researchers began to explore how trauma impacts the most vulnerable brain—that of a child. In the past 20 years, those who work with traumatized children began to understand that the brain of a child who has been exposed to severe trauma is often seriously damaged and changed. In short, the chaos of the outside world becomes the chaos of the inner world as trauma overwhelms and reshapes the young brain.

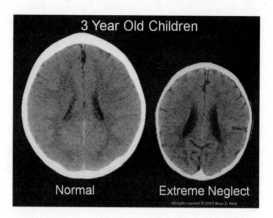

These images illustrate the impact of neglect on the developing brain. The CT scan on the left is from a healthy 3-year-old child with an average head size (50th percentile). The image on the right is from a 3-year-old following total global neglect during early childhood; the brain is significantly smaller than average and has abnormal development of cortical, limbic, and midbrain structures.

Source: From studies by Bruce D. Perry, MD, PhD, at The ChildTrauma Academy (www.ChildTrauma.org); Perry, B. D., "Childhood Experience and the Expression of Genetic Potential: What Childhood Neglect Tells Us about Nature and Nurture," Brain and Mind 3 (2002): 79–100.

Researchers today are able to document—literally—how trauma alters the growth of a child's brain, skews its chemistry, and compromises its ability to function well. Bruce Perry, MD, PhD, a renowned neuroscientist and child psychiatrist, has taken dramatic images (using a CT scan) that show how trauma and neglect can actually *stunt* brain growth. In them, the brain of a severely traumatized 3-year-old child is significantly smaller than that of an average 3-year-old. In effect, the brain of the traumatized child has quite literally atrophied. This kind of severe brain damage is rare, but Dr. Perry's visual documentation shows conclusively how much trauma impacts the brain.

The duration, intensity, and frequency of trauma have a significant impact on the structure and chemical configuration of the brain. Trauma is the cruelest tool of all when it comes to the sculpting of a young brain. In terms of the physical structures in the brain, we know that trauma may cause abnormal development of the hippocampus (the area that involves cognition and memory) and the amygdala (part of the limbic system, where emotions and feelings are located), weaken the connection between the two hemispheres (which has been linked to ADHD-like symptoms), and cause poor development of the left hemisphere (which creates a vulnerability to depression) and underdevelopment of the cerebral cortex (the seat of reasoned thinking). When any of these structures are damaged, the result is a cascading effect, and the young brain is unable to function optimally. Dr. Perry and his colleagues have shown how trauma also inhibits neuron growth and development and how it floods the brain with chemicals that inhibit optimal neuron function. Trauma, therefore, delivers a one-two punch to the young brain, causing it to suffer both physically and chemically.

One aspect of Dr. Perry's work that I find poignant and devastating is the acknowledgment that when a child's brain is exposed to chronic trauma, it becomes acclimated to the unhealthy, aroused state the trauma induces. For children who exist in this mode of chronic fear, with high levels of stress hormones coursing through their brains, this awful state becomes "normal." These children inhabit a world that has literally been turned upside down by their brain chemistry: What is unsafe and damaging is what is most familiar to them. And these children don't know how to turn off the "red alert" when they're no longer in a dangerous environment. For them, the natural "fight or flight" response becomes depressed, and they suffer from chronic impaired brain function. It is heartbreaking to encounter children who live in this disabled state.

THE IMPACT OF TRAUMA ON CHILDHOOD DEVELOPMENT

Basic development for children who suffer from trauma is often disrupted in profound ways. If a child is under siege, it's nearly impossible for her to acquire age-appropriate skills. Survivors of childhood trauma exhibit deficits (from mild to severe) in developing areas such as these.

- Being able to regulate their emotions

- Being able to perceive the world as a safe place

- Trusting others

- Being able to engage in logical, organized thinking

- Being able to avoid danger or exploitation

In a child in whom these skills are poorly developed, it begins to look as if he has "symptoms" of a mental disorder instead of the natural effects of trauma. Obviously then, he is more likely to be mislabeled and incorrectly treated.

THE GREAT MASQUERADER

Trauma is a tricky source of stress because even when the event is over, the victim may continue to reexperience the trauma over and over again. The old adage "time heals all wounds" simply does not apply to trauma. Time may pass, but the residue of traumatic experience may linger, as we learned from Vietnam vets suffering from PTSD.

One of the aspects of treating childhood trauma that confounds experts is how different the response to trauma can be from child to child. One child who grows up in an impoverished, chaotic environment may recover quite rapidly from years of abuse and neglect, while another may display maladaptive tendencies long after she has been removed from the offending environment. We do know that a child who has at least one healthy relationship with an adult does better than a child whose primary caregivers are unavailable emotionally for her. Trust is crucial in treating trauma because one's sense of safety has usually been severely damaged, and trust can exist only when there is a close, healthy relationship in place.

We also know that the perception of the trauma—and the impact it has on self-esteem and world view—can vary greatly from child to child. The way a child processes a trauma will determine the best course of treatment in that specific case.

In other words, the internal damage caused by trauma is unique to each child, and it takes great skill, patience, and a lot of love to do the difficult but necessary work of getting beyond the symptoms, identifying the source, and helping a child move past it. Here are some common symptoms seen in traumatized children.

- Hyperarousal
- Regressive behavior
- Withdrawn or avoidant behavior (or both)
- Impaired concentration
- Hyperactivity
- Anxiety
- Fearfulness
- Poor sleep
- Depression
- Aggression and anger
- Suicidal thinking
- Dissociation (disconnection from reality)
- Sexual acting out
- Posttraumatic stress disorder

As you can see, the *symptoms* of traumatic injury look an awful lot like those of mental or emotional disorders. It's important that those treating children who have experienced trauma don't get caught up in addressing only the symptoms. This is why using medication to treat trauma survivors can be a double-edged sword. Although drugs may help initially, they can also cause the true source of the problems to go unrecognized and untreated.

Consider this example of how using medication to treat the symptoms of trauma actually hindered a child's recovery.

Charlie

Charlie, a streetwise 16-year-old, found his way into our adolescent program after becoming enraged and violent with his mother. She had grounded him for ditching school, and his response was to threaten her, kick a door, and break some furniture. The police were called, they took Charlie to the emergency room, and he was admitted to the hospital.

Charlie grew up rough and early. His father was a petty criminal and alcoholic who left the family when Charlie was about 10. His mother, who was poorly educated, was overwhelmed by two jobs and raising four kids on her own. Charlie began running the streets early. By 14, he was smoking pot and drinking alcohol regularly. By 15, he had spent some time in our local juvenile correctional facility for assaulting a peer in a gang fight.

He had been treated once before, at a local community mental health facility, where the staff psychiatrist put him on lithium (a mood stabilizer) and Zyprexa (olanzapine, an antipsychotic commonly used to treat aggression). The medications did make Charlie less aggressive, but he hated the flat, dopey feeling they gave him, so he refused to take them. He had never talked to anyone professionally trained to deal with adolescent mental health issues. Once Charlie was stabilized and released from the hospital after the more recent incident, his parole officer referred him into our adolescent day treatment program with the understanding that he had to participate or he would be sent to a residential facility for 1 to 2 years. That got his attention.

Wiry and lean, Charlie looked rough. He had tattoos on his arms and wore some of the clothing favored by our local gangster crowd: baggy jeans that nearly fell off his hips, unlaced sneakers, and a giant gold chain around his neck. He shuffled more than walked. His bravado was so strong it hit you before he said a word. His speech was crude, at times vulgar, and riddled with slang.

In spite of his rough bravado, we grew to love Charlie, who began to shed his gangster persona as he began to trust us. We discovered that he had a very dry sense of humor and a big heart. He loved little kids and took some of our younger kids under his wing, helping them along.

Most of all, Charlie was very emotional. Under the cold persona he hid behind as a defense against the world, he was hurting. We learned that his father had beaten him for years before abandoning the family right around Charlie's 10th birthday. His feelings about his father were a toxic mixture of hurt and hate. He poured his heart out in group therapy, and the other kids helped him heal. After 6 months, he was a different person.

He started to take an interest in his own future and expressed a true desire to move beyond the gangs and drugs that had been his support system for the past few years. His relationship with his mother improved significantly, and just as we hoped, his volatile aggression gave way once we were able to identify and address the trauma he had suffered. Four years later, he was working as a roofer, was married, and had a young son, whom he doted upon. He was taking no medication and hadn't had another violent episode.

Charlie is a great illustration of how powerful intensive intervention can be when treating trauma. When he came to us, he was raw and unable to hide his pain. I can't help feeling that his refusal to take his meds was actually the first step on a course of treatment that healed him in ways that drugs never could. Had he been compliant and stayed on the medication, he might not ever have truly dealt with his father's abuse and abandonment.

Charlie is a great example of how children who survive trauma often exhibit a cluster of symptoms or different symptoms under different circumstances. Kids have very distinct responses to trauma based on gender. Boys tend toward more aggressive behavior, often reenacting the traumatic event, or display agitated affect, which may look like ADD or hyperactivity. Girls, on the other hand, tend to become numb, withdrawn, and emotionally shut down. Dr. Perry makes the very astute observation that this kind of withholding in girls may even look like resilience to us, but we have to resist thinking that this kind of stoicism is healthy. It's important that parents work to read the signals a child is giving off, especially if they know there has been trauma. Here's a story about a girl who tried to be stoic in the face of great loss.

Lauren

Not long ago, Annette Wilson, MD, one of the best family doctors in my community, phoned me. "Scott," she said, "I know your practice is closed to new patients, but I have a 16-year-old I want you to see. Her name's Lauren. Another psychiatrist diagnosed her with depression. She's clearly depressed, but I don't think that's the whole story."

I agreed to make time for Lauren the following week. I telephoned her mother, Sue, to gather some background information. She told me that Lauren had always been an easy, happy child who did well in school, was quite popular, and was loved for her easygoing charm and sharp wit. Over the past 2 years, however, she had begun to change. Once almost blissfully unaware of her body, Lauren had taken to radical dieting and lost almost 20 pounds. She had also dropped out of several extracurricular activities and had taken to spending more and more time alone and less time with her large, outgoing circle of friends.

Everything Sue said confirmed the diagnosis of depression,

except the detail about Lauren's dieting. I got the impression that she was trying to control something in her life and that there might be a vital piece of information missing from Sue's history. Finally, Sue told me that they had put Lauren on an antidepressant about a year ago but that it didn't seem to help. I thanked her for all the information and told her that I was looking forward to meeting her and Lauren in a few days.

Lauren and Sue arrived for our appointment promptly. I was immediately struck by how exhausted, gaunt, and down Lauren looked. We sat down together and began to chat. I asked Lauren what her life was like, and she told me about her friends, her school, and her family, using a sunny vocabulary that just didn't match up with how miserable she looked. She seemed to be expending a great amount of energy trying to "hold it together," as though she was supposed to keep some kind of stiff upper lip.

Toward the end of the first hour of our meeting, I asked Lauren if anything of significance had changed in her life recently. She murmured no, then glanced at her mother, who sat silently. Then Lauren started to cry. At this point, I asked Sue if she would mind giving Lauren and me a moment alone, and she agreed.

I sat with Lauren as she cried silently for another few minutes. When the tears had subsided some, she looked at me and said, "My best friend was killed in a car accident 2 years ago. I know I should be over it, but it still feels like it just happened yesterday. Everyone else seemed to get over it pretty quickly, and I feel like something must be wrong with me since I haven't been able to get past it."

I learned that Lauren's friend Pam had been in a car with her mother, who also died in the crash. Pam's mother had been one of Sue's best friends. I asked Lauren if she and her mother had been able to process this loss. She told me that she and her mother became very close right after the accident. At the time, they talked a lot about their loss and attended the funeral together, and Sue had even helped Lauren create a "memory book" for her beloved friend. But just a couple of weeks after the funeral, Sue became impatient with Lauren's grief and abruptly shut her out. Lauren was given the message that the appropriate grieving time had ended and that she needed to move on.

This was when she began to withdraw into herself and became obsessed with her diet. As time passed, Lauren—and everyone around her, including her mother—lost sight of the event that had caused her grief in the first place. With each passing month, Lauren internalized her loss as a relentlessly self-critical voice that manifested itself as a weight-control fiend. To those around her, Lauren had inexplicably changed, and her symptoms had become her problem.

I asked Sue to rejoin us. I told her that Lauren was basically "stuck" because she hadn't been able to publicly and fully complete the grieving process for her dead friend and that this was behind her depression. I told her I was confident that with the right kind of treatment, we would get Lauren off the antidepressant medication and back to her former happy self. I also told them both that I felt confident that as Lauren's grief was addressed, her need to diet so vigilantly would subside. I then sketched out a comprehensive treatment plan that included grief counseling for Lauren and a rigorous nutritional plan that would feed her overstressed brain, and I recommended that the family attend therapy in order to reopen vital lines of communication so that Lauren's loss (and Sue's) could be openly and adequately addressed. Over the next several months, I watched as Lauren was able to work through her grief, shed the negative feelings about herself she had taken on, and regain her trust in herself and the world around her.

Losing a friend is a major loss and a significant trauma for anyone, but what about the situations that our kids encounter daily that may look like no big deal but may in fact be sources of trauma for them? How do we learn to identify and help our children cope with everyday trauma, such as bullying?

BULLYING

In American society today, millions of kids are affected each day by bullying and teasing, and both, in my experience, can be very traumatic. In fact, kids cite bullying as the number one problem they face at school, trumping issues like alcohol or drug abuse and the pressure to have sex. But there is a weird disconnect between what our kids are telling us and what we parents (and teachers) are willing to hear. Bullying, bizarrely, is often sanctioned by adults in that they often ignore it.

One need only think of the massacre in 1999 at Columbine High School, here in my home state of Colorado, to understand how isolating and damaging being bullied, teased, or otherwise marginalized can be for kids—and how easily the adults around them can overlook it. The psychologists working on behalf of the FBI published a report after Columbine that focused almost exclusively on the mental states of the two students who attacked the school. They didn't, however, look at the school environment itself in order to understand how that might have affected the behavior of the two disturbed students.

Most mental health experts understand that kids who are troubled—even this unimaginably troubled—do not become that way in a vacuum. A close look at the school environment after the tragedy showed it was rife with severe unchecked social problems, including rampant bullying. The kids doing the bullying were privileged, white athletes who ridiculed, tormented, and abused kids of different races, ethnic groups, and social cliques. School officials and teachers turned a blind eye to this abuse and did not see the many red flags that went up prior to the massacre. The two kids who attacked the school were, many students and faculty members later admitted, among those who were most bullied and tormented.

Bullying is an act of aggression, an abuse of power. Bullies usually target kids they think are weaker than they, including those who are shy, passive, or have disabilities. In the short term, kids who are bullied lose confidence, worry more, experience anxiety, and otherwise suffer from the stress of being targeted and abused. In the long term, they suffer from depression, low self-esteem, chronic anxiety, and other serious mental or emotional conditions that can dog them for life.

Bullying is a form of violence, so even kids who witness bullying suffer, as they often stand by helplessly while one kid abuses another. I would argue that even the bully deserves our compassion and help: Kids who bully often end up as dropouts, have criminal records, and are prone to a lifetime of mental health problems.

Even taunting and teasing, which adults often mistake as "fun" or "play," leave an indelible mark on kids and are really just subtler forms of bullying. Kids who are bullied feel a lot of shame, so they try to hide what's going on, and this can make identifying bullying or teasing particularly tough for parents. Here are some signs to look out for if you suspect your child may be the victim of bullying or another form of social abuse.

- She becomes passive or withdrawn, seeming to lose interest in normal activities.

- She cries frequently.

- You notice she is missing some personal property (a jacket, a purse, jewelry).

- She complains of headaches, stomachaches, or other ailments that then take her out of her normal routine.

- There is a sudden drop in her grades, or a problem academic area becomes exacerbated.

- She just doesn't want to go to school.

- She has trouble sleeping.

- She has trouble concentrating.

- Her social life drops away: Friends stop calling and invitations stop coming.

- Her speech changes: She begins to reference herself and others in negative ways, referring to herself as a "loser" and her former best friend as a "jerk."

All of these changes in behavior or affect may point to a child who is no longer socially comfortable at school, and there's a good chance that bullying (which includes subtle, seemingly acceptable behaviors such as gossiping or shunning) is taking place. It is a parent's job to help the child cope with the situation. Here are a few suggestions for things you can do when your child is being bullied.

- Be a good listener; trust your child and believe him.

- Provide comfort and support; be sure to reassure your child that he isn't to blame.

- Don't show your anger. Instead, show your child that remaining calm and detached is important. Reacting to aggression with aggression is never the answer.

- Don't rush in to rescue (unless your child is in physical danger). Instead, encourage him to work through the feelings and situation on his own, with your role being one of consistent, loving support.

- Help your child "try on" various coping strategies. For a young child, perhaps use puppets to illustrate how one "walks away" from such abuse; for an older child, talk through various ways to handle the situation that will empower him.

- Model esteem-building behaviors when confronted with social conflict yourself.

- Get professional help if you think your child needs it.

We parents frequently underestimate how traumatic even daily social interactions can be for our kids. Think of the teenage girl who is afraid to walk into the lunchroom because she feels "fat"; or the shy prepubescent boy who hides his trombone, believing that carrying it to class will signal that he's uncool; or the seemingly "perfect" senior who is riddled with anxiety because she's being pressured to have sex and isn't ready. Every day, our kids may experience humiliation, pressure, or stress that remains hidden from us unless we ask about their social lives—and really listen to what they tell us.

Even when kids speak up, however, it's sometimes difficult for us to step outside of our own realm of experience and put ourselves in their shoes. This interesting story was shared with me by a teacher colleague.

Ellen

Ellen was a first grader who loved school and had many friends. She was also by far the smallest kid in her class, and she was somewhat shy. Yet she had a magnetism that drew people to her, often to her great distress (she was so tiny that adults would often pick her up as though she were a doll). One day, Ellen was surprised by a classmate named Robin who pulled her into a corner, put her face right up to hers, and told her, "I'm going take you home and lock you in my closet and never let you go." Terrified, Ellen pushed past Robin and ran away.

The next day, the same thing happened, but it escalated a bit. This time, Robin waited for Ellen at the end of the school day and grabbed her hand. "I'm going to take you home, and you will never see your mother again!" Robin shouted into Ellen's face. At this, Ellen burst into tears and begged to be let go. Robin finally relented. Ellen ran straight home and told her mother what had just happened, but her mother, who was busy making dinner for the family (Ellen was one of five kids who were all in elementary school together), responded without looking up from her work. "Don't be silly, Ellen. I'm sure she just wants to play with you." With those words, Ellen fell silent.

Usually chatty and animated, Ellen sat through dinner that night without saying a word. She also slipped off to bed without anyone noticing. Once in bed, however, she couldn't sleep; visions of being locked in a dark closet, in a strange house, haunted her. She was racked with terror the entire night.

The next morning, she was distracted while she dressed for school, barely touched her breakfast, and walked to school on her own instead of with her siblings and neighborhood friends as she usually did. She was totally preoccupied with whether she would have another run-in with Robin. That day, Robin didn't approach her, and Ellen was relieved. She thought "Maybe my mother was right; maybe I'm silly." But the next day, Robin was back, and this time was the worst of all. Robin steered clear of Ellen all day, but at the end of the day, she hid in the bushes outside the school and grabbed Ellen when she walked by. This time, she didn't let go, even as Ellen screamed for help. She managed to drag Ellen many blocks from the school yard before a group of older kids saw what was happening and made her release the smaller child.

Robin let go, and Ellen stumbled home, lost and beside herself with fear. Once home, she again stayed quiet. Again she had a sleepless night, and the next morning after breakfast, she tucked a butter knife into her coat pocket. When she arrived at school and went to hang up her coat, the knife fell out, and another student told Ellen's teacher, who took her aside and gently asked her why she had brought a knife to school. That was when this story emerged.

A New Way to Help Traumatized Kids

Traumatized children are particularly prone to exhibiting the symptoms of attachment disorders, such as being rageful, being depressed, having a poor attention span, being oppositional, being violent, or expressing their hurt in various other ways that are quite problematic.

Because of the work of Bruce Perry, MD, PhD, a renowned neuroscientist and child psychiatrist, as well as the work of others, we now know that the brain of a traumatized child does not function like that of a typical child.

When restressed, the traumatized brain becomes further disorganized and isn't capable of reasoned thought or appropriate decision-making. Yet, when traumatized children misbehave, our first response is often to mete out some pretty severe punishment by giving them timeouts, using harsh words, ignoring them, or even spanking them.

Trying to change the behavior of traumatized children with this kind of rigid response only exacerbates the stress that they're already experiencing. Unknowingly, we may actually be reinforcing traumatic response when we think that we're getting bad behavior under control.

Brian Post, PhD, a psychologist who was also traumatized as a child, has developed an innovative alternative for addressing the behavioral problems of traumatized kids. At the Post Institute, they teach a style of care and treatment that emphasizes reducing stress and enhancing a sense of safety and security. When a child feels safe and connected, his brain begins to calm, a problem can be solved, and learning can take place.

Treating traumatized kids gently and compassionately is the only way to allow their brains to heal. When we do that with loving gentleness, their behavior will improve—often without the need to use powerful drugs.

The teacher realized that Ellen had truly been terrorized by Robin and had asked for help by telling her mother but believed that no help was forthcoming. Ellen decided that the only way she could protect herself from Robin was to arm herself with a knife. Ellen's teacher, a friend of mine who shared this story, had the compassion and insight to call Ellen's mother, explain the situation, and share how serious she thought it was. Fortunately, Ellen's mother responded well and expressed her horror at how dismissive she had been of her daughter. My friend assured her that the school would take up the issue with Robin appropriately, and she ended the call by saying she hoped Ellen wasn't too traumatized by the experience and that she was there to help if needed.

This was a wakeup call for Ellen's busy, overextended mother, who had no idea her young daughter was so traumatized. Her response to Ellen when she came home from school that night was far different than it had been before: This time, she made a point of putting aside her chores and spending some quality quiet time with her daughter. She encouraged Ellen to share the whole story with her, and she listened carefully. She worked hard to show genuine concern for Ellen's welfare and safety and apologized to her for not being more responsive sooner. That night, Ellen was able to sleep soundly.

This example shows how even parents who are usually in tune with their kids can view a situation through a faulty lens— the lens of maturity and adulthood. We have to make sure, especially when a child is suffering, that we work hard to see the world from the child's point of view.

LABELS ON THE INSIDE: WHAT TRAUMA DOES TO A CHILD'S SENSE OF SELF

One of the most noxious side effects of trauma is what it does to a child's sense of self. Children who survive trauma (particularly those who survive chronic abuse at the hands of a trusted care-giver) are prone to internalizing the harm done to them in insid-ious, damaging ways. They can't process information about the world with the same kind of sophistication as adults, so often they can't separate themselves from the event at hand and blame themselves when bad things happen to them as a way of explain-ing the unexplainable. For instance, a young boy who is punished by being hit may come to believe he has somehow "asked for it" each time his father strikes him; a young girl with a disability who is taunted by her classmates may come to view herself as being "less than"; and even a child who loses a loved one in an accident may be able to make sense of the tragedy only by taking responsibility for it ("If I had obeyed Mommy, she wouldn't be dead").

The tendency of children of trauma to take on the burden of the violence done to them makes a perverse kind of sense: Trauma, by its very definition, is overwhelming. The mind, espe-cially the vulnerable mind of a child, naturally makes every effort to make sense of that which will never make sense. Often, the only way a child's brain can do this is to internalize the trauma and make it its own. When this happens, a child's iden-tity becomes inexorably linked to the trauma, and this is when labels become the most damaging of all.

TREATING TRAUMA: WHAT A CHILD NEEDS

Trauma doesn't just damage a child's brain; it wreaks havoc on his overall sense of well-being. For a child who has endured trauma, the world is no longer a safe place, and often self-care becomes utterly compromised for such a child. In order to recover from traumatic injury, a child truly does need a village: He needs to be surrounded and supported by a community that is committed to his recovery. In order to recover from trauma, a child needs:

▪ Safety

▪ Nurturance

▪ Stability

▪ Predictability

▪ Understanding

When these elements are in place, a child (and his brain) may begin to release traumatic stress and regain alignment with the nonviolent, nonthreatening world that exists beyond the trauma. Then his brain will begin to heal, and he will begin to regain his equilibrium in terms of mental and emotional health. Parents can do a great deal to help their children recover from trauma.

▪ Establish safety and security for your child, because only a child who feels safe from further harm can recover from trauma.

▪ Listen actively and nonjudgmentally. Your child may need to discuss the traumatic event over and over again. Listen well each time.

▪ Answer your child's questions openly and honestly.

▪ Work to clear up misunderstandings about the trauma, especially those that lead to guilt, shame, self-loathing, and so on.

▪ Validate and respect your child's feelings.

▪ Allow for mourning.

▪ Expect setbacks (and regression).

▪ Seek out appropriate professional support.

▪ Communicate with other family members, school personnel, and other important people in your child's life so there is clear understanding of what your child is coping with.

▪ Above all, love your child. Words may fail us, but genuine love and concern never do.

Trauma is probably the number one hidden cause of mental and emotional upset in our kids. It is our job, as parents and practitioners, to address childhood trauma with patience, tenderness, and empathy. Only then will children feel safe and secure enough to work through the traumatic injury and regain their full potential for emotional and mental health. In the next chapter, I'll discuss the powerful role parenting plays in shaping a child's mental and emotional development.

CHAPTER 9

Parenting for Emotional and Mental Health

R aising a child is an enormously complex and challenging task. Parenting pushes us to the edge of everything we think we know about ourselves, the world, and others. We are called on to access and use the fullest array of cognitive and emotional skills we have. But at the heart of good parenting lies a great paradox that isn't often discussed: We need to be close to our children in order to let go.

This paradox is what I refer to as the yin and yang of parenting. Yin and yang, in ancient Chinese philosophy, is the concept that there are two opposing yet complementary forces at work in all things in the universe. That's certainly true of parenting! The yin, or the feminine, is internally oriented and contemplative and is symbolized by the moon. The yang, or the masculine, is externally oriented and active and is symbolized by the sun. The early years of caring for a child are the yin years and are marked by devotion to the other, to the process of being actively attuned, to bonding, and to forming a deep and abiding attachment. The later years of childrearing are the yang years, in which we learn to loosen our emotional grip on our children and step back, allowing them to emerge as autonomous individuals. These two truths (the need to bond and the need to let go) are actually at play from the moment of birth, and the dance of parenting is learning how to balance these two objectives in a fluid, loving way.

As a child begins to grow and mature, we see the "roots" of the yin energy take on a powerful weight as her sense of self and value, her burgeoning awareness of her solid place in the world, strengthens. This yin energy, like the roots of a strong tree, provides the foundation on which an emotionally healthy child may grow, stretch, and reach for life. The yang energy is the bright, outward reflection of the strong sense of self our child has developed thanks to the strong attachment we've forged with her.

The symbol of yin and yang is also a helpful metaphor for parenting because it conveys the eternal dance that takes place between these two elemental forces: dependence and independence for the child, nurturance and letting go for the parent. The fluid energy that flows between these two tensions is what makes parenting so dynamic—and so challenging.

The first few years of parenting involve a level of commitment and dedication to another that is unparalleled in any other area of life. Once a child begins to mature and strive for independence, we have to gently begin to let go. One of the great ironies of parenting is that the better we bond and attach with our young children, the easier it is for them to individuate, mature, and establish a healthy identity beyond us. But letting go of such well-nurtured kids isn't so easy for parents!

On the other hand, parents who haven't formed strong attachments with their children have an easier time letting go, even as their children tend to be less equipped or prepared for healthy separation. When our children reach adolescence and early adulthood, our work involves learning to trust their ability to care for themselves and to champion their choices and decisions, even if we don't fully agree with them. (I'm in the middle of this process now as my youngest prepares to go off to college.) This stage is when parents really learn what they're made of, in terms of selflessness, generosity, and true confidence.

This final chapter offers parents a guide to how to let go in the most effective and healthy way for you and your child. For optimal mental and emotional health, this process begins early in parenting, and when it occurs organically, it's guided by the developmental pace of the child. We see this kind of healthy promotion of individuality when mother lets a toddler choose the toy she'll play with, when the father of an 8-year-old lets his son pay for the movie tickets, or when parents extend a teen's curfew to 11:00 p.m. on a special weekend and know that she'll be safe. Every time we step back and let a child make a healthy choice on his own behalf, we're helping him develop the skills and traits he'll need for enjoying a lifetime of emotional and mental health.

Knowing that a child's brain grows and develops in response to the quality of the parent-child relationship revolutionizes our understanding of how we may parent a child toward optimal mental and emotional health. Once we've provided our children with a stable, healthy foundation of secure attachment, and we're committed to working on "fit" (by parenting with lots of temperamental compassion), we can focus on helping our children develop the following three core traits they will need in order to appropriately separate from us and take their place in the world as healthy individuals.

- A strong sense of self-identity
- The ability to self-regulate
- An inner core of resilience

HELPING YOUR CHILD DEVELOP
A STRONG SENSE OF SELF-IDENTITY

Each child comes into the world as a unique, valuable individual, but gaining awareness of this and establishing a sense of self-identity is a complex process that takes place over time. The interactions (the mirroring, moments of bonding, and so forth) that occur between a baby and a primary caregiver, beginning at birth, are the gestures that begin this process. When a baby's needs are well met, when she enjoys consistent, caring responsiveness and her presence is treated with love and respect, she begins to view herself as having value and being worthy of love. This awareness on the part of the infant marks the burgeoning of a healthy sense of self-identity. Children who experience insecure attachment, who live an unpredictable world, are limited in this regard. They have to struggle to develop a sense of self-worth and to view themselves as being lovable.

Children who feel secure and well attached then try to replicate this pleasant state throughout their lives. Feeling good (and good about themselves) becomes wired into these kids, and they strive to constantly restore this core sense of well-being as they tackle life's challenges. Securely attached kids develop balanced awareness of who they are, meaning that they can identify and accept their own weaknesses and limitations as well as their strengths. These kids grow and develop with the true understanding that their presence in the world matters, that they can make positive things happen (even things such as eliciting a smile from a busy mother), and that they are valuable.

Securely attached infants become confident children, especially when we appropriately respect their autonomy and their vast capability to connect, problem-solve, learn, grow, and love.

Children who enjoy unconditional positive regard from their parents, which is the by-product of a healthy, mutually satisfying attachment, are aware of their inherent value and thus enjoy an organic sense of their own self-worth. Every child deserves to experience this. In my practice, I use the expression "understanding is loving, but acceptance is love" to help parents grasp how crucial it is to really accept and love a child for who he is—not who we wish him to be. Children deserve to be treated with dignity and respect at all times, but this isn't always easy to do. It takes commitment on the part of the parent to constantly work on being understanding, to constantly strive to be fully accepting. This is probably the most difficult and taxing work of parenting and arguably the most important.

Practicing Forgiveness

All of us make mistakes. Our children make mistakes, we make mistakes—no one is exempt. But mistakes aren't the mark of a deficient character or an unacceptable temperament—and they certainly aren't the mark of a faulty or broken "self." The mistakes we make in our relationships offer great opportunities for us to rethink the way we react and learn new ways of relating, but we can learn from our mistakes only if we acknowledge them. Let me give you a brief example.

Brian

Brian was a 10-year-old with a very high activity level. From birth, he moved at warp speed. This was quite literally how he was wired. His mother, Emma, knew that this was part of who Brian was. But she sometimes forgot.

One afternoon, Brian came tearing through the house and roared into the living room at such high speed that he knocked a brand-new vase to the floor, and it smashed to bits. Emma's first response was anger. She shouted at Brian for being so reckless, and then she sent him to his room. As she swept up the fragments of her broken vase, though, she began to doubt her response. She knew that Brian didn't intentionally break the vase, and she knew that he was a child with a high activity level. It hadn't been wise, she realized, to put the vase in such a high-traffic place, given Brian's style. So why, then, did she punish him?

Emma realized that she had made a mistake and that she needed to apologize to Brian, to ask his forgiveness. She needed to convey to him with love and true regret that she had responded inappropriately to what happened. She immediately went to his room and apologized, and the two came back downstairs hugging. Brian even helped Emma clean up the mess, secure in his understanding that the accident was not a reflection of his self-worth. The act of forgiveness was, for Emma and Brian, a gesture of true acceptance.

In order for a child to develop a positive sense of self, parents must provide a safe, consistent, and well-structured environment for the child while also respecting his autonomy (boundaries), emotional life, and style. In other words, although we parents need to provide for our children emotionally and spiritually as well as physically, we also need to respectfully give them room to grow. This may seem like a mixed message, and I encounter many parents who are confused in their understanding of how "hands-off" or "hands-on" they should be.

Allowing Your Child's Self-Identity to Emerge

As our children grow, their sense of self-identity—and our awareness of their individuality—grows, too. The infant who used to coo at you while being nursed is now the spirited toddler who throws food from his high chair with delight. The shy kindergartener is now president of her sixth-grade class. The middle-schooler who seemed to mimic everything his friends did (good or bad) is now a high-schooler who prefers training for 5-Ks to hanging out in the school yard on nights and weekends. All of these kids, at various stages of emotional and social development, are able to key in to who they really are precisely because they are accepted by their parents.

Parents who wish to foster their children's sense of self and help them attain age-appropriate levels of autonomy and independence ought to use these strategies.

Express appreciation for who a child is, not for what he does. This is an important distinction: Too many children get the message that they are their actions. The toddler who throws food and is scolded as "bad" comes to believe that *he* is bad; the shy girl who is labeled as "sullen" will never have the confidence to run for school office; the middle-schooler who follows the pack may never develop the joy and sense of accomplishment and autonomy he finds in running if his parents convey the message that he's "invisible," just one of the pack. Similarly, children who garner praise or warm parental attention only when they accomplish something are not appreciated for who they essentially are. I see many children whose senses of self-worth are seriously compromised because they are praised or "loved" only when they have accomplished something. Too many children are crumbling inside under the burden of high parental expectation and feel "worthless" or "bad" if they can't always perform as expected.

Don't confuse *discipline* with *punishment*. These two terms are closely related but have crucial differences that I want to highlight. All children need rules, boundaries, and correction when they do things that will harm themselves or others. But many parents believe that punishing poor behavior will teach a child something positive. Actually, what punishment does is frighten her into giving up a behavior. Punishment is very hard not to take personally (given that it is based on harsh judgment) and can have a very corrosive effect on a child's positive feelings about herself and on your relationship with her. Punishment is reactive and doesn't teach a child that his actions will have either positive or negative consequences.

Discipline, on the other hand, is the process of providing corrective intervention that will teach a child how to behave in ways that ought to enhance her sense of self and provide insight into the link between actions and consequences. By discipline, I mean establishing consistent rituals and rules that teach a child how to modify and moderate his behavior in ways that make him feel good about himself. For example, telling your toddler that hitting hurts and that it's not acceptable behavior builds esteem, whereas either hitting back or expelling your child from the scene for a timeout isn't.

Disciplining (rather than punishing) takes a lot of work: It is repetitive, tiresome, and at times frustrating. But the net result of being committed to disciplining your child well is that he will learn to give up undesirable behaviors without giving up his sense of self-worth. Holding your teenager to a regular curfew because you wish to keep her safe, ensure that she is well rested, and allow for adequate homework time, free time, or family time is an appropriate and esteem-building form of discipline. Threatening your child with a curfew because you don't like the company she keeps is a form of punishment. Resorting to punishment is a power play, whereas healthy discipline conveys to your child that you are helping her mature and build responsibility and move toward real freedom. Discipline becomes a reminder to make good choices and is a cooperation builder.

Ultimately, the greatest downside to the reward/punishment style of parenting comes from the corrosive effect it has on the parent-child relationship. At its core, the main difference between the punishment approach and the discipline approach is how it affects the nature of this relationship.

In the reward/punishment style, parents approach correcting undesirable behavior with the belief that the only way to get a child to do something is to force him. I frequently see parents who use a reward/punishment model fall into a few traps. First, they approach their child with anger, so whether they are spanking, verbally reprimanding, or putting a child into a timeout, the interaction is laced with a tone of animosity and rejection. Often, a child who is punished feels shamed, belittled, criticized, and humiliated. The other trap of the reward/punishment mindset involves manipulating for convenience. (We've all done it: "Hey, I really want you to quiet down right now. I will buy you this toy if you keep quiet.") This technique, though occasionally effective, undermines your relationship to the child in that the parent-child connection becomes a commodity to bargain for. I see this pattern very commonly in the most behaviorally difficult children I encounter. A father wants his 6-year-old son to cooperate in the grocery store, but a tantrum develops when the boy refuses. Ultimately, the father bargains with him by offering to buy him something in exchange for appropriate behavior. At this point, the relationship is up for sale in the child's eyes. They are no longer communicating from a place of mutual respect and connectedness, and although the child may quiet down, it is at a price.

Discipline, on the other hand, shores up the parent-child bond rather than tearing away at it. Let's look again at the example I used above. A father is in the grocery store with his 6-year-old son, who erupts in anger when he doesn't get to buy the treat he wants. This father, who is committed to disciplining rather than punishing or bargaining, leaves his grocery cart and walks his son outside, then sits down with the child and discusses what is happening. The boy vents his anger at not getting his way. The father acknowledges that he understands that his son is upset and calmly explains why this isn't the time for a treat. When the boy is calm, they agree that they can finish their shopping, and they go back into the store.

When you work to discipline your child, you impart the message, "We are working together toward this goal" versus "I will make you do this because I said so." Make no mistake, though, being authoritative is crucial to disciplining well. Although the goals of discipline are shared, the parent still must have the final word.

Maximize the do's and limit the don'ts. We discipline our children in two ways: by encouraging them to do something ("Please wash your hands") and discouraging them from doing something ("Don't take my keys"). Your child will become confident and comfortable in the "do" zone and will work to maintain this state (which will reinforce her sense of self-worth) and thus will learn to prefer to engage in these actions instead of "don't" actions.

Affirm your child's autonomy at all times. Parents have to do a mindful dance of providing structure and discipline for their children while giving them enough "room" to use their own judgment and problem-solving skills. This can be very hard to do, especially when we don't "agree" with our child's thinking.

A child's autonomy matures as his brain and body do, so gauging when it's time to step back and when it's time to stay close can be a real challenge. Here are the best ways to show your child that you value her autonomy.

- Ask for, value, and resist judging your child's opinion.

- Encourage your child to express himself authentically, which means accepting his words, facial expressions, and body language as well as his likes and dislikes.

- Work to promote your child's individuality, even if this means that at times you have to tolerate it.

Set appropriate reasonable limits, rules, and boundaries. If you create a safe, structured environment around your child, she will thrive within it. I even encourage parents to include kids in the discussion. Explain your concerns, hopes, and fears as you discuss this with your spouse in front of your child. Help her to embrace the rationale behind the decisions you make as a family.

Ask her opinion, but make it clear that as parents, you make the final decisions. As she matures, she will offer more and more relevant feedback. This will enable her to more quickly imitate and internalize the caretaking process that you've established.

Encourage and support your child at all times. Be patient and let your child find his own pace, his own solutions, and his own successes. Let him know that you are behind him every step of the way by honoring his process in appropriate ways. When your young child is taking his time to order from the menu at a restaurant, for example, resist the impulse to push him along or order for him. Or suppose your college-age son tells you he's going to take a year off to travel in Asia before he starts college. Although you may not agree with a decision, honor his wishes if his choice won't bring harm to himself or anyone else.

Support your child's burgeoning independence. As children mature, they have opportunities to take on challenges away from home and parents. Encourage this by sending your child to summer camp when she is ready, let her make independent visits to relatives or family friends, and champion school trips that also provide this opportunity. Process the experience with your child when she returns.

HELPING YOUR CHILD DEVELOP THE ABILITY TO SELF-REGULATE

Babies are the great communicators in life. They spontaneously express all their feelings without any inhibition. But what would our world be like if we all had the emotional spontaneity of infants? It would be a crazy, chaotic, and loud place, where meaningful communication and the transactions of daily life would be impossible. Acquiring the ability to regulate emotions is the result of healthy brain growth, secure attachment, and the achievement of physical, psychological, and socio-emotional milestones over time.

The Downside of "Good Job!"

Self-esteem has become a buzzword in parenting today. I believe we spend too much time worrying about our children's self-esteem when we simply don't need to. Children who have a strong sense of self-identity and a strong awareness of their inherent self-worth will naturally have self-esteem. It's part of the package.

Children absolutely need encouragement and support to feel good about themselves, but praising them for routine or appropriate behavior (something I see a lot of) can actually weaken a child's sense of self-worth. I run into parents all the time who mindlessly say "good job!" whenever a child does absolutely anything, even things as mundane as finishing a meal, using the toilet, or following a simple command (such as "Please close the door"). Relating to your child only in this way gives her the message that just functioning nominally is, in your mind, somehow a great accomplishment. Believe it or not, you actually set fairly low expectations for her when you do this. ("Damning with faint praise" is the expression that comes to mind.) When children who are pelted with this message (however well intentioned) actually do achieve something that marks a significant developmental step toward autonomy and independence, there is simply no adequate language available for the parent to use. When it comes to helping to foster self-esteem in your child, remember to be encouraging at all times, but save excessive praise for the moments that truly merit it.

We are all born with the full spectrum of emotions, but it takes time (even a lifetime for some) to become fully acquainted with our emotional repertoire and be able to express our emotions clearly and appropriately. A big part of what attentive, attuned parents help babies develop is an awareness of their own feelings. When we mirror back to a baby what he is showing us (his joy, his anguish, his tiredness), we help him begin to separate, identify, and understand his own feelings.

As he moves into toddlerhood and begins to acquire language, he becomes capable of expressing even more complex emotions, though he's still not yet able to regulate them. This stage is when appropriate discipline and setting limits takes on a whole new level of importance and meaning for attuned parents. Without the right kind of modeling ("Do what I do, not what I say"), positive reinforcement, and social guidance, acquiring the ability to regulate emotions will be tough for any kid. This is why I see so many children (especially in the middle years) who are labeled as having behavioral problems and disorders: They simply haven't yet reached a level of cognitive or physical maturity that allows them to effectively regulate their emotions.

A child's ability to self-regulate has clearly demarcated developmental milestones, just as cognitive skill does. Babies cry—a lot. This is an important way for them to express themselves. Toddlers, when angry or frustrated, have tantrums. Tantrums are normal and even healthy for a 3-year-old, but they aren't a sign of strong emotional health in a 10-year-old. A toddler's brain does not yet have the maturity to respond to stress (or distress) in any other way, but a 10-year-old who has a secure attachment and is being well disciplined ought to have this kind of emotional control. In our label-happy society, we tend to label and medicate kids who don't yet have the requisite tools (or brain structure) to self-regulate instead of addressing these issues from a more appropriate social/relational point of view. Here are some strategies to help you help your child learn to self-regulate.

Maintain a serene, safe, clean home environment. Stress (including noise, pollution, and discord) is the enemy of self-regulation. When the brain is on "high alert" and distracted by stress, the ability to identify emotions and express them appropriately is greatly impaired.

Model self-control and healthy self-regulation. Your child needs to see you handle your full spectrum of emotions well. If you feel overwhelmed by your feelings, walk away, regroup, and then come back to your child; otherwise, she will be overwhelmed by your feelings, too. Appropriate role modeling is a big part of how children learn. While imitation comes long before the development of true skill mastery, these steps are connected in many crucial ways.

Know and respect your child's "triggers." This is another way of saying know your child's temperament, style, and limitations. If your child tends to be emotionally overwhelmed by large groups of people, make sure he gets one-on-one play dates instead of expecting him to simply navigate the playground crowds. If your child's pace is slow, try very hard not to rush him; instead, add extra time so he can accomplish things at a natural, peaceful rate.

Respect your child's feelings at all times. Stop and look at any given situation from your child's vantage point before you judge or negate her feelings. You may think the clown at the circus is funny; your daughter may find him terrifying.

Encourage your child to express—not hide—her feelings. We live in a culture that is uncomfortable with feelings, especially any outward expression of them. This societal emotional repression isn't good for anyone's emotional and mental health. Break the pattern: Help your child feel comfortable with experiencing and sharing the full range of his emotions. After a big disappointment with a friend in junior high, give your son the room to calm down, then sit down and discuss his feelings with him. Ask questions and listen. Don't give directions or criticize; the goal is to really understand your son's feelings.

Develop an emotional vocabulary. Encourage your child to put her feelings, responses, and reactions into words. A fun way to help younger kids build an emotional vocabulary is to create a chart with many feeling words and draw faces that correspond to these states. As they mature, help them add new words to their emotional repertoire, such as *exhilarated, disappointed,* or *apprehensive.* Challenge them to seek out the nuances in their inner state and to share with you the subtle differences in how they feel. This kind of vocabulary building helps children look within and learn to "read" their inner barometers. This skill will help them to seek their own counsel first in life. Once a child feels confident that he is reading his own emotional state well, he'll be in a much better position to interact appropriately with others. Children with behavioral problems typically lack the ability to identify and name their feelings well.

Seek help. If you feel overwhelmed by your own feelings or your child's, seek professional help (in particular, some type of talk therapy).

Learning emotional self-regulation is a gratifying process for children that reinforces their sense of control and mastery in life. Kids who have a healthy acceptance of their own feelings and know how to express them appropriately have better relationships with others, are more empathetic and compassionate, and enjoy stronger emotional and mental health.

HELPING YOUR CHILD DEVELOP RESILIENCE

Resilience, as discussed in Chapter 6, is the ability to bounce back in the face of adversity. Resilience is also flexibility, adaptability, and the ability to embrace—not fear—change. Without resilience, life for a child can seem forbidding and overwhelming. With it, life becomes an exhilarating succession of one well-met challenge after another.

The human brain, by its very nature, is highly resilient. The only organ that continues to grow and change throughout a lifetime, the brain is designed to absorb and respond to the human condition, which is constantly in a state of flux and transition. No brain is more resilient than that of a child. Parents who know this are able to relax, understanding that parenting (like life) is made up of trial-and-error experiences and that no well-intentioned parental gesture or decision can take away a child's ability to bounce back, grow, change, and be resilient.

One of the most prominent researchers on resilience, Bonnie Benard, has written that "the development of resiliency is none other than the process of healthy human development." Resilience is the ability to encounter stress, trauma, or conflict and come out wiser and stronger as a result. The development of resilience is also the development of a healthy brain, and the presence of resilience in a child is a great predicator of emotional and mental health. Benard, who understands that "we shrink kids when we give them labels," has been a passionate crusader for shifting our focus away from a child's weakness (the area we are most likely to label) and focus instead on a child's strengths. She understands that resilience protects children from labels, even those that may be well intentioned (for example, "he is a victim of Hurricane Katrina" or "she is a survivor of 9/11").

I share Benard's view that any kind of label—especially those that in any way define a child as a victim—fosters a sense of helplessness and undermines a child's belief that she can take action and is not simply acted upon. When we resist the urge to label and instead focus on nurturing a child's ability to handle stress, we are in effect helping to create everyday heroes, helping to raise young people who know that they can overcome all kinds of adversity and create truly meaningful lives for themselves.

Kids who have a sense of their own resilience, who believe that they have control or influence over the course of their lives, have the capacity to become deeply committed to themselves and their activities. Resilient kids view change as an exciting challenge and not something to be feared. Resilient kids are successful—and happy—kids. They tend to share the following traits.

Possessing an internal locus of control. Resilient kids believe that they have control over their lives and that they are not helpless. They believe in their ability to effect change. A boy who admires another boy's strong character reaches out and establishes a rewarding friendship based on his risk-taking action. A teen struggling with algebra asks the teacher for help and in turn develops a new area of competence. Encourage your child to take risks to reach her goals. Validate her when taking risks leads to positive results in her life. This will strengthen her internal locus of control.

Having good problem-solving skills. Resilient kids thrive on challenge. They enjoy seeking solutions and don't give up easily. The tougher the problem, the more kids with good problem-solving skills seem to enjoy it. They realize tough problems take time and effort to solve, and they accept that. Best of all, they can enjoy the process. Be respectful of this process, and you will enjoy a child who can face all of life's problems head-on.

Knowing how to ask for help. A resilient child knows how to find appropriate support (even outside of the family) and seems to grasp intuitively that enlisting help is a sign of healthy independence. Sadly, our culture tends to view asking for help as a sign of weakness. Praise your child for his efforts to find the support he needs to succeed.

Having an optimistic view of life. A resilient kid views challenges, even hardships, as opportunities and has faith that things will "work out." Optimistic kids don't see failures as setbacks but just as part of life. They take advantage of being given the chance to try again or to shift gears entirely. They tend to "roll with the punches" and are not afraid of change.

Liking to help others. A resilient child tends toward "compassionate action" and wants to help others through difficult times (just as she accepts such help when she is in need). I encourage parents to get involved in service projects that can involve kids as well. Encourage your child to volunteer at the local soup kitchen or humane society and revel in the good feelings that come from helping others.

Having strong communication skills. Can your child effectively make his needs, desires, and opinions known? Does he listen well to others? Children who are listened to tend to be great communicators and to enjoy the most successful relationships. Role-playing is a great way to help younger kids learn to communicate well. Talking to your teen about everything (politics, sex, sports, feelings) will help him stay open and communicative.

Knowing who they are. Resilient children aren't just among the gifted or intellectually elite. They are kids from all areas of the cognitive spectrum who know how to maximize their strengths and compensate for their weaknesses. To accomplish this, they must be comfortable with self-examination and reflection. Encourage this type of dialogue. Ask, "So, what do you think your strengths are?" Strongly support any attempt at honest self-appraisal. Don't let your child beat herself up; compassionate treatment must be modeled.

THE TRUE JOB OF PARENTING

Once we've done the hard work of raising a resilient, self-regulating kid with a clear sense of self-identity, we begin the process of letting go. One parent I know likened this to spending years filling the coal bin of a locomotive: His back was bent from shoveling. Finally, when the coal bin was full, the train chugged off, leaving him behind. Part of the process of letting go of our children, of launching them into adulthood, is preparing ourselves for this transition. You would be amazed at how many parents unintentionally fight this part of the process, and I see many troubled teenagers who are suffering because their parents have such great difficulty letting them go. Here are some useful reminders about letting go for parents of children of all ages.

1. Remind yourself frequently that this youngster is a person that you're raising, not something you own. Your child belongs to God, the universe, the world—use whatever metaphor feels right for you.

2. Know that all the hard work you've done as a parent is also meant to transform you—not just your child. Prepare yourself for the change in responsibility that launching your child into adulthood will bring. Now you get to enjoy the friendship with your child that you've been cultivating for years.

3. Try not to overprotect your child from life. I've discussed how important it is for children to experience failure, and this is also true for adolescents and young adults. The tendency to overprotect seems to really come on strong for parents when children are leaving the nest. Resist this as best you can.

4. Keep your focus on who your child is, not what she does or what she might become. When a child is ready to leave home, all sorts of unfulfilled hopes and wishes often begin to emerge for parents. Your daughter decides to become an artist instead of a lawyer like you. Your son decides he doesn't want to marry, so you have to give up the fantasy you've had of being involved in a big wedding. Don't lose sight of who your child is simply because she makes choices that are different from yours.

5. Don't be afraid to be vulnerable and honest with your child. When a child is preparing to leave home, the feelings you have will be genuine and intense. Don't be afraid to say, "I love you; I'll miss you." Children need to hear these things from us, just as we needed to hear them throughout the years.

6. Be aware of and work on your own issues. Whenever you reach a point of conflict or disagreement with your child,

stop and ask yourself, "Is this situation about me and my need to take control?" (I strongly recommend the book *Parenting from the Inside Out,* by Daniel Siegel, MD, and Mary Hartzell. It thoughtfully explores how our own childhood experiences and expectations affect us as parents.)

7. Convey to your child that your interest in his life will remain consistent, loving, and supportive. Some parents make the mistake of thinking that once a child leaves home, his life is no longer their business. This is anything but true for kids who have been close to their parents. Now, as in any adult relationship, there will be a reciprocal expression of interest, and your relationship will take on the new rhythm of friendship. You may phone your son at college, and he may not return your call right away. If you respect his independence, this won't upset you. In fact, when he calls back a few days later, you'll enjoy catching up on all the news.

8. Show interest in your child's future. Frequently ask your child what she foresees for herself as a young adult. Help her envision positive scenarios for herself in the future. Most labeled kids have little sense of a positive future. Don't get caught up in whether your child's dreams are realistic or not. Instead, encourage the dream. This shows that you'll support your child to become who she really hopes to be and will also allow you to get to know your child in new ways.

9. Work on your own inner life. Being a great parent demands a lot of personal growth, including spiritual growth (whether you are religious or not). As you learn to move beyond your own issues and put your child's welfare first, you can't help growing spiritually. Embrace this process.

10. Prepare to have an empty nest. Develop hobbies and interests that you can enjoy once your kids have left home. Many fine

parents struggle after the kids leave because they were so devoted to the job of parenting that they didn't prepare themselves.

11. Enhance your relationships with other adults. Deepen your connection with your spouse or partner or with friends. Parenting is a hugely time-consuming and emotionally taxing endeavor. When your child is reaching adulthood, you have the chance to renew your relationships with other adults and deepen your intimacy with your partner or spouse. Seize this opportunity!

THE REWARD

When your 18-year-old packs up the car and moves on to college or a job and a place of his own, don't be surprised if you shed a few tears—tears of joy, sorrow, relief, and satisfaction. You have just spent many years of your life helping another person to grow and flourish, and the result is nothing short of miraculous.

You loved, nurtured, and supported your child through good times and tough times, working diligently to identify and address the stressors that may have periodically challenged his emotional and mental health. But you understood the power of the infant brain to grow, adapt, and respond, and you had faith that the secure, attached relationship you established with your baby would serve him well as he grew.

At times, you struggled to "fit" with your child, but you hung in there and worked hard to stay attuned and in sync with this child, who you knew from day one was a person very different from you. You understood that in terms of brain development, the relationships this young person had were more important than anything he would ever read in a book, so you worked hard to ensure that he fit well with teachers, friends, and others and that he moved in healthy environments beyond the home. You provided a safe, harmonious home environment in which your child (and his young brain) could grow optimally, and you nourished his body with brain-building foods. You were aware of the impact media and culture had on your child. You couldn't protect him from all harm, and so when trauma came into his life, you addressed it appropriately and compassionately.

Very early on, you stood by in amazement as you watched him develop the awesome skills of resilience and self-regulation. You felt pride as his sense of self-identity grew steadily over the years. All the while, you rejoiced as he developed a growing and progressive sense of independence that made today's transition not only possible but natural.

When we parent our kids toward authentic self-acceptance and a deep appreciation for their own self-worth, we are fortifying them against ever being victimized by debilitating and demeaning labels, wherever they may come from. We are also fulfilling our truest parental obligation, which is to nourish and support another being while he grows toward glorious autonomy and healthy maturity. Parenting is the perpetual process of getting out of the way, of letting go. When we do it well, our children are exquisitely capable of taking care of themselves.

When you raise a child with the three core traits—a strong self-identity, the ability to self-regulate, and resilience—you raise a child who will probably enjoy a lifetime of strong emotional and mental health. You also raise a child who will be "label resistant," a true individual. Children who have strong emotional and mental health become leaders, innovators, and dynamic contributors to society. They also enjoy better overall physical health and healthier relationships.

It is my great hope that we will take advantage of the knowledge and understanding we have about the way a child's brain works and consciously strive to move into a future where all children live without labels. We all want to raise healthy, happy children, and we all want to be good parents. Every child desires nothing more than to be loved and accepted. In the end, the work of parenting involves learning to love well. We must learn the many different ways that our children ask for our loving attention. Every time we're able to do this, another label dissolves.

Where there is love, there are no labels.

The Most-Common Psychiatric Labels Given to Children

Today, children are diagnosed with a staggering array of psychiatric disorders. The following list includes the labels that I see most frequently in my day-to-day practice and are the disorders that seem to be the most common nationwide.

ANXIETY DISORDERS

Anxiety disorders is the term that is used to describe a wide range of fear-based disorders that affect a large part of the American population, including children. They can range from specific phobias (such as fear of snakes, heights, closed spaces, water, and so forth) and generalized symptoms of anxiety that severely inhibit the quality of everyday life to obsessive-compulsive disorder.

Generalized Anxiety Disorder (GAD)

Kids with GAD worry about everything: about homework and the family finances, about Dad driving home in the rain, and about global warming. GAD is officially diagnosed when a child compulsively worries for at least 6 months, and the worry interferes with normal daily functioning.

GAD affects about 3 to 5 percent of adults and appears to be much more prevalent in children. In my practice, I have found it to be underrecognized in school-age children. I even performed a small research study in our local school district that confirmed my suspicions. Eight percent of the children that I surveyed (first and sixth graders) had three or more symptoms of chronic anxiety, but only 1 percent were being treated. The child often internalizes the worry, so it's hidden from parents and other adults in the child's life.

Treatment is often twofold: cognitive behavioral therapy and medications. Kids respond well to treatment, and many grow out of GAD as they mature. Depression can be a common side effect since GAD can be limiting to the child and cause a great deal of distress. I work with diet, supplements, and supportive counseling. These kids really appreciate being able to talk about their concerns, and they benefit from counseling. When treating GAD, it's important to look for undisclosed trauma/posttraumatic stress disorder as well.

Obsessive-Compulsive Disorder (OCD)

OCD is characterized by recurrent obsessions and/or compulsions that are intense enough to cause severe discomfort. Obsessions are recurrent and persistent unwanted thoughts, impulses, or images that cause marked anxiety or distress; compulsions are the repeated behaviors and rituals employed to control the obsessions. Although OCD usually begins in adolescence or young adulthood, it is seen in as many as 1 in 200 children (people up to age 18) in this country. Research has shown that OCD tends to run in families, but this doesn't mean that a child with a family history of OCD will definitely develop symptoms, and a child with no previous family history may develop the disorder. Recent studies have also shown that OCD may develop or worsen after a strep infection.

Children and adolescents with OCD often feel ashamed and embarrassed. Many fear that they are crazy. OCD in children is often treated with medication and behavior therapy. The best of the latter is exposure and response prevention (ERP), a behavioral approach that helps the child by interrupting compulsive responses to common triggers. With help, they learn to choose different responses, thereby overriding the habitual pattern. The most severe cases seem to benefit from a combination of ERP and antidepressant medications.

Even though OCD may be one of the most biological of mental disorders, its course waxes and wanes. Over 3 or 4 years, as many as a third of patients will have spontaneous remission.

Panic Disorder

Anxiety and panic are two completely different things, yet most people equate them. Anxiety is uncomfortable psychological and physical tension that builds in response to some external process. For example, people with a fear of flying become progressively more anxious as they approach the airport and their flight. Panic, on the other hand, is a full-blown body/mind state of total fear that occurs without warning. Panic episodes can last for 5 to 30 minutes. Children and adults often end up in an emergency room for assessment since the symptoms of a panic attack mimic those of heart attack, stroke, or something equally as serious. Catastrophic thinking may actually be one cause of this disorder, which is also thought to have a genetic component.

These attacks can be so overwhelming that people limit their behavior in order to avoid triggering one. Panic disorder affects about 1 percent of Americans and often starts in childhood. Drug and alcohol abuse can develop as the person tries—ineffectively—to cope with the disorder.

Treatment often involves cognitive behavioral therapy (CBT) and medications, often those in the selective serotonin reuptake inhibitor (SSRI) class of antidepressants. Treatment can be very successful if the person is able to stay engaged. Most forms of traditional psychotherapy aren't very effective, so when choosing a therapist, be sure he has been trained in CBT. I find that in addition to CBT, many anxiety-reducing supplements, such as inositol and valerian, can be helpful in treating panic disorder. Those with panic disorder should also eliminate all caffeine from their diets.

Posttraumatic Stress Disorder (PTSD)

PTSD occurs in people who have experienced significant trauma. The hallmarks in adults are overarousal, flashbacks, insomnia, anxiety, and nightmares as well as an increased incidence of depression, suicide attempts, and substance abuse. In children, the syndrome is much more variable and more complicated to diagnose. PTSD can develop when a child has experienced a significant traumatic event (a car accident) or ongoing trauma over time (war). We now know that a child raised in a chaotic or violent home can develop PTSD even if he has only witnessed trauma and not experienced it directly.

In PTSD, kids develop altered cortisol (stress hormone) levels, which in turn can impair neurological growth and development. This creates a situation in which PTSD can look like almost any other psychiatric illness, and it's commonly missed or misdiagnosed in children. Also, much of the abuse that children experience happens without any common awareness of it. Children may repress or dissociate the actual memory and have no conscious awareness of it. Abuse also commonly occurs before children are old enough to have clear adult-like memories of it or to have the cognitive ability to comprehend it.

In my experience, the most common labels that traumatized kids are given erroneously are attention deficit hyperactivity disorder, bipolar disorder, depression, generalized anxiety disorder, panic disorder, and oppositional defiant disorder. If I think that significant trauma has occurred in a child's past, I will approach her primarily as a PTSD patient.

ATTENTION DEFICIT HYPERACTIVITY DISORDER (ADHD)

More than four million American children have been diagnosed with ADHD, and most of them are taking medication for it. The current edition of *The Diagnostic and Statistical Manual of Mental Disorders* (*DSM*-IV) states that the principal characteristics of ADHD, which was first identified in 1945, are inattention, hyperactivity, and impulsivity. These symptoms arise in young children, usually before the age of 7, although they often go unrecognized until a child enters school and the characteristics become more pronounced.

Everyone, of course, is inattentive, hyperactive, and impulsive at times, but when the characteristics are severe, many physicians and other experts on ADHD believe that a child has a full-blown disorder or illness. I happen to disagree with this way of thinking. Unlike illnesses such as diabetes, arthritis, or epilepsy, there is no physiological or pathological evidence for ADHD. The diagnosis is entirely subjective and is based on how we interpret a collection of symptomatic behaviors. Too often, we doctors get it wrong and misdiagnose ADHD when we fail to identify and treat the underlying stress that may be causing ADHD-like behaviors. For instance, a child may have a thyroid problem, a brain injury, or a genetic disorder such as fragile X syndrome, all of which are true illnesses that cause ADHD-like symptoms in children.

Other stressors that can cause this type of behavior in children include a sudden change in a child's life (including the loss of a parent or beloved guardian, a divorce, a move, or a parent losing a job), undetected seizures, an iron deficiency, an unacknowledged learning disability, or a medical disorder that affects brain function. Almost daily, I treat children who have been diagnosed with ADHD but are actually suffering the effects of severe trauma or abuse or are battling undiagnosed disorders like depression or anxiety.

Although I think we use ADHD as a catchall label for a vast array of symptoms that could indicate myriad true illnesses, I don't dispute how effective the use of stimulants can be in treating these symptoms. The problem for me is that by labeling and treating only the symptoms—what we call ADHD—the true underlying problem may go unrecognized and untreated.

AUTISTIC SPECTRUM DISORDERS

Autism is a severe neurobehavioral disorder characterized by impaired social, language, and cognitive skills. Seizures and mental retardation commonly occur. Autism may be the most devastating developmental illness of childhood.

This illness has clear biological roots and strikes some families more than others. Boys are affected four times more frequently than girls. The behaviors can be so difficult that many of these kids are institutionalized. Autism is lifelong, but some progress can be made if intensive treatment begins early in childhood.

The onset typically occurs in early childhood. In the most common scenario, a child develops normally until about 1 year of age. The parents then see an abrupt regression of behavior and learning, and from then on, the child behaves quite differently. He becomes detached and devoid of affection. Whereas he was previously cuddly, he may now arch his back and resist even being held.

He often avoids eye contact altogether and may develop odd mannerisms, such as hand flapping or twirling things in front of his eyes. Language development comes to an abrupt halt as he stops using words and starts pointing at objects or dragging a parent or caregiver to whatever it is that he wants.

An autistic child inhabits his own world and becomes stuck in odd, peculiar interests. A 6-year-old may become preoccupied with pencils and collect hundreds of them. Sameness and constancy become a crucial comfort. If his pencil collection is moved in any way, he may scream for hours. He may even cry for an hour if his mother takes a different route home from preschool.

Social skills are remarkably absent. His voice takes on a dreary monotone, and he treats other kids like objects. An autistic child does not develop relationships as we know them.

Some people with autism have remarkable cognitive skills. The movie *Rain Man* tells the story of one such savant, as people with this characteristic are called. One of my patients correctly calculated in his head on which day of the week I was born within 10 seconds of finding out my birth date. Another memorizes all the license plates in the parking lot as he walks into the office to see me.

Researchers have documented a horrific rise in autistic spectrum disorders in the past 20 years. Researchers at the Centers for Disease Control and Prevention in Atlanta published a survey in 2003 that documented a tenfold rise in autism rates over 10 years. This study echoed other, smaller studies. No one knows why this has occurred, but it's estimated that 425,000 American children have this disorder.

The conventional treatment is a combination of social skills training, language development, and management with medication. There are no specific medications for autism; the drugs that are used are for specific symptoms, such as hyperactivity or volatile anger. Nonconventional approaches involve supplements like vitamin B$_6$, magnesium, and specific diets (dairy-free and gluten-free). For information from the Autism Research Institute and the Center for the Study of Autism, visit www.autismwebsite.com/ari/index.htm and www.autism.org. The most common nonconventional approach is the DAN (Defeat Autism Now) protocol found on these sites.

Asperger syndrome (Asperger's disorder) is a neurobiological disorder that's often described as an autistic spectrum disorder because there are similarities between the two conditions. Those with Asperger syndrome (named for a Viennese physician, Hans Asperger) have normal intelligence and language skills but also exhibit autistic-like behaviors, including deficiencies in social skills. Asperger's was added to the *DSM*-IV in 1994, and it's only been recognized by professionals and parents within the past few years.

People with Asperger's can exhibit a variety of characteristics, and the disorder can range from mild to severe. They show marked deficiencies in social skills, have difficulty with transitions or changes, and prefer sameness. They often have obsessive routines and may be preoccupied with a particular subject of interest. They have a great deal of difficulty reading nonverbal cues (body language) and very often have difficulty with physical boundaries. They are often quite sensitive to sounds, tastes, smells, and sights.

Kids with Asperger's are the "odd ducks" or eccentrics who speak like little adults but have real problems fitting in with peers. They come at the world from a vantage point that's very different from that of most other kids, and this needs to be recognized and honored. The condition usually coexists with other issues, such as ADHD, depression, anxiety, and obsessive-compulsive disorder. Treatment for Asperger's, as for autism, is multipronged, and life-skill–building therapies are central.

CHILDHOOD-ONSET BIPOLAR DISORDER (BD)

Bipolar disorder is also known as manic-depressive illness, and until recently, very few children were diagnosed with this severe mood disorder. However, one recent study found that hospitalization rates for this disorder rose fivefold over the last decade. It's characterized by severe, unpredictable swings from agitated, high-energy states to flat, almost affectless periods during which the patient can barely function. In children, the symptoms of BD are often mistaken for ADHD (and vice versa) since BD expresses itself as mood cycling dysregulation with elements of elation, depression, and irritability.

BD is a devastating lifelong illness that needs aggressive and ongoing medical treatment. Joseph Biederman, MD, a leading pediatric psychopharmacologist and professor at Harvard, estimates that as many as 1 percent of American children may have this disorder. Dr. Biederman also contends that treating depressed children with certain types of antidepressants (selective serotonin reuptake inhibitors, or SSRIs) may trigger mania. He also believes that those prone to childhood depression are also at higher risk of developing full-blown BD. The fact that more and more of our children have this disorder is indisputable, but what stressors are causing this rise in such a serious mood disorder? I believe we must look at the causes while seeking the cure.

I believe a lack of essential fatty acids, vitamins, and minerals in kids' diets contributes to these symptoms. The rise in bipolar disorder makes me think of an illness called pellagra that was rampant in the American South more than 100 years ago. Pellagra was found in rural, poor communities; the symptoms included aggression, insomnia, mental confusion, and eventually, dementia and death. It was originally thought to be a peculiar psychiatric disorder, but it turned out to be a deficiency of niacin (vitamin B_3) and protein. The poor in the rural South ate mainly corn and little else. Once essential nutrients were restored to their diets, the illness abated completely. I treat many "bipolar" patients who respond so well to nutritional therapy that I can't help believing that what we're now calling childhood-onset bipolar disorder is more likely a reflection of a nutrient-deficient diet.

DEPRESSION

What we call depression is the expression of behavioral or emotional symptoms that arise when a person has experienced a loss or trauma and hasn't been able to overcome the normal attendant sorrow of that loss. In more clinical terms, depression is the mental state of excessive sadness characterized by persistently low mood or extensive loss of pleasure and interest. To be considered a clinical condition that merits treatment with therapy, medication, or both, the symptoms of depression must have lasted at least 2 weeks and include weight loss or gain, agitated or sluggish behavior, and disturbances in sleep, appetite, and/or concentration. Depression can be mild (dysthymia) or severe (major depression), and the impact it can have on someone's life can be devastating. No one knows for sure what causes it or exactly how to best treat it. Because depression is so difficult to identify, it often goes undiagnosed, especially in children.

Although we know more about depression now than we ever have before, we're still in the early stages of understanding it. The unhappy fact is that it afflicts more and more of us—at younger and younger ages. Not long ago (within the last half century), it was thought that children simply did not suffer from depression. Today, it's the number one emotional disorder diagnosed in children of all ages.

Antidepressant medications have fared poorly in tests to evaluate their effectiveness in kids. While there's a variety of antidepressants on the market that work on the brain in various ways, only Prozac (fluoxetine) has been found to be effective in children. All antidepressants now carry the most severe FDA warning about safety (a "black box" warning), cautioning about the increased risk of suicidal behavior in children who take these drugs. Medications are one option, but they may not be the best one.

INTERMITTENT EXPLOSIVE DISORDER

This is an uncommon diagnosis that I believe that we will hear more about in the coming years. It consists of explosions of violent anger out of proportion to the precipitating events and is not better accounted for by another diagnosis. If this diagnosis sounds vague and nonspecific to you, that's because it is. Children with this disorder periodically explode in aggressive or destructive episodes of anger. Typically, children that I see with this pattern tend to explode more at home with parents and less often elsewhere. Often, these kids have some underlying mood, trauma, or parent-child issues that affect the situation. My efforts are usually to work with nutrients and supplements like magnesium and fish oil while addressing the family dynamics or past history.

OPPOSITIONAL DEFIANT DISORDER (ODD)

All kids are oppositional or defiant at times, but when that's the primary way a child relates to the world, it becomes problematic—and pathologized. The child often becomes labeled when the main style of coping they possess is a refusal to cooperate. These kids feel angry, disconnected, and insecure in the world. They grasp at a sense of control by using defiance in spite of how much it costs them. Often right below the surface is a sense of hopelessness. I do see many similarities to depression in these kids who often have issues with the parent-child relationship. Parents might be either too harsh and distant or too lenient and enabling. Actually, both may occur in the same family with a triangle of three created between the mother, the father, and the child. Symptoms of ODD include being argumentative, having frequent tantrums, refusing to comply with rules and requests, blaming others for mistakes or behavior, having chronic anger or resentment, using mean language when upset, being vengeful, and deliberately upsetting others. It's estimated that 5 to 15 percent of all school-age children have ODD, and it can be difficult to detect, as it often co-exists with other conditions, such as ADHD, depression, anxiety, or a learning disability.

There are no drug therapies for ODD. Instead of drugs, these kids need allies who will try to reach them and help them learn the coping skills they'll need for life. The standard treatment is behavioral therapy, in which limits, rules, and consequences are set. Very often, children with ODD have learning challenges or poor social skills that trigger frequent failures. The weakness that's usually present in the parent-child bond also needs to be addressed. If this key relationship doesn't improve, behavioral therapies will only delay the onset of additional symptoms.

Glossary of Mental Health Therapies

T his is a comprehensive list of therapies from a wide range of disciplines. I've found that each of these offers relief from mental and emotional symptoms and that when combined, several forms of therapy can ameliorate even the worst symptoms—often without the use of medication.

Acupuncture: An ancient Chinese medical system using needles and herbs. Comprehensive scientific data supports this as an effective treatment. I recommend it for pain, headaches, anxiety, and occasionally depression.

Animal-assisted therapy: Many people can make huge gains by connecting with animals, such as dogs, horses, or dolphins. I'm often surprised by the variety of children who find animals a key to opening up emotionally. I often recommend this for kids who don't like to talk or discuss feelings.

Aromatherapy: A health care system that applies the scientific use of aromatic and volatile oils for their beneficial effects. I often encourage people to explore its gentle environmental influence to aid ADHD or anxiety.

Art therapy: This evocative therapy fosters emotional healing and relief through the use of personal art expression. I find it very helpful for people who don't do well with verbally oriented talk therapies, such as is the case with many young boys.

Biofeedback: This well-researched technique uses instruments to give the participants information about their bodies. This in turn gives them the ability to control physiological functions ranging from brainwaves to muscle tension. I find it helpful in treating the symptoms of ADHD, anxiety, and some types of pain, such as headaches.

Bodywork: This broad term is used to describe all types of hands-on work with the soft tissue of the body. Massage is the most common type. I find it useful with recovery from sexual and physical abuse as well as anxiety and depression.

Chiropractic: A health care system that employs manipulation of the spine to improve health and well-being. I recommend it for some back pain and neck problems.

Cognitive behavioral therapy (CBT): This well-researched psychotherapy helps to rewrite inappropriate assumptions and generalizations that predispose people to depression or anxiety. I find it useful for treating some types of depression.

Cranial manipulation: This offshoot of osteopathy involves extremely gentle manipulation of the skull. I find it useful for kids with a history of birth trauma, head injuries, explosive temper, or developmental disabilities.

Dialectical behavior therapy (DBT): This recent innovation combines CBT with some facets of mindfulness meditation. I find it helpful for people with mood swings, anger management issues, and bipolar-type symptoms.

Exercise: Vigorous physical activity. Many studies demonstrate that exercise is as good as any prescription antidepressant, with fewer side effects and better long-term results. I recommend that all of my depressed patients increase their activity levels.

Experiential therapy: This therapy involves adventurous outdoor activities such as those promoted by Outward Bound, National Outdoor Leadership School (NOLS), and other organizations. I find them helpful for many types of teen depression or behavioral problems.

Eye movement desensitization and reprocessing (EMDR): This is another recent innovation that involves eye movements to reduce emotional intensity related to trauma or fear. I recommend it routinely for kids with posttraumatic stress disorder or anxiety issues.

Family therapy: This has been a cornerstone of child and adolescent therapy for decades. Sadly, I find it to be underused. I employ it when there are issues of fit, parent-child conflict, or poor interfamily communication.

Group therapy: An honored tradition in psychiatry and psychology, this may the single most powerful technique for working with teens. Unfortunately, it can be very hard to find a good group when you need one, but doing the legwork is worth it.

Hakomi: Another recent innovation in psychotherapy. This gentle technique skillfully blends mindfulness with other exploratory skills. I have found it to be valuable for treating anxiety and for use with highly sensitive, thoughtful patients.

Homeopathy: As a 200-year-old medical science, homeopathy challenges our current paradigm more than any other approach. Many studies document its clinical claims. I recommend it for people who are resistant to other approaches or those with unusual symptoms, such as odd sensations, peculiar cravings, or very specific physical symptoms.

Journaling: Simply writing down one's thoughts each day greatly enhances self-awareness. I especially encourage teens to keep journals if they are struggling with communicating, have self-image issues, are depressed, or are overwhelmed by life.

Light therapy: We now know that light has the ability to reduce depression and improve learning. Light boxes with high-intensity bulbs make this work. I encourage anyone with a seasonal pattern of low moods or chronic depression to give it a try.

Martial arts: This term describes a broad range of practices that develop "warrior skills" in practitioners. They are grounded in respect and discipline and promote self-control and physical confidence. I find them to be highly therapeutic, especially for boys.

Massage therapy: An ancient and honored form of bodywork that uses gentle strokes and oils to soothe the body and mind. I routinely encourage anyone with anxiety or depression to try it.

Mindfulness meditation: This form of mental skill builds self-awareness and insight. Studies show a broad range of physical, mental, and spiritual benefits from this practice. I recommend it frequently, avoiding it only when there are serious psychotic symptoms present, such as hallucinations.

Music therapy: Many have found value in applying music to emotional or mental issues. Music therapy employs both listening to and creating music to foster healing. I have found it helpful for the right person with depression. Young kids with ADHD often do well in music/drumming groups.

Naturopathy: This health care tradition is more than 100 years old and is based on the healing powers of nature; diet, nutrition, herbs, acupuncture, and homeopathy form the foundation. Many states now recognize naturopaths as primary care providers. I refer patients to them when I want more help with lifestyle, nutrition, or chronic illness issues.

Osteopathy: A medical system based on promoting health by focusing on the structures (bones, muscles, blood vessels, tissues) of the body. Body work is at the core of osteopathy, as the practice is built on the understanding that when the systems of the body are in sync, health will be achieved and maintained. I find osteopathic cranial work to be a godsend for many conditions and refer patients to osteopaths for musculoskeletal problems.

Play therapy: A fundamental therapy in child psychiatry that is based on the belief that children express themselves most freely through play rather than with words. Skilled therapists use games, dolls, role-playing, and other techniques and materials to support a child in expressing feelings or problems. It's invaluable for helping young children with psychiatric distress, especially those who have suffered trauma or have anxiety.

Process work: This therapy comes to us from Carl Jung, who understood the spiritual nature of man. It involves seeing life as a dream that we live out with many choices just below our awareness. It employs the healing power of the Self that lies within all of us and is a wonderful form of exploration for people wanting to go deep within.

Psychodrama: An action-oriented psychotherapeutic technique that uses community to address longstanding relational problems from the past or present. Each member of a psychodrama group serves a therapeutic function, and the role-playing is led and monitored by a well-trained professional. It facilitates much catharsis and resolution. I have found that teens love this and do well with it.

Psychosynthesis: An understanding of human/personal growth that came out of Italy at the time of Freud's work, its goal is to achieve development and integration, a sense of personal wholeness. It is an optimistic and empowering philosophy, and I find it very helpful for people who are interested in developing self-awareness.

Role-playing: This basic technique is used in many forms of therapy (including Gestalt). Many teens love to role-play while in group therapy. Its use can make therapy fun and effective.

Tai chi: A slow and gentle martial art from China, tai chi is a great form of "moving" meditation. I recommend tai chi classes for kids who need to slow down. It can be a wonderful tool for anxiety or concentration issues.

Yoga: This ancient Hindu discipline aligns body and mind through a series of physical postures and awareness of the quality of "breath" to promote a meditative state of mind. There are many varieties of yoga, but all promote quieting the mind and strengthening/awareness of the body. I recommend it to kids who are stressed out and need this kind of peaceful, restorative "timeout." It also provides structure and a commitment to wellness that kids who need grounding can easily latch onto. It's an empowering activity that suits kids well and that they can engage in for a lifetime.

Glossary of Supplements

'm a true believer in the power of food to heal, and know that nutritional support is crucial for mental and emotional health. Here is a list of the nutritional supplements I use most frequently and find to be most effective. Of course, consult your physician before using any of these supplements with your child.

5-HTP: A precursor of the neurotransmitter serotonin, 5-HTP comes from tryptophan, an amino acid. This compound has a sedating, antianxiety effect and has been proven to improve depression. I find it helpful for treating insomnia, depression, and anxiety. 5-HTP comes in capsules and is available at health food stores. It should not be used with selective serotonin reuptake inhibitors (SSRIs).

Amino acids: These form when proteins are broken down into their smaller components by digestion. They're found in all foods that contain protein, especially meats, and are crucial for building all structures in the body and for energy metabolism.

Used supplementally, amino acids help boost energy, balance mood, or induce sleep. Supplements are available in capsules or powders and are sold separately or in combination.

B-complex vitamins: These are cofactors that are needed to maintain the energy and metabolic activities of the body and brain. B vitamins can be found in high concentrations in yeast and many other foods. Taken together, these water-soluble vitamins stabilize mood and promote vitality and mental clarity. I find them extremely useful in treating almost every mental or emotional complaint. They are sold separately, in multivitamins, or as B complex. I prefer a B-50 form that is more potent.

Calcium: The most abundant mineral in the body, calcium is crucial for building bones and teeth. It's also critical to the regulation of enzymes and the release of neurotransmitters. I find calcium to be helpful for regulating moods, reducing anxiety, and improving sleep. Found in dairy products, tofu, kale, and other leafy green vegetables, calcium is also sold as powders, capsules, liquids, or pills.

Choline: An essential nutrient found throughout the body, choline is needed for the manufacture of neurotransmitters and cell membranes in the brain and is crucial for fat metabolism. I find it helpful for bipolar symptoms and thought disorders. Choline is found in grains, legumes, and egg yolks and is sold as free choline and phosphatidylcholine. Lecithin also contains choline. You can buy choline supplements in the form of capsules.

Chromium: A mineral crucial for sugar and energy metabolism in the body, chromium helps regulate blood sugar levels and maintain energy. I have found it useful for treating depression, food cravings, and fatigue. Found in yeast, whole wheat bread, and potatoes, chromium is sold in capsules and tablets and as GTF (glucose tolerance factor).

Digestive enzymes: Our bodies produce chemicals called enzymes to digest or break down all foods, including proteins, fats, and carbohydrates. These chemicals break down food into its smaller components so that we can absorb them. I find enzymes useful for kids with developmental or absorption issues that affect brain functioning. They are found in some plants like papaya or derived from animal sources and are sold as tablets and capsules to be taken after eating.

Docosohexaenoic acid (DHA): DHA is an omega-3 essential fatty acid found in fish oil. It forms the most crucial building block for an infant's developing brain and plays a crucial role in membranes and neurons. It has been proven to be helpful in a variety of developmental issues. I prescribe it for attention problems, coordination issues, and learning problems. Wild game, flaxseed, and walnuts contain DHA precursors, and it is sold in gel-caps, fish oil, and flavored supplements.

Eicosapentaenoic acid (EPA): Another essential fatty acid, EPA comes from omega-3 oils and forms one of the two most crucial building blocks of the developing brain. I find it useful for treating depression, bipolar symptoms, and aggression. It can be found in cold-water fish, grass-fed game, and red algae and is sold as liquids and gel-caps. Be sure to buy a quality product, or you may belch and burp it up.

EMPower: A Canadian animal nutritionist and a father with two treatment-resistant bipolar patients developed this natural supplement, which contains high doses of 13 vitamins and 17 minerals/trace elements. There is a growing body of research to support this compound's effectiveness in treating psychiatric illnesses. I have found it extremely useful for treating bipolar symptoms, agitation, aggression, and even depression. It's available on the Internet (at www.truehope.com) as capsules or powder. (Please note: I have no financial ties to this or any other company.)

Ginkgo biloba: This herb comes from the leaves of a tree found all over the world. It has a stimulating effect and has been found useful for treating cognitive decline in the elderly. I use this herb with kids for depression, ADHD symptoms, and fatigue. It is sold as tablets and capsules containing various concentrations of the herb. Look for standardized concentrations and amounts, since quality counts for herbs and oils. Do not use this herb if bipolar symptoms are present.

Gotu kola: Also called centella, this herb is found in India and Africa. It has been used for promoting mental clarity and reducing stress. I use it for some symptoms of ADHD with good success. It's sold in capsules.

Inositol: A member of the B vitamin family, inositol is a relative of glucose. It works inside the cells and enhances cell membranes as well. I find this sweet-tasting powder to be very helpful for a variety of problems, including anxiety, stress, depression, OCD, and bipolar-type symptoms. It is found in a number of foods, especially grains that have bran, and is sold as capsules, but I favor the powder in bulk form.

Iron: This mineral/metal is critical for human life. All humans use iron in hemoglobin to transport oxygen into our cells. Iron also plays a crucial role in energy production and metabolism. I test kids with learning and mood issues to make sure they have enough iron. Iron can be found in high amounts in kelp, yeast, bran, liver, beef, and seeds.

Lemon balm: A wonderful calming herb that I use for anxiety and stress issues in children, lemon balm can be found in capsule or liquid form.

Magnesium: This is a very important mineral in which Americans are profoundly deficient. Magnesium helps reduce tension, agitation, and insomnia. I use it for anxiety, aggression, and mood disorders. I prefer powder over capsules. It's often used in combination with calcium.

Melatonin: This natural hormone made by the pineal gland has a sleep-inducing effect and helps the immune system as well. Melatonin can aid sleep problems like insomnia and jet lag. I use it for anxiety and insomnia. This supplement typically comes from animal sources and is sold as capsules, tablets, and sublingual lozenges.

Milk thistle: This herb helps the liver detoxify foreign substances such as psychiatric medications. I use it for people who are experiencing toxic effects from medications. It's found mainly in capsule form.

Rhodiola rosea: This herb from Russia works as an adaptogen like ginseng (an energizing traditional Chinese herb noted for its antiaging benefits). As an adaptogen, rhodiola is very helpful in reducing the negative effects of stress on the body. It also works well for chronic depression and seasonal affective disorder. I prescribe it in capsule form.

St. John's wort: This herb, which I have growing in my backyard, has been used for centuries for depression. I find it very useful for minor to moderate depression in kids. It comes as capsules or liquid concentrates.

SAMe: This naturally occurring substance is a potent stimulating antidepressant. It functions in many crucial chemical reactions inside the body. I frequently use it for slowed or lethargic depression. I avoid it when there are bipolar-type symptoms or a family history of bipolar disorder. It's available in foil-sealed tablets and can be costly.

Theonine: This compound comes from tea and has been found to be calming and soothing. I use it for anxiety or sleep problems in children. I find it mainly in tablet form.

Valerian: This herb grows nicely in my garden in Colorado. It has been proven to reduce anxiety and improve sleep; the only issue is its strong smell. It's widely available in capsule or liquid form.

Vitamin C: Essential for protein synthesis in the human body, vitamin C requirements vary enormously from one person to another. I recommend it for everyone. It is found naturally in citrus and fresh fruit and is sold in powders, capsules, and tablets.

Zinc: This mineral is another that Americans typically lack. Zinc is crucial for wound healing, immune system function, learning, and neuronal metabolism. Anytime I see focus or learning issues, I think about zinc. It is available in tablets and lozenges.

Family Stress Index

This questionnaire was designed to help assess the level of stress that you and your family experience. I find that using questionnaires like this one can be invaluable to parents who often don't (or can't) slow down enough to truly assess the stress in their lives. Looking at the facts of your situation in black and white is often the first step toward positive action and change.

Answer the following questions using this scale.

> 0 = never true
> 1 = rarely true
> 2 = often true
> 3 = always true

Respond with the first answer that comes to you; don't ponder it for a long time.

1. I feel that I work too much.	0	1	2	3
2. The kids are doing well in school.	0	1	2	3
3. I don't enjoy things the way I used to.	0	1	2	3

4. We have fun on our vacations.	0	1	2	3
5. It seems as if we argue a lot.	0	1	2	3
6. I feel appreciated.	0	1	2	3
7. I feel rushed for time.	0	1	2	3
8. I exercise regularly to manage stress.	0	1	2	3
9. I feel alone and without friends.	0	1	2	3
10. I am glad that I have kids.	0	1	2	3
11. I feel as if my child doesn't like me.	0	1	2	3
12. Everybody does their fair share around here.	0	1	2	3
13. I feel trapped by my responsibilities.	0	1	2	3
14. We often talk about our feelings.	0	1	2	3
15. I feel that I can't handle things very well.	0	1	2	3
16. We have meals together regularly.	0	1	2	3
17. Sometimes marriage is disappointing.	0	1	2	3
18. I feel good about my role as a parent.	0	1	2	3
19. My child doesn't respect me.	0	1	2	3
20. My marriage is strong (couples), or I am comfortable being single (single parents).	0	1	2	3

Scoring: Add your scores for even-numbered and odd-numbered questions separately.

Even-numbered questions

26–30 = You are doing well. Congratulations.

16–25 = You have moderate concerns. Work to build positives.

11–15 = You have serious concerns. Manage your stress, or symptoms will appear in your family.

10 or less = Seek professional help quickly. You are floundering.

Odd-numbered questions

0–5 = You have minimal issues. Continue your strong efforts to manage stress.

6–15 = These are moderate indicators of stress. Strive to acknowledge the underlying issues and address them.

16–20 = These are significant warning signs. It's crucial that you take care of them, or someone is likely to be labeled soon.

21–30 = This is a crisis situation. Call someone today for help.

Trauma Questionnaire

like this questionnaire, created by the good people at the Triad Trauma Centre in Ontario, Canada. It's a great aid in helping parents understand the scope of traumatic experience for children. If you know or suspect that your child has had a traumatic experience, using this questionnaire in conjunction with a practitioner who has expertise in treating childhood trauma can help facilitate swift and effective treatment.

Has the child:

1. Directly experienced one or more of the following?

   - Physical abuse

   - Sexual abuse

   - Verbal abuse

   - Emotional abuse

2. Witnessed family violence and/or abusive behavior involving their caregiver(s)?

3. Lost a mother, father, sibling, or friend to sudden death or a chronic, debilitating illness such as cancer?

4. Experienced an unplanned separation from their primary caregiver for longer than 3 days?

5. Experienced the adoption process?

6. Experienced a real or perceived threat to the life or safety of their primary caregiver?

7. Experienced one or more foster home placements?

8. Experienced abandonment by a caregiver?

9. Experienced neglect by a caregiver?

10. Experienced a frightening or protracted hospital stay?

11. Experienced a serious illness?

12. Experienced an unexpected move?

13. Experienced inconsistent visits by one of their caregivers because visits are frequently canceled or appointments aren't kept?

14. Been discovered to have been touched inappropriately or been found touching another child inappropriately (even if approximately the same age)?

If the answer to any of these questions is yes, it may indicate that your child is experiencing an inordinate amount of stress and may need support and possibly treatment. Remember that trauma is a form of stress that can easily go "underground." Naming the trauma and treating it are essential for your child's emotional and mental health.

Resources and Recommended Reading

CHAPTER 1: THE HIGH COST OF LABELING

Armstrong, Thomas. *The Myth of the ADD Child: 50 Ways to Improve Your Child's Behavior and Attention Span without Drugs, Labels, or Coercion* (Plume, 1997). The author questions the diagnosis of ADD and offers 50 methods to improve attention span.

Diller, Lawrence. *Running on Ritalin: A Physician Reflects on Children, Society, and Performance in a Pill* (Bantam, 1998). An inquisitive pediatrician explores a variety of issues behind why we medicate children and the vagaries of the ADHD diagnosis.

———. *Should I Medicate My Child?: Sane Solutions for Troubled Kids with— and without—Psychiatric Drugs* (Basic, 2002). A thoughtful tour of behavioral, educational, and pharmaceutical options for parents.

———. *The Last Normal Child: Essays on the Intersection of Kids, Culture, and Psychiatric Drugs* (Praeger, 2006). A wonderful look at many of the issues I explore.

Maté, Gabor. *Scattered: How Attention Deficit Disorder Originates and What You Can Do about It* (Plume, 2000). This Canadian physician and ADHD patient questions the cause and treatments of his own illness.

CHAPTER 2: HOW YOUR CHILD'S BRAIN GROWS

Eliot, Lise. *What's Going On in There?: How the Brain and Mind Develop in the First Five Years of Life* (Bantam, 2000). Eliot, a mother of three and a neuroscientist, provides a detailed look at early brain development.

Restak, Richard. *The Secret Life of the Brain* (National Academies Press, 2001). A large-format companion to the excellent PBS series of the same name, this book offers a nice overview of the growth and development of the human brain.

Siegel, Daniel. *The Developing Mind: How Relationships and the Brain Interact to Shape Who We Are* (Guilford, 1999). A surprisingly readable look at how relationships direct the growth of the young brain.

Schwartz, Jeffrey, and Sharon Begley. *The Mind and the Brain: Neuroplasticity and the Power of Mental Force* (HarperCollins, 2002). A wonderful exploration of how our interests, activities, and willpower change our brains.

CHAPTER 3: RELATIONSHIPS AND THE YOUNG BRAIN

Chess, Stella, and Alexander Thomas. *Know Your Child: An Authoritative Guide for Today's Parents* (Basic, 1989). Chess and Thomas are grandparents, child psychiatrists, and researchers who pioneered temperament studies.

Karen, Robert. *Becoming Attached: First Relationships and How They Shape Our Capacity to Love* (Oxford University Press, 1998). A detailed exploration of how our early relationships determine our capacity to love.

Neville, Helen, and Diane Clark Johnson. *Temperament Tools: Working with Your Child's Inborn Traits* (Parenting Press, 1997). Simple and practical, this book offers lots of tips for parenting with an understanding temperament and fit.

Turecki, Stanley. *The Difficult Child* (Bantam, 2000). This classic book offers Turecki's deep understanding of temperament and behavior issues.

CHAPTER 4: FEEDING YOUR CHILD'S BRAIN
FOR EMOTIONAL AND MENTAL HEALTH

Evers, Connie Liakos. *How to Teach Nutrition to Kids* (24 Carrot Press, 2003). A nutritionist offers a variety of tools to teach nutrition and fitness to kids ages 6 to 12.

Graimes, Nicola. *Brain Foods for Kids: Over 100 Recipes to Boost Your Child's Intelligence* (Delta, 2005). The author offers brain-boosting recipes and advice about what to avoid.

Joachim, David, and Rochelle Davis. *Fresh Choices: More Than 100 Easy Recipes for Pure Food When You Can't Buy 100% Organic* (Rodale, 2004). Practical help for parents who want to prepare very simple, healthy food.

Schmidt, Michael. *Brain-Building Nutrition: The Healing Power of Fats and Oils* (North Atlantic Books, 2001). An experienced nutritionally oriented pediatrician offers advice from his years of practice and research.

Stoll, Andrew. *The Omega-3 Connection: The Groundbreaking Antidepression Diet and Brain Program* (Simon & Schuster, 2001). A Harvard psychiatrist takes you on a tour of the emotional benefits of omega oils and his research.

Stordy, B. Jacqueline, and Malcolm Nicholl. *The LCP Solution: The Remarkable Nutritional Treatment for ADHD, Dyslexia, and Dyspraxia* (Ballantine, 2000). The author explains how omega-3 oils can correct what we label as illness.

www.keepkidshealthy.com/nutrition. Great information for parents on good food.

www.kidshealth.org. This is a site for parents, kids, and teens.

www.kidsnutrition.org. More sound information and advice.

www.nordicnaturals.com. A great source of information on the value of omega-3 oils in the diet.

www.truehope.com. This is the EMPower Web site, which offers explanation and research on the nutritional treatment of bipolar disorder for interested parents.

CHAPTER 5: ENVIRONMENTAL CAUSES OF DISHARMONY IN OUR KIDS

Garbarino, James. *Raising Children in a Socially Toxic Environment* (Jossey Bass, 1999). The author acts as both a social critic and a child advocate.

Gaynor, Mitchell. *Nurture Nature, Nurture Health: Your Health and the Environment* (Nurture Nature Press, 2005). Gaynor, an oncologist, presents information about the unhealthy aspects of our world and what we can do about them.

Landrigan, Phillip; Herbert Needleman; and Mary Landrigan. *Raising Healthy Children in a Toxic World: 101 Smart Solutions for Every Family* (Rodale, 2002). The authors present a variety of options for parents who want to create a healthier home for their kids.

Louv, Richard. *Last Child in the Woods: Saving Our Children from Nature-Deficit Disorder* (Algonquin, 2006). An eloquent call to reunite our children with nature in order to restore their physical and emotional health.

www.mediafamily.org. This is the National Institute on Media and the Family site. It offers useful ratings of current movies and videogames with respect to violence and sexual content.

www.organicconsumers.org. This organization advocates for food safety and sustainability.

www.scorecard.org. This site provides detailed toxic chemical and pollution data for various areas, based on ZIP code.

CHAPTER 6: THE FAMILY SYSTEM AND FIT: SCHOOL, INTELLIGENCE, AND LEARNING STYLE

Brazelton, T. Berry, and Joshua Sparrow. *Understanding Sibling Rivalry: The Brazelton Way* (Da Capo, 2005). This book offers more wonderful stuff by the acclaimed pediatrician. Check out the nice section on newborns and sibling reactions.

Kabat-Zinn, Jon. *Wherever You Go, There You Are: Mindfulness Meditation in Everyday Life* (Hyperion, 2005). This nondenominational and very practical book is a wonderful introduction to the practice of mindfulness and meditation.

Higgins, Gina O'Connell. *Resilient Adults: Overcoming a Cruel Past* (Jossey Bass, 1994). This is an inspiring book about people who have moved beyond early abuse and neglect to succeed on every level. The real story here is about the power of love and relationships.

Long, Nicholas, and Rex Forehand. *Making Divorce Easier on Your Child: 50 Effective Ways to Help Children Adjust* (McGraw-Hill, 2002). The authors provide advice for helping kids through this difficult process.

Neuman, M. Gary. *Helping Your Kids Cope with Divorce the Sandcastles Way* (Random House, 1999). This book is based on a proven clinical program for assisting kids ages 8 to 17 through divorce.

Thayer, Elizabeth, and Jeffrey Zimmerman. *The Co-Parenting Survival Guide: Letting Go of Conflict after a Difficult Divorce* (New Harbinger Press, 2001). Advice for putting children first in an adversarial divorce.

Wallerstein, Judith. *What about the Kids?: Raising Your Children before, during, and after Divorce* (Hyperion, 2003). The famous divorce researcher helps parents caught up in divorce take care of their kids.

CHAPTER 7: SCHOOL, LEARNING, AND THE YOUNG BRAIN

Gardner, Howard. *Frames of Mind: The Theory of Multiple Intelligences* (Basic, 1983). This is the classic book by the man who popularized this concept.

Goldstein, Sam, and Nancy Mather. *Overcoming Underachieving: An Action Guide to Helping Your Child Succeed in School* (Wiley, 1998). This book offers many wonderful insights about how to support a child who is struggling in school.

Levine, Mel. *Keeping a Head in School: A Students' Book about Learning Abilities and Learning Disorders* (Educators Publishing Services, 1990). A nice book for kids about how to succeed in school.

————. *A Mind at a Time: America's Top Learning Expert Shows How Every Child Can Succeed* (Simon & Schuster, 2002). An in-depth and valuable look at learning differences and solutions.

————. *Educational Care: A System for Understanding and Helping Children with Learning Problems at Home and in School* (Educators Publishing Services, 2002). A useful overview of schools and how to navigate the resources to get what your child needs.

Silver, Larry. *The Misunderstood Child: Understanding and Coping with Your Child's Learning Disabilities* (Crown, 1998). An excellent primer on managing learning challenges.

www.allkindsofminds.org. This site connects you to Mel Levine's nonprofit organization, All Kinds of Minds, dedicated to helping students with learning differences.

www.ldonline.org. This is an interactive guide to learning differences for parents, teachers, and children.

www.schwablearning.org. A parents' guide to learning and school issues for kids.

www.smallschoolsproject.org; www.smallschoolsworkshop.org. Both of these sites provide information, direction, and support for those interested in the small schools concept.

CHAPTER 8: UNDERSTANDING TRAUMA

Alexander, Debra. *Children Changed by Trauma: A Healing Guide* (New Harbinger, 1999). A nice overview of what happens to children who have been traumatized and what parents can do about it.

Terr, Lenore. *Too Scared to Cry: Psychic Trauma in Childhood* (Basic, 1990). This is a more formal look at childhood trauma by a famous researcher and child psychiatrist.

www.beyondconsequences.com. Offers a trauma- and stress-oriented treatment program developed by clinicians for behavior problems in kids.

www.childtrauma.org. This is the home site of Bruce Perry's Child Trauma Academy, a great nonprofit organization dedicated to teaching about the consequences of childhood trauma and abuse.

www.emdr.com. This is the home site for EMDR, a highly effective eye movement treatment for any type of trauma or anxiety.

www.traumatreatment.ca. This is the site of an innovative Canadian clinician and researcher who provides family-centered care for trauma victims.

CHAPTER 9: PARENTING FOR EMOTIONAL AND MENTAL HEALTH

Brooks, Robert, and Sam Goldstein. *Raising Resilient Children: Fostering Strength, Hope, and Optimism in Your Child* (McGraw-Hill, 2002). Two child psychologists give solid direction for steering kids toward the habits of resilience.

Kohn, Alfie. *Unconditional Parenting: Moving from Rewards and Punishments to Love and Reason* (Atria, 2005). I couldn't have said it better.

Prather, Hugh, and Gayle Prather. *Spiritual Parenting: A Guide to Understanding and Nurturing the Heart of Your Child* (Harmony, 1996). A nondenominational and insightful look at the deeper aspects of parenting.

Seligman, Martin. *The Optimistic Child: A Proven Program to Safeguard Children against Depression and Build Lifelong Resilience* (Harper, 1996). One of our most influential psychologists teaches about the power of optimism.

Siegel, Daniel, and Mary Hartzell. *Parenting from the Inside Out: How a Deeper Self-Understanding Can Help You Raise Children Who Thrive* (Tarcher, 2004). The authors strongly believe, as I do, that who we are determines our parenting, and thus, inner work brings deep benefits. Strongly recommended.

Steinberg, Laurence. *Crossing Paths: How Your Child's Adolescence Triggers Your Own Crisis* (Fireside, 1994). The subtitle says it all.

Choosing a Practitioner

Finding the right doctors, therapists, and other practitioners to best help our children can be a real challenge. I've put together a list of things parents can do that will make this process less stressful and, I hope, more fruitful and efficient. Aside from credentials, philosophy, and other considerations, the most important issue is that you feel you and your child "fit" with any professional you hire.

1. Find someone who works mainly with children. Many adult therapists will see only an occasional child and often don't have the skill set needed to work effectively with kids' issues. This is particularly important for children under age 12.

2. Degrees aren't crucial; heart is crucial. Look for chemistry and fit. I'm not concerned with whether a practitioner is a psychiatrist, psychologist, or master's-level counselor. Does your child like him and relate easily to him? Does he seem to understand your child and exude compassion?

3. Ask if the practitioner will meet with you to assess fit before you commit. After this, ask your child if he likes and feels he can trust the therapist.

4. Does the practitioner spend time with you, the parents? The younger the child, the more time parents need to be involved in the process for it to be successful. With a 6- or 8-year-old, a therapist may need to spend as much as half of the clinical time with the parents, giving feedback and directions. As kids move into their teen years, this falls off so that by age 14, the child may see the therapist alone 100 percent of the time.

5. Before you go, assess your own role in your child's upset honestly. Be willing to focus on the changes that would be helpful for you to make in order for your child to get better. If such feedback isn't offered, ask for suggestions.

6. Assess your child's strengths carefully and make a list before you go. Share that information with the practitioner early on and request that she work from a strength-based approach.

7. Tell practitioners that you are dubious of labels in kids and want to downplay the role they have in treatment. Ask instead to identify key problem areas/challenges. For example, instead of settling on a label such as ADHD, have the therapist address specific challenges, such as difficulty staying seated in class or completing specific tasks.

8. Ask the practitioner to develop a simple treatment plan that's built around the child's strengths and includes specific goals and challenges. Get a written copy of this plan so you can monitor your child's progress.

9. Be a demanding consumer. Don't be afraid to be assertive and direct: Your child depends on you. Not all practitioners are good or effective, and you may need to shop around to find someone skilled in the ways you and your child need.

Ask people you respect for recommendations. Always feel comfortable getting a second (or third) opinion.

10. Finally, before you select any practitioner, examine your own beliefs about mental and emotional health and how to achieve it. Include your spouse and your child/teen. Are you pro-medication? Antimedication? Do you have a more natural or ecological mindset with an emphasis on nutrition and holistic treatments? Do you want a conventional, mainstream approach? Selecting someone who shares your family's worldview is crucial. The goal is to work with a practitioner who will be empathetic and supportive of your child and your family.

Here are some resources to help you locate a mental health practitioner near you.

American Association for Marriage and Family Therapy

www.aamft.org
703-838-9808

This group supports the value of marriage and family work that is crucial to the healing of a child.

American Psychological Association

www.apa.org
800-374-2721

These practitioners have doctorates in psychology (PhD, PsyD, or EdD) and can do psychological testing and therapy. If your child is under age 14, find someone who specializes in working only with kids. Psychologists have a wide range of styles and approaches. Explore their orientation and approach before you start to make sure it matches yours.

Eye Movement Desensitization and Reprocessing Institute, Inc.

www.emdr.com
831-761-1040

This new therapy is very helpful for trauma, abuse, and anxiety of any kind.

National Association of Social Workers

www.socialworkers.org

202-408-8600

Social workers focus on working with family systems and have the most systems-oriented philosophy in all of mental health. They can be helpful with marital issues as well.

Locating Other Professionals

The best approach for children is often multidisciplinary. A child's condition can often improve more effectively if the primary treatment, working with a therapist or psychiatrist, is supported by other modalities. Here are some helpful resources to steer you toward finding practitioners from other disciplines to help your child.

American Academy of Child and Adolescent Psychiatry

www.aacap.org

202-966-7300

I come from this background. Training involves a minimum of 5 years after medical school. Child psychiatry has narrowed considerably in the past two decades and has been increasingly focused on diagnosing disorders and prescribing medications. Try to find someone who is progressive and open minded about alternative treatments. Ask about the use of supplements, nutritional therapies, and other nonmedical treatments.

American Association of Naturopathic Physicians

www.naturopathic.org

866-538-2267

Naturopaths have a 4-year ND degree and are licensed in many states as primary care physicians. They work extensively with diet, herbs, and natural methods.

American Holistic Medical Association

www.holisticmedicine.org

425-967-0737

This group, founded in 1978, honors the whole person and shares many of my core beliefs about health care. I was a founding member and remain involved. Our members come from all medical specialties and regions of the country.

The Cranial Academy

www.cranialacademy.org

317-594-0411

These practitioners are osteopaths (DOs) who are skilled in the manipulation of the bones of the skull. In my experience, this wonderful skill is quite useful for developmental issues, learning problems, explosive temper, and headaches.

Society for Developmental and Behavioral Pediatrics

www.sdbp.org

703-556-9222

The pediatricians in this group have additional training and are skilled in the treatment of kids with a variety of severe issues related to behavior or abnormal development. They tend to be less focused on medications and have a fairly broad perspective. There aren't many of them.

INDEX

Boldface page references indicate photographs and illustrations.
Underscored references indicate boxed text.

A

Abuse, child, 228–29
Academic pressure, 159.
    See also Learning; School
Activity level temperament trait,
    60
Acupuncture, 237
Adaptability of brain, 27
Adaptability temperament trait,
    60
Adderall (amphetamine-
    dextroamphetamine), 4
Addictive behaviors, 85
Adelsheim, Steven, 175
ADHD
    case studies, 10–11, 13–14
    causes of, 229–30
    as common label, 10, 229–30
    definition of, 229
    food allergies and, 80
    incidence of, 3, 8, 10, 229
    iron deficiency and, 70
    mercury exposure and, 127
    nature and, exposure to, 120
    nutrition and, 68, 70
    other problems missed and, 9
    pesticide exposure and, 127
    posttraumatic stress disorder
        and, 229
    psychiatric diagnosis and, 7–8
    psychiatric medications for, 3
    requirements, 103–4
    rise in, 7–8
    sleep deprivation and, 103
    stigma of, 10–11

symptoms of, 230
trauma and, 183
Adolescence
    brain in, 31
    nutrition in, 93–99
    sleep deprivation in, 105–6
    sleep requirements in, 104–5
Affective education, 174–76
Aggressive behaviors, 85, 116
Allergies, food, 80
Altruism, 217–18
American Academy of Child and
    Adolescent Psychiatry, 266
American Academy of Pediatrics,
    37
American Association for
    Marriage and Family
    Therapy, 265
American Association of
    Naturopathic Physicians,
    266
American Holistic Medical
    Association, 266
American Psychological
    Association, 265
Amino acids, 243–44
Amygdala, 39, 182–83
Animal-assisted therapy, 237
Antidepressants. *See also specific*
    type
    for bipolar disorder, 233
    for depression, 234–35
    for obsessive-compulsive
        disorder, 227
    overlabeling and, 3

Environment *(cont.)*
  toxins *(cont.)*
    occurrences of, 121
    pesticides, 127–28
    pregnancy and, 40
    risks of, 121–22
Environmental Protection
      Agency (EPA), 122, 124
EPA (eicosapentaenoic acid), 76,
      245
EPA (Environmental Protection
      Agency), 122, 124
ERP, 227
Essential fatty acids (EFAs),
      72–73, 74–76, 87
Exercise, 239
Experiential therapy, 239
Exposure and response
      prevention (ERP), 227
Express Scripts Inc. study (2004),
      3
Eye movement desensitization
      and reprocessing (EMDR),
      239
Eye Movement Desensitization
      and Reprocessing Institute,
      Inc., 265

F

Family. *See also* Parenting;
      Relationships
  appreciation of, 150
  closeness of, 151
  commitment of, 150
  discipline versus punishment
      and, 207–10
  father-child relationships, 57,
      57
  health of child and, 30–31
  importance of, 131–32, 150
  imprinting and, 131–32
  mental and emotional disorders
      and, 132–34
  mother-child relationships,
      45–51, 57
  optimal brain development and,
      43
  parent-child relationships, 57,
      62–66, 64

predictability of, 151
resilience and, 145–49
resourcefulness of, in crisis, 151
school and, 176–78
spiritual awareness of, 150–51
steadiness of, 151
stress in
  causes of, 138–39
  divorce, 139–42
  excessive, 137–38
  index for, 249–51
  management, 142–45, 150
  occurrences of, 137
  resilience and, 145–49
  as school stress cause, 158
strong, 150–51
systems, 132–37
therapy, 239
Father-child relationships, 57, 57
Fats, dietary, 69, 71, 72–73, 74–76
FDA, 4, 21, 235
Fear-based disorders. *See* Anxiety
      disorders
Federal Trade Commission
      (FTC), 37
Feelings. *See* Emotions
Fish, 75–76, 78, 128
"Fit" of parent-child
      temperament, 62–66, 221
5-HTP, 243
Folate, 70, 74
Folic acid, 70, 74
Food. *See* Nutrition; *specific type*
Food allergies, 80
Food Pyramid, 68
Forgiveness, 205–6
Fried food, 79
Frontal lobe of brain, 31
Fruits, 73, 78, 128
FTC, 37

G

GAD, 226, 229
Gardner, Howard, 156–57, 160
Generalized anxiety disorder
      (GAD), 226, 229
Genes, 27, 52, 58–59, 61
Genetics, 27
GI, 91